STUDIA POST-BIBLICA

VOLUMEN SEPTIMUM DECIMUM

STUDIA POST-BIBLICA

INSTITUTA A P. A. H. DE BOER

ADIUVANTIBUS

T. JANSMA ET J. SMIT SIBINGA

EDIDIT

J. C. H. LEBRAM

VOLUMEN SEPTIMUM DECIMUM

LEIDEN
E. J. BRILL
1970

THE FORMATION OF THE BABYLONIAN TALMUD

STUDIES IN THE ACHIEVEMENTS OF LATE NINETEENTH AND TWENTIETH CENTURY HISTORICAL AND LITERARY-CRITICAL RESEARCH

EDITED BY

JACOB NEUSNER

Professor of Religious Studies
Brown University

TUTA SUB AEGIDE PALLAS · EJB ·

LEIDEN
E. J. BRILL
1970

PRINTED IN THE NETHERLANDS

For

Wendell S. Dietrich

and

Horst R. Moehring

TABLE OF CONTENTS

Part Three

BY WAY OF COMPARISON

Part Four

THE SUGYA

FOREWORD

The Babylonian Talmud is the primary source for Jewish law and theology. Completed in the fifth and sixth centuries, the Talmud has been studied ever since, not only because it was and remains widely accepted as the compendium of the Oral Torah which, together with the Written Torah, constitutes Judaism's decisive authority, but also because it is one of the most engaging, indeed fascinating, works of the human spirit. The endless difficulties of content, conception, dialectical argument—these have provoked one generation after another to contribute commentaries. But the greater number of students of the Talmud produced no written treatises. The shape of their lives, lived in perpetual response to the document and its wisdom, was their contribution to study of "Torah". The study of Judaism, its history, ideas and ideals, begins now, as for the past fifteen centuries, in the pages of the Babylonian Talmud. Whatever one has studied, if he has not studied the Talmud, he knows nothing of later Judaism. If he has studied the Talmud, then everything else is merely commentary.

The origins of the Oral Torah in its written form, the history of the Babylonian Talmud, the contributions made by each of the generations of Babylonian masters (*Amoraim*)—these questions were asked almost as soon as the document itself had attained final form. R. Sherira Gaon of Pumbedita, the school which, as we shall see, is primarily responsible for the Babylonian Talmud, wrote the first great treatise on the history of the Talmud and of the period in which it was written. Living in the tenth century, he made use of traditions of his own school. All subsequent studies drew upon what Sherira had to say. In the Babylonian Talmud itself is an enigmatic statement (b. B.M. 86a) that Rabina and R. Ashi were the end of "instruction" (*hora'ah*), and the meaning of that saying was subjected to many analyses.

With the development of Jewish scholarship in the modern, Western mode, generally referred to as "Jewish science", the question of the origins of the Talmud was asked with renewed interest. If scholars hoped to make use of Talmudic sources, they needed a critical theory as to the period and context in which the sources were shaped. Furthermore, the history of Jewry and of Judaism in the period in which the Talmud was taking shape, and concerning which the Talmud is the primary testimony, attracted new interest as part of the renaissance of the writing of the history of the Jews. All general histories, beginning with Abraham and extending to contemporary life, naturally treated the Jews in late antiquity in general, and in Babylonia in particular; and each contains an account of the literary history of the Babylonian Talmud. Still a third stimulus was the development of new modes of study of the Talmud itself, which emphasized the meaning of Talmudic sayings and stories in their own age and setting, rather than their implications for law and theology viewed under the aspect of eternity. Philological and historical disciplines, shaped in the critical study of other ancient literatures, were brought to bear upon Talmudic literature as well.

These papers, originally prepared for my seminar in Talmudic studies at Brown University and then revised for publication, offer an account of the achievements of some of the more important late nineteenth and twentieth century historians and literary critics. We have concentrated on a single fundamental question, namely, how and when did the Babylonian Talmud take shape. It seemed to us that all other issues depend upon the answer to this first one. Furthermore, with the increasing use by New Testament and other scholars of Talmudic literature, it becomes important to provide students of various topics in late antiquity with a summary of scholarship which is pertinent to their inquiry, but not widely available, because it is written mostly in Hebrew. Since no survey of the state of so vital a question as the formation of the Babylonian Talmud existed, we determined to provide a preliminary and modest beginning.

It quickly became clear that two quite separate sorts of studies have been made. Historians of the period tended to rely solely upon the evidence they regarded as "historical", meaning the few germane sayings in the Babylonian Talmud, on the one hand, and the letter of R. Sherira on the other. These materials were repeatedly cited, and some scholars, particularly Y. I. Halevy, subjected them to close and careful analysis. But because they paid little, if any, attention to the internal evidence exhibited by the Talmud itself, these historians succeeded only in rehearsing over and over again the few plausible theories capable of accounting for the little corpus of pertinent sayings. The limitations of the historical method practiced by these men are spelled out in each relevant study. The evidence they thought relevant was inadequate to answer the question they posed, and reliance on it led them inevitably to inadequate results.

Literary critics, that is, students of Talmudic literature who concentrated on precise text-study by means of modern, critical methods, have made impressive progress in the analysis of the Babylonian Talmud, along with other ancient rabbinic documents. But most of the literary critics have had slight, if any, interest in historical questions; they never translated the results of their literary criticism into historical categories of inquiry. Their accounts of the formation of the Babylonian Talmud rarely exhibit much sustained interest in the question to begin with. Y. N. Epstein, certainly the doyen of modern critical study of Talmudic literature, produced no coherent account, and his results, difficult to come by, are garbled and incomplete.

Only two recent scholars faced the problem of literary history and answered it with requisite care, in sustained and cogent style, and in articulated, methodologically self-conscious manner. These are Saul Lieberman and Abraham Weiss. Lieberman's research on the formation of the first stratum of the Palestinian Talmud sets the standard by which any such inquiry is to be measured.[1]

The sole scholar to provide for the Babylonian Talmudic problem an answer which we found persuasive, not arbitrary or enigmatic, and genuinely fruitful comes at the end. Abraham Weiss seems to us to provide the sole account worth taking seriously and building upon for historical purposes. Weiss has had a modest audience. Outside of Yeshiva University, where he taught for nearly three decades, his books have not been widely read, though with the appearance of M. S. Feldblum's summary and précis of them in English, Weiss has begun to reach a somewhat larger circle of readers. Still, the examination of his theories in the context of those that went before must further enhance appreciation for his achievements.

For our seminar, he came as a climax, after successive disappointments. I certainly did not plan it that way. I could not, at the outset, have predicted that we should be left unpersuaded by the earlier scholars, by their arbitrary definitions, circular arguments, loose, often slovenly formulations, practically private and esoteric framework of discourse, exhibited in most, though not all, studies in varying ways and degrees. Yet such was the case. Even so sophisticated a scholar as Hyman Klein solves at least one major problem by postulating that the master to whom a saying was explicitly attributed never said it at all. This is somewhat like the old style of biblical scholars, a style

[1] Saul Lieberman, "The Talmud of Caesarea—Jerusalem Tractate Neziqin", *Tarbiz*, 1931, Supplement II, 4.

characterized by promiscuous emendations as the solution of all problems. It is not that emendations are invariably false, or that postulating a well-known master out of existence is always unpersuasive. Much in talmudic literature is pseudepigraphic. But the definition of what is, and is not, pseudepigraphic is more impressive when it does not serve to solve a single difficulty of logic or interpretation.

The final section is devoted to the study of the *sugya*, the building-block of the Babylonian Talmud. Some attention is paid to Ḥanokh Albeck's essays on this subject, but the larger part of our study was devoted to David Weiss Halivni, *Meqorot uMesorot. Bi'urim baTalmud leSeder Nashim* (Tel Aviv, 1968). Halivni's monumental work demands and deserves extended study, item by item. Here we have tried to systematize some of his conceptual and methodological contributions, and to indicate why and how he shows the way for future research. But the reader should not imagine that the three papers exhaust all that is to be learned from Halivni. They are meant only to call attention to his importance.

For most readers, the literary critics will prove more difficult to comprehend than the historians. This is natural, for the latter deal in an ordinary way with commonplace problems. The former concentrate on a literature which is doubtless unfamiliar to a wide audience. We hope that the papers are sufficiently lucid and self-contained, depending on no outside texts or information, so that at least the fundamental concepts of the literary critics will become clear. If talmudic studies are to make their way in the context of humanistic scholarship in universities, as I believe they can and should for the sake both of the humanities and of the Talmud alike, then we shall have to strive for the greatest possible simplicity and clarity in conveying our results. It is my hope that the present writers have attained in this respect a measure of success.

JACOB NEUSNER

Providence, Rhode Island
5 Sivan 5729, 'Erev Shavu'ot
May 22, 1969.

ABBREVIATIONS

TALMUDIC TRACTATES

ʿArakh. = ʿArakhin
A.Z. = ʿAvodah Zarah
B.B. = Bava' Batra'
B.M. = Bava' Meẓiʿa'
B.Q. = Bava' Qamma'
Ber. = Berakhot
Bekh. = Bekhorot
Bez. = Beẓah
Bik. = Bikkurim
Ed. = ʿEduyot
ʿEruv. = ʿEruvin
Git. = Giṭṭin
Hag. = Ḥagigah
Hul. = Ḥullin
Hal. = Ḥallah
Hor. = Horayot
Ket. = Ketuvot
Kel. = Kelim
Kil. = Kila'yim
M.Q. = Moʿed Qatan
M.S. = Maʿaser Sheni
Ma. = Maʿaserot
Mak. = Makkot
Meg. = Megillah
Men. = Menaḥot
Mid. = Middot
Miq. = Miqva'ot
Naz. = Nazir
Ned. = Nedarim
Neg. = Negaʿim
Nid. = Niddah
Oh. = Ohalot
Par. = Parah
Pes. = Pesaḥim
Qid. = Qiddushin
R.H. = Rosh Hashanah
Sanh. = Sanhedrin
Shab. = Shabbat
Sheq. = Sheqalim
Shev. = Sheviʿit
Sot. = Soṭah
Suk. = Sukkah
Ter. = Terumot
Toh. = Ṭoharot
Yad. = Yadaim
Yev. = Yevamot
Zev. = Zevaḥim

OTHER ABBREVIATIONS

b., BT = Babylonian Talmud
ESG = Epistle of R. Sherira Gaon
IAL = J. N. Epstein, *Introductions to Amoraic Literature*
ITM = J. N. Epstein, *Introductions to the Text of the Mishnah*
JQR = Jewish Quarterly Review
M. = Mishnah
MT = Mishnah Tamid
RST = B. M. Lewin, *Rabbanan Savora'ē veTalmudam*
TC = Talmud of Caesarea
y., PT = Palestinian Talmud

I

HISTORIANS

I

HEINRICH GRAETZ AND ZE'EV JAWITZ

BY

Herman J. Blumberg

i

Heinrich Graetz was born in Xions, Germany, in 1817.[1] His work as an historian began when in 1883 he moved to Berlin, delivered lectures on Jewish history and began publication of his *magnum opus*, *Geschichte der Juden von dem ältesten Zeiten bis zur Gegenwart*. During this period he began teaching at the newly-founded Jewish Theological Seminary in Breslau and founded the Jewish Theological Society which promoted the scientific study of Judaism, but maintained a middle of the road position between Orthodoxy and Reform. Throughout his career he exhibited a hostility to German Reform Judaism.

His main achievement is his *Geschichte* which he produced over a period of twenty-three years. He also produced a more popular three-volume history, *Volkstümliche Geschichte*, wrote other historical books and essays which appeared primarily in the Breslau Seminary publication and in the *Monatsschrift*. In examining Graetz's account of the redaction of the Babylonian Talmud, I will attempt to show how his preconceptions were imposed upon the source material, resulting in a dramatic, moving account of the Talmud's compilation, which is also highly forced and artificial and leaves more problems than it resolves.

Salo Baron sets forth the chief characteristics of Graetz as historian.[2] In seeking a controlling idea for his history, he found in the Jewish past an "inner spiritual evolution" and proceeded to interpret all of Jewish history to show its dynamic presence. Graetz is a national historian; he isolated the Jew from the surrounding world and explained history mainly through internal factors which originate and

[1] Salo Baron, "H. H. Graetz 1817-1891—A biographical sketch", *History and Jewish Historians*, pp. 263ff.

[2] *Ibid.*, "Graetz and Ranke—A Methodological Study", pp. 269ff.

disappear from within the Jewish people. Graetz's treatment of history is primarily biographical. He attempted to interpret events by probing the actions and attitudes of individual leaders. Moreover, Baron suggests that he preferred to present characters congenial to his own personality. He was a rationalist and focused upon Jewish personalities of intellectual ability. Finally, while he was the first Jewish historian to use a long array of modern and ancient sources for resolving historical problems, setting his history on a solid foundation, he stressed sources which told the story of Jewish suffering and scholars. The introduction to Volume V of his *Geschichte* speaks of his history as the "history of persecutions and scholarship",[1] and in fact this becomes the dominant motif for his history.

The "inner spiritual evolution" gives impetus to the rabbis to fix the traditions and order the great mass of Talmudic material. Mid-fourth century Jewish leaders realized the eternal character of the Jewish people. In response to general unrest in the world the leaders felt the need to bring together the traditions of the past so that they might be preserved for future generations sure to survive whatever tragedy the immediate present might bring.[2]

We are immediately upon the heart of the problem in Graetz's methodology: the imposition of general theory upon non-existant historical facts. There is simply no direct evidence that the Arab (Tai) invasion of 309-325 or the internal policies of Shapur II or the Persian-Roman confrontation, or, more generally, the collapse of the Roman Empire, seriously altered Jewish life in mid-fourth century Babylonia. With the exception of the invasion of 363 the Jewish community was not appreciably effected by internal or external events. More important, Jews were not singled out for persecution and after 363 a situation of peace prevailed. Talmudic accounts of persecution must be measured against the realities of the actual events, an exercise which Graetz fails to do. He relies solely upon, and accepts uncritically, whatever Talmudic evidence is available.

Rav Ashi (d. 427) represented this new tendency for compilation and arrangement. With power concentrated in his hand in the academy at Sura, which he restored to the status it had enjoyed in the time of Rav, R. Ashi began the process of "collecting and arranging the explanations, deductions and amplifications of the Mishnah which were

---

[1] *Ibid.*, p. 273.

[2] H. Graetz, *History of the Jews*, Volume II, p. 605.

included in the name 'Talmud'."[1] Graetz repeats the familiar account of the semi-annual *Kallot* where selected tractates of the Mishnah were discussed together with corollaries which had been excluded from Judah the Prince's Mishnah and explanations offered in the first generations of the Amoraim. Rav Ashi's fifty-two years in office permitted the double review of each tractate. The net result: "What remained after the double process of winnowing and testing was accepted as of binding force."[2]

Graetz accepts the parallel drawn in the Talmud between Judah the Prince and Rav Ashi. In addition to the similarities in their careers (wealth, position of authority, status as scholar), they engaged in similar types of activity: compiling the mass of laws and traditions, sifting and ordering them into a body of material which became the cornerstone for future generations. However, he regards R. Ashi as the greater of the two, a creative scholar—as were others in his generation—who, in addition to the achievement of compilation, resolved unanswered questions and doubtful conclusions.

While Graetz follows Talmudic sources in viewing R. Ashi as the principal editor of the Talmud, he also respects the Geonic tradition that the work of redaction continued after R. Ashi until the death of Rabina. Here he reintroduces his persecution theme, suggesting that the total effort of R. Ashi's successors was to complete the Talmud, fixing it as a full and complete body of tradition, immune to "the approaching storm". Of R. Ashi's son (Mar bar R. Ashi) and his contemporaries, he says: "[They] felt themselves all the more impelled to complete the work of compilation as the persecution they had gone through made them feel that the future was precarious."[3] Similarly when the academies were reopened under Rabina and R. Yosi toward the end of the fifth century following Peroz's death, Graetz reminds us that they had one purpose: to complete the work begun by Ashi. Graetz accepts the date of 499 suggested by Rav Sherira for the death of Rabina with Yosi continuing until 520. Graetz also acknowledges that although the term *sof hora'ah* (end of instruction) is assigned to Rabina and Yosi, the Amoraic period extends to the members of their academies.[4]

Graetz draws the sharp line between Amoraic activity and the work

[1] *Ibid.*, p. 607.
[2] *Ibid.*, p. 608.
[3] *Ibid.*, p. 628.
[4] *Ibid.*, p. 631.

of the Saboraim. The latter were not originators. They limited themselves, Graetz suggests, to reviewing various opinions (*sabora*), establishing final, valid laws in order to make the Talmud available for practical use as a law book. They removed remaining doubts and uncertainties and established fixed rules for legal and religious practices. The Saboraim also committed the Talmud to writing.

One immediately suspects any account which links the development of the Talmud so closely to *anticipated* persecutions of the Jewish community. At the same time, Graetz's account raises three specific questions which other historians have attempted to deal with:

1. Is it probable that there was no significant redactional activity between the time of Judah the Prince and R. Ashi? While this corresponds to the Talmudic account itself, one immediately points to the other Mishnah-collections which were available to Judah when he ordered his work. Personality portraits make it easy to write history, but history is not simply a series of brilliant, creative, isolated geniuses.

2. Graetz does not reconcile the Geonic tradition that has R. Ashi and Rabina as *sof hora'ah* (end of instruction) with his admission that considerable redactional activity was carried on for seventy years after R. Ashi's death.

3. Finally, the line drawn between Saboraim and Amoraim is highly artificial. The work of the Saboraim described by Graetz is far from ordinary. Moreover, contemporaries of Rabina bar R. Huna, the last of the Amoraim, are considered Saboraim, though their main work was accomplished during the lifetime of Rabina before the close of Talmud.[1]

ii

Ze'ev Jawitz's concept of history is described as "a purely theological one, ... based entirely on tradition".[2] He was an Orthodox Jew, a Zionist, and a severe critic of the Jewish Enlightenment. His education and his life efforts—like his history—were limited to the resources of Jewish tradition.

Before settling into his life work in 1871 as an historian, he distinguished himself as a Hebrew author and religious Zionist. Born in Kolno, Poland, in 1848, he emigrated to Palestine at the age of 20 where he served as Rabbi, author, publisher and an advocate of

[1] J. Kaplan, *The Redaction of the Babylonian Talmud.*
[2] "Zeeb Wolfe Jawitz", *Universal Jewish Encyclopedia*, Vol. VI, p. 48.

modern Hebrew language and culture. He returned to Vilna in 1898 where he founded the *Mizraḥi* wing of Zionism and began to work on historical studies and his *magnum opus*, *Sefer Toledot Yisra'el*, a ten-volume history. He lived intermittently in several central and western European capital cities. He wrote readers and textbooks for children, a liturgical work, and descriptions of life in Palestine. He died in 1924.

Ze'ev Jawitz follows the general scheme for the redaction of the Talmud set forth by Y. I. Halevy (below). The Talmud represents a continuous process of development beginning around the time of the completion of Judah the Prince's Mishnah, reaching a major peak in the generation of Rava and Abaye and an almost final conclusion in the time of Rav Ashi and Rabina II. The entire Saboraic period—even allowing for a clear distinction between the more active first generation and the work of the later generations which is of secondary importance—is a period of little or no creative effort.

The first period begins with the ordering of *Mishnayot* omitted from Judah the Prince's collection into an order corresponding to the sections of the Mishnah. The first Amoraim sifted through and evaluated these extra *Mishnayot*, retaining those which served to explain the Mishnah and to resolve its contradictions.[1] These extra-Mishnaic sources became the "corner stone" of the Talmud and the model for its legal decisions.[2] This activity was pursued in Palestine and in Babylonia, where the first generations of Babylonian Amoraim added their solutions to problems, answers to contemporary questions and other new materials to the Talmud. This process reached a first peak in the generation of Abaye and Rava at Pumbedita. These men and their schools edited oral traditions, clarifying them and arranging them into their final form, placed contradictory oral traditions (*Qushiyot*) together, discussing them and resolving them where possible.[3]

Jawitz pays special attention to Rav Naḥman bar Yiẓḥaq. Naḥman had a particular sense for setting discussions in proper order and for bringing to the text mnemonic devices. Jawitz also singles out the effort of Rav Ḥama, who succeeded Rav Naḥman and eventually led the academy at Nehardea. Rav Ḥama excelled at arranging and fixing the body of the argument and arriving at final decisions. Thus during this early period the basic outline of the Talmud is fixed. Jawitz, with

---

[1] Z. Jawitz, *Sefer Toledot Yisra'el*, Vol. VII, p. 150.

[2] *Ibid.*, p. 153.

[3] *Ibid.*, p. 161.

Halevy, refers to this period as "the day of the beginning of the order of the Talmud".[1]

As noted, Jawitz cites Halevy and follows him in attributing considerable activity to the generations proceeding Rav Ashi. The arguments for this early redactional activity are based on internal analysis of the *Sugyot* or pericopae. Following the traditional sources, Rav Ashi is seen as the major redactor of the Talmud. His colleagues delegated to him the responsibility to "seal" (*ḥtm*) the Talmud, "adding to it whatever there was to add; clarifying whatever needed to be clarified".[2] They constituted what is called a "consistery", and each brought before R. Ashi his oral tradition and opinions. In what appears as a totally democratic process, R. Ashi and his colleagues selected materials to be added to the gemara. Here again Jawitz turns to Halevy for support; he does not feel constrained to buttress Halevy and the traditional sources with fresh evidence.

Jawitz, perhaps more than Halevy, underscores the continuous nature of the redaction-process and the importance of the third and fourth generations of Amoraim. Thus, while R. Ashi is recognized as the final major redactor of the Talmud, his work was seen as a direct continuation of the effort of Abaye and Raba. It is misleading, Jawitz insists, to consider them as separate groups:

> The work of completing the Talmud undertaken by Rav Ashi and Rabina is nothing more than an additional ordering; Abaye and Rav and their colleagues fixed the order of the Talmud ... they were connected strands in one extended and continuous chain.[3]

As proof for this thesis he cites a Geonic source which states that whatever was not attributed to Abaye and Raba or the Amoraim who followed them may be credited to R. Ashi and his colleague, Rabina II. Jawitz concludes from this that the Geonim considered their work as a single effort.[4]

Jawitz also stresses the way in which unordered Amoraic traditions from Palestine were incorporated into the Babylonian discussions.[5] Here he joins Halevy and other pietistic historians in affirming the superior quality and authority of the Babylonian Talmud. Everything good in the Palestinian Talmud was brought from Palestine by the

---

[1] *Ibid.*, p. 162.
[2] *Ibid.*, p. 163.
[3] *Ibid.*, p. 165.
[4] *Ibid.*, p. 165, footnote 2.
[5] *Ibid.*, p. 165.

scholars fleeing persecution, and incorporated into the Babylonian one. The proof for this assertion is rooted in the history of the period. The Roman persecution, particularly after Constantine, so "darkened their situation" that they were unable to convene meetings to explain and order Talmudic materials. Thus the Palestinian Talmud remains an unfinished, unordered literature.[1]

The activity of those who followed Rav Ashi was more limited in scope. They concentrated in weighing the opinions of various generations and determining the law.[2] The generation of Rav Ashi closes with the death in 474 of Rabina II (bar R. Huna). Here Jawitz follows Halevy who considers Rav Sherira's date of 500 for the death of Rabina II a scribal error. He accepts Halevy's resolution of R. Sherira's apparent contradiction: R. Ashi and Ravina I mentioned in b. B.B. 86a are understood as the "*generation* of R. Ashi and Ravina I is *sof hora'ah*" while Rabina II is the "last redactor of the Babylonian Talmud", as indicated in Rav Sherira's statements that identify him as *sof hora'ah*.

Jawitz also follows Halevy in minimizing the contribution of the Saboraim. In a moving description he compares the development of Torah to the seasons of the year: Spring brings the creative prophetic spirit: the birth of Torah. In the summer season the Tannaim and Amoraim care for fruit of Torah and cause it to ripen. The Saboraim are the harvesters, gathering all the fruit grown by previous generations into storehouses to be guarded and sustained during the dark winter days ahead.[3] Thus the Saboraim once again examined the structure of the Talmud, but added very little of importance. Graetz limits the Saboraic period to between 40 and 68 years, following Rav Sherira's statement that most of the Saboraim died within a relatively short period of time. However, Jawitz distinguishes four generations of Saboraic activity, extending approximately 115 years from the death of Rabina II in 474 to the time of the first *gaon*, Rav Ḥanan ben Askai in 589. He suggests that Graetz and others who define a short period for Saboraic activity were misled by focusing exclusively on the first generation.[4]

Jawitz discusses at length the transition from the Amoraic to the Saboraic period. A major tension—never resolved—is created by his

---

[1] *Ibid.*, p. 164.
[2] *Ibid.*, p. 146.
[3] *Ibid.*, p. 146.
[4] Jawitz, *op. cit.*, Volume IX, p. 214.

maintaining a sharp distinction between Amoraic activity, ending with Rabina, and Saboraic activity, beginning with R. Yosi,[1] while pointing to the obvious fact that the first Saboraim lived during the time of the last Amoraim and participated in their discussions. Thus he maintains the validity of Geonic sources which identify R. Yosi as the first of the Saboraim, explaining that when Sherira says of R. Yosi, *beyomo sof hora'ah* (in his day was the end of instruction), he means that Yosi engaged in creative redactional activity until Rabina II's death. Jawitz maintains that the statement only means to buttress R. Yosi's importance: a highly forced, unwarranted conclusion. This permits Jawitz to maintain that the activity of the first generation of Saboraim was limited to explaining insignificant matters, issues unresolved by the last generation of Amoraim.

The obvious problem in this reconstruction of the redaction-process is the historian's inability to bring new understanding to the Saboraic period, particularly the transition period after the death of Rabina II. An adequate definition of *Sebara* has not been presented. Jawitz attempts to force a firm and artificial distinction upon a process which must have been gradual. His reading of Talmudic and Geonic sources is arbitrary and highly subjective. This failure is particularly striking in light of what may be his most original and sound suggestion: namely the positing of a continuous process of redaction in the Amoraic period, with notable peaks or turning points in the generations of Raba and Abaye and R. Ashi.

[1] *Ibid.*, p. 7.

II

I. H. WEISS AND J. S. ZURI

BY

SHAMAI KANTER

Isaac Hirsch Weiss and Jacob Samuel Zuri represent, in their lives and work, the geographical and intellectual movement from East to West characteristic of a century of Jewish scholarship. Both men received intensive grounding in traditional methods of the study of Talmud from their native *Yeshivot* and later acquired the scholarly techniques used in the European universities, for application to the materials they had come to know so thoroughly. In the case of Weiss, it was the application of late nineteenth-century historical studies to the history of the Talmud; for Zuri, it was the use of early twentieth-century sociology and comparative law.

i

Isaac Hirsch Weiss (1815-1905) was born in Gross Meseritch, Moravia, and received his elementary Jewish education and traditional rabbinical Talmudic training in various *Yeshivot* in Moravia and Hungary. Since Moravia fell within the orbit of German cultural influence, the German language provided access to contemporary secular culture as well. Weiss' secular studies were carried on through private tutoring and reading. Though he had prepared himself at one point for entrance into the University of Eisenstadt, Hungary, he decided against it. While still in Moravia, Weiss published a number of Talmudic studies, and contributed to Hebrew periodicals in the fields of poetry and biography.

In 1858, Weiss settled in Vienna, first working for a publishing house and then, in 1864, receiving an appointment as lecturer in the Bet HaMidrash founded by Adolph Jellinek, a position he was to hold for over forty years. In his new post, Weiss had opportunity for more sustained literary activity. His works include, besides pamphlets and essays in periodicals, critical editions of the Talmud, Sifra and Mekhilta, and a volume on the language of the Mishnah, *Mishpat Leshon HaMishnah* (1867).

Weiss' *magnum opus*, *The History of Jewish Tradition* (*Zur Geschichte der jüdischen Tradition*, Hebrew title: *Dor Dor VeDorshav*) was published in five volumes over the twenty year period, 1871-1891. It is a history of Jewish oral tradition, primarily focused on *halakhah* (law) but including *aggadah* (lore), from the time of the Pentateuch to the *Shulḥan 'Arukh*, Joseph Karo's sixteenth-century legal codification of Talmudic Law.

A strong *tendenz* is evident in *The History of Jewish Tradition.* The work reflects the nineteenth-century battle over the application of evolutionary ideas to Jewish history. It also both participates in, and defends against, the nineteenth-century rationalist critique of rabbinical legends and logic. Weiss stresses the evolutionary character of the *halakhah*, and lauds those authorities of "independent, critical, scientific spirit" who responded to the challenges of their age with new contributions and new institutions, within the general pattern of the Law. He heavily emphasizes that this development never ceased, and that early scholars never viewed their work as establishing an unchanging, eternal form. He is severely critical (as were some of his own teachers) of *pilpul*, an exhibitionist dialectics which could create either difficulty or harmony where it did not exist in the text of the Talmud or its commentaries. Yet though Weiss adopted an evolutionary view of the Oral Tradition, he assumed the unity and Mosaic authorship of the Pentateuch. He held that since the latter was accompanied from its birth by unwritten laws and interpretations, contradictions between the Pentateuch and later Biblical books are evidence of varying interpretations of the law in later generations.

Weiss' work thus drew fire from scholars like Abraham Geiger for being too traditional and uncritical. He was also condemned by Orthodox groups as heretical. One individual even purchased the original plates of an earlier compendium of Jewish ritual laws, by Weiss, so that he could have them destroyed![1] Nevertheless, the centrality of his achievement within Talmudic scholarship was soon attested to by the *Jewish Encyclopedia*: "The work (was) adopted by the majority of Talmudic Scholars as the standard history of the oral law".[2] *The History of Jewish Tradition* stimulated the composition of a number of works in reply, among them Isaac Halevy's *Dorot HaRishonim*.

---

[1] L. Ginzberg, *Students, Scholars and Saints*, p. 226.

[2] Vol. XII, p. 497.

The problem of the redaction of the Babylonian Talmud occupies but a small part of the scope of Weiss' *History*. The author basically accepts the Geonic tradition of Rav Ashi's editorship, while explaining or harmonizing the minor contradictions of that tradition. He is more concerned with establishing such points as these: that Rav Ashi's role in history was similar to that of Rabbi Judah the Prince, since both sifted a vast traditional lore in order to preserve its most valuable parts; or, that the oral law was indeed reduced to writing by Rav Ashi, on the basis of earlier written materials (here Weiss counters the prestigious view of Rashi); or, that later rabbinical generations continued contributing to the developing legal tradition. Nevertheless, Weiss does submit the Geonic tradition to scrutiny along the way of his narration, and offers some internal Talmudic evidence to support his views.

As Weiss narrates the story[1], the time of the Persian King Yazdagird II (d. 420) and the Exilarch Huna bar Nathan was externally peaceful for the Jewish community. But a crisis for scholarship existed, implicit in the very success of the various academies. They had been teaching and discussing the Mishnah of Rabbi Judah the Prince over the previous two centuries. Comment and interpretation had flourished; every academy had, in effect, its own Talmud. It was imperative that someone stabilize the great mass of knowledge which had accumulated, someone who would not only preserve, but who, like Rabbi Judah, would select the valuable material from that which could be allowed to slip into oblivion. The man was Rav Ashi bar Shimi, who like Rabbi Judah combined "Torah and worldly greatness within one person" (b. Git. 59a)[2].

Rav Ashi, Weiss continues, rebuilt the school at Sura with his own funds and under his own supervision. It was not merely a place of instruction for students, but a center where scholars could engage in the great work of collation and redaction which the times demanded. Rav Ashi's complaint about the lessening powers of memory in his generation (as noted by N. Brüll) recorded on b. ʿEruv. 53a, is not to be explained by any lessening of intellectual ability. It was rather his comment on the "explosion of knowledge" which necessitated such a work of editorship.[3]

There is no clear statement of Rav Ashi's editorship in the Talmud;

[1] I. H. Weiss, *Zur Geschichte der jüdischen Tradition*, Vol. IV, pp. 183-190.
[2] *Ibid.*, pp. 185-186, following ESG and b. B.B. 3b.
[3] *Ibid.*, p. 185, note 7.

however, there are two "clear hints". First, there is the *aggadic* passage (b. B.M. 86a) which draws the parallel between "Rabbi [Judah] and Rabbi Nathan conclude the Mishnah" and "Rav Ashi and Ravina conclude [authentic] teaching (*hora'ah*)." This "poetic expression" tells us that Rav Ashi brought the Amoraic period to a close by editing the Talmud, just as Rabbi Judah completed the age of the Tannaim with his Mishnah. The tradition of his editorship was preserved in the records of the Geonim.[1]

The second "hint" lies in a passage in b. B.B. 157b:

> Ravina said: In the first version, R. Ashi told us (that) the first (creditor) acquired (the right over the land); the second version of R. Ashi (however) told us (that the land was) to be divided.

Ravina refers to two "versions" or "editions" (*mahadura'*) of Rav Ashi's teaching on a question of property rights. Rabbi Judah the Prince edited his Mishnah in two such revisions; Rabbi Yosi edited the Jerusalem Talmud in the same way.

Weiss also cites two kinds of evidence, internal to the Talmud, reflecting the editorial function of Rav Ashi. First, there are "many places" (two examples being cited) where an Amoraic discussion is interrupted by a parenthetical explanatory comment in Rav Ashi's name, and then resumes—a clear indication of the editorial process[2]:

> And how do you know that if two are sitting and studying the Torah together the Divine presence is with them? For it is said: *Then they that feared the Lord spoke with one another; and the Lord hearkened and heard, and a book of remembrance was written before Him, for them that feared the Lord and thought upon His name* (Mal. 3:16). (What does it mean: '*And thought upon His name*'? R. Ashi says: If a man thought to fulfill a commandment, and he did not do it because he was prevented by force or accident, then Scripture credits it to him as if he had performed it.) And how do you know that if even one man sits and studies the Torah the Divine Presence is with him? ...
>
> (b. Ber. 6a)

> R. Isaac said: Just as a vessel may not be placed under a fowl to receive her eggs, so may a vessel not be overturned upon (the egg) that it should not be broken. He holds that a vessel may be handled only for the sake of that which itself may be handled on the Sabbath. All of the foregoing objections were raised; and he answered, it means that its place is required ...
>
> Come and hear: one may spread mats over bee-hives on the Sabbath;

[1] *Ibid.*, p. 186.
[2] *Ibid.*, p. 186, note 8.

in the sun on account of the sun and in the rain on account of the rain, providing he has no intention of capturing (the bees)? The circumstances are that they contain honey.

(Said R. ʿUqba of Mesene to R. Ashi: That is correct of summer when there is honey; but what can be said of winter, when it does not contain honey? It is in respect of two loaves. But they are muqẓeh? It means that he designated them? It is forbidden! ... R. Ashi said: Is it then taught, 'in summer' and 'in winter'? Surely it is stated, 'in the sun because of the sun and in the rain because of rain'. (That means in the days of Nisan and Tishri, when there is sun, rain and honey.)

R. Shesheth said to them (his disciples): Go forth and tell R. Isaac, R. Huna has already stated your ruling in Babylonia.

(b. Shab. 43a-b)

In the latter passage, from b. Shab. 43, the exchange between R. ʿUqba of Mesene and Rav Ashi is a digression. It explains the specific choice of language of the *beraita* quoted as an objection to R. Isaac. The passage continues directly with R. Shesheth's statement to his disciples. Thus one can see that the comments of R. ʿUqba to Ashi were added to the previously formed *sugya'* (pericope).

As his second type of internal evidence Weiss presents the great number of discussions which culminate either in (a) a decision by Rav Ashi, or in (b) his declaration, "The question stands (*teiqu*)" or "This is a difficulty (*qushya'*)":

(a) Our Rabbis taught: The night has four watches. These are the words of Rabbi. R. Nathan says: Three ... And R. Nathan? He is of the opinion of R. Joshua, as we have learned: R. Joshua says: Until the third hour, for such is the custom of kings, to rise in the third hour. Six hours of the night and two hours of the day amount to two watches. R. Ashi says: One watch and a half are also spoken of as 'watches'. (b. Ber. 3b)

(b) Abaye said: He must utter his thanksgiving in the presence of ten, as it is written: *Let them exalt Him in the assembly of the people* (Ps. 107: 32). Mar Zutra said: And two of them must be rabbis, as it says, *And praise Him in the seat of the elders*. R. Ashi demurred to this: You might as well say (he remarked) that all should be rabbis! Is it written 'in the assembly of the elders'? It is written, 'in the assembly of the people'! Let us say then, in the presence of ten ordinary people and two rabbis (in addition)?—This is a difficulty. (b. Ber. 54b)

This also indicates editorial activity on the part of Rav Ashi: "Anyone who looks at the *sugyot* of the Talmud with a discerning eye will recognize this almost immediately."[1]

[1] *Ibid.*, p. 186, note 7.

On reviewing this evidence, one question must first be decided: Does an editor include statements in his own name, or does he include his own decisions anonymously? Julius Kaplan[1] notes a contradiction in Weiss' approach to this question. When discussing Rabbi Judah the Prince and the Mishnah, Weiss objects to the idea that an editor would include material in his own name. Therefore he calls every quotation in the name of Rabbi Judah an interpolation by another person. On the other hand, Weiss makes no such objection to statements in Rav Ashi's name; he assumes them to indicate Rav Ashi's own work, though one might argue a later editorship, on the same grounds.

Let us re-examine the four points raised by Weiss in order. The passage in b. B.M. 86a about the end of instruction presents more of a problem than a solution. One must presuppose Rav Ashi's editorship in order to derive support from it. Like the Geonic tradition, it does indicate that an important peak of authority was reached with him, but its nature is unclear.

Unclear too is the meaning of the passage in b. B.B. 157b mentioning the two "versions" or "editions" by Rav Ashi. It can refer to the revision of his own decisions and teachings. It can refer to a more extensive ordering and editing of halakhic material by him. But certainly the fact that it is mentioned by Ravina in a discussion of a point of law implies that the final form of *that sugya'* was edited by someone later than Ravina. It can be argued, on the one hand, that this passage alone reflects a later editing while pointing to the bulk of the Talmud as Rav Ashi's work. But it can equally well be argued that Rav Ashi's work was *not* the final form of the Talmud. Once again we are thrown back upon the reliability of Geonic tradition.

Similar reasoning can be applied to the passages cited by Weiss in which a parenthetical comment involving Rav Ashi interrupts the flow of the Amoraic discussion. Weiss understands this as the editorial work of Rav Ashi; but it can be interpreted as the work of a subsequent generation, incorporating material from his school.

More convincing, however, is the second type of evidence indicated by Weiss. The decisions rendered, in some cases in opposition to previous authorities,[2] and especially the numerous questions culminating in *qushya'*, "it is a difficulty", or *teiqu*, "the question stands", do point to significant redactional activity by Rav Ashi. They would

[1] J. Kaplan, *The Redaction of the Babylonian Talmud*, p. 15.
[2] Weiss, *Zur Geschichte*, p. 185, note 6.

indicate an effort by him to resolve a large number of questions previously left unresolved. In view of the fact that the rabbis who followed him, as heads of the academy at Sura, contributed far less altogether to the Talmud than did he, it is not unreasonable to infer some motive of completion of the work of previous generations on his part, at least as a decisor. The question of "final redaction" must remain open, and it remains open to some degree, even in Weiss' own account.

In his discussion of the sources of the Talmud[1], Weiss emphasezis that the editing and arrangement of the Talmud was based on written, not oral sources. Though Rashi, in his comment on the reference to the *Megillat Taʿanit*, the Scroll of Fast Days (b. ʿEruv 62b) declares: "No word of *halakhah* was written down, not even one letter", this view is based only upon a pious acceptance of statements in b. Git. 60b and b. Tem. 14b that the oral tradition was not to be submitted to writing:

> (Concerning Ex. 34:27, *Write thou these words*) A Tanna of the School of R. Ishmael taught: (It is written) *These*, thou mayest write, but thou mayest not write *halakhot*.
>
> (b. Git. 60b)

> And the Tanna of the School of R. Ishmael taught: Scripture says, *Write thou these words*, implying that *these* words you may write but you may not write *halakhot*.
>
> (b. Tem. 14b)

In addition to pointing out the simple impossibility for anyone to commit to memory the totality of rabbinical tradition, both *halakhah* and *aggadah*, Weiss cites the Geonim and many Spanish and German scholars, all of whom disagree with Rashi on this point. More important, the Talmud itself (b. Shab. 6b, b. Sanh. 57b, b. Yev. 21b) makes reference to scrolls containing compilations of laws from the schools of Rav Ḥiyya and of Rav. Weiss' quotation from Rabbenu Nissim b. Jacob of Kairwan (11th c.) sums up the Geonic view: "(Rav Ashi) and the sages of his generation decided to write the explanation of the Mishnah, ... but those who wrote it down, cite it orally." Further, asks Weiss, how can one think of an "edition" (b. B.B. 157b) except in written form?[2]

Returning to Weiss' narration: the revitalized Sura academy became the leading center of learning under Rav Ashi's direction. The yearly gathering honoring the Exilarch was moved there from its previous

[1] *Ibid.*, pp. 215-220.
[2] *Ibid.*, p. 185, note 5.

locations in Nehardea and Pumbedita. The *Kallah* month gatherings attracted large crowds once again. While previously these months of Adar and Ellul had been used to instruct students in holiday laws, Rav Ashi shifted their purpose to the public teaching of the tractates which had been carefully edited during the previous months. Thus his editorial schedule was to complete two tractates per year, with the projected editing and revision to take thirty years. Rav Ashi almost accomplished this goal.

From here on, one might describe the author's purpose to be as much exegetical as historical. If we accept Rav Ashi's editorship, based on the Epistle of Rav Sherira Gaon (= ESG), how then do we interpret other equally reliable statements there? Ravina is also called "the end of (authentic) teaching." And further, ESG states: "Rav Yosi was the first of the Rabbanan Saborai, the end of (authentic) teaching, and in his days the Talmud was completed (*nistayyem*)."

The explanation, in Weiss' rather opaque account, is as follows[1]: Rav Ashi indeed composed and edited the Talmud, completing one edition and almost completing the second edition before his death. A succession of undistinguished leaders of the academy of Sura continued his work, adding material of Rav Ashi's, of Ravina II, his student and colleague, and of their own generation. This succession, which included Mar, son of Rav Ashi, culminated in the leadership of Rabbah Tosfa'ah, colleague of Ravina bar Huna (or Ravina III, as implied by Weiss). (He does not accept the possibility that the Ravina who died fifteen years after Rabbah Tosfa'ah, 68 years after Rav Ashi, was also the student-colleague of Rav Ashi.[2])

After the death of Ravina bar Huna, who can thus be described as the last Amora, in whose days the Talmud was "completed" (*nishlam*, i.e., made whole in the sense of completing Rav Ashi's master plan) Rav Yosi and the Rabbanan Saborai "completed" (*siyyemu*) the Talmud in the sense of making corrections in the text, and adding some of their own discussions, not to mention possibly some of the materials Rav Ashi had seen fit to omit. Rav Yosi and his generation agreed that no more material would be added to the Talmud; hence their successors would not be "Amoraim", interpreters of the Mishnah, but rather "Saboraim", explainers of the Talmud.

Nevertheless, Weiss is quick to add, though the Talmud as an entity was complete, this does not imply that it represented in any way a

[1] *Ibid.*, pp. 187-188.
[2] *Ibid.*, p. 187, note 9, and p. 189, note 12.

fixed or final form of the process of the legal tradition. The process of discussion and decision by authorities of each generation was to continue; the concept of the Talmud as final and total authority was to be a dogma imposed by a later generation. Weiss' reconstruction of the history of the redaction of the Talmud rests securely in the framework of Geonic tradition. Talmudic evidence adduced is comparatively slight, and comes as illustration rather than as proof. In some instances, Weiss' narration of the details of the story is completely conjectural (for example, that Rav Ashi rebuilt the academy at Sura with his own funds is unwarranted by our sources, which merely state that he had the *synagogue* at Sura rebuilt, and that he supervised the construction). He also uses a concept like "the needs of the times" to explain historical events, something tautological at best.

Yet it must be re-emphasized, as stated earlier, that Weiss' treatment of this question represents only a few pages of his complete work, whose purpose was to chart the total development of rabbinical tradition. It must be seen in that perspective. The view of J. S. Zuri, though similar in conclusions to Weiss, is based upon a more extensive marshalling of literary evidence, in order to reveal the hand of the Editor at work.

ii

Jacob S. Zuri (Szezak [1884-1943]) received a traditional yeshivah education in Poland, country of his birth, and pursued higher studies in Germany and France, in the fields of sociology, history and law. Though he lived in Palestine for two periods of his life, Zuri's work in comparative law led him to spend most of his mature working years in Paris and London.

Samuel Landman's short biographical essay on Zuri[1] notes a single, continuing purpose to the thirty-one scholarly works Zuri published.[2] Zuri keenly felt the absence of an appreciation of the basic principles of Jewish law in the scholarship of Europe, which abounded in studies of Greek, Roman and even Islamic law. He wanted to present a full understanding of the underlying structure of Talmudic law, and to show its value as a product of human civilization. This apologetic

[1] Samuel Landman, "Jacob Samuel Zuri", *Mezuda*, Vol. 2, reprinted in J. S. Zuri, *Hypotheka*, pp. 1-5.

[2] A bibliography was prepared by M. Sanders, in J. S. Zuri, *Hypotheka* (London, 1944).

purpose, shared with much of the scholarship of the Jewish Enlightenment, might seem to be contravened by his choice to publish all of his works in Hebrew, especially since Zuri controlled both the French and German languages. But here another purpose was at work. As a Zionist, Zuri hoped that his studies in Jewish law would help to lay the foundation of legal principles for the system of legislation of the Jewish state which he felt was sure to come.

Zuri's description of the redaction of the Talmud is found in his biography of Rav Ashi, to whom that redaction is credited. His approach to the problem is more directly connected with the total scope of his work in biography and history, rather than what we have seen to be the case with Weiss. Indeed, the acceptance of his analysis would seem to imply an acceptance of his more inclusive views.

In the biography entitled *Rav* and in a number of Talmudic studies, among them *Mishpat HaTalmud* (Talmudic Law), *Torat HaDeromim* (The *Torah* of the Southerners), and *Toledot Darkhei HaLimud* (The History of Methods of Learning), Zuri draws a comprehensive picture of two "main currents of rabbinical thought" permeating all halakhic literature. Zuri distinguishes between thought-patterns of the scholars of Judea ("the South") and of Galilee ("the north"), characteristic methods of thinking which were transmitted to the Babylonian schools of Sura and Nehardea-Pumbedita, respectively.[1] Southern (Suran) thinking tends to have a greater affinity for general, abstract ideas. It analyzes problems by searching out the underlying unity beneath surface differences. When it compares the differences between individual cases, it does so in terms of general categories, or types. In the discussion of a Mishnah, the Southern scholar will seek to relate the view of an anonymous Mishnah to the total view of some Tannaitic authority, or to some abstract principle. The great work of Rav, according to Zuri, was the development of this approach to its fullest, bringing out all the abstract principles implicit in the Mishnah. Northern (Nehardean-Pumbeditan) thinking represents a reverse intellectual style. It relates itself to the specific characteristics of the cases under discussion, and tends to see fine individual differences. Where there is a difference of viewpoints in the Mishnah, it would seek an explanation in the different circumstances of two individual cases rather than in an underlying difference of principle.

In short, Zuri describes the "Northern" scholars as the "nominalists"

---

[1] Zuri, *Rav Ashi*, pp. 94-95.

of rabbinical thought, while the "Southerners" are its "realists". He claims that it is especially characteristic of Rav Ashi to analyze the Mishnah in the "Northern" manner, on the basis of fine distinctions of language or of cases. Therefore he is able to assign many anonymous passages of the Talmud to Rav Ashi's composition, on the grounds of style.

As Zuri narrates the story of the formation of the Talmud, it is a process of gradual differentiation and diffusion through the increasing number of academies. Different kinds of Amoraic material can be distinguished. There are discrete Amoraic statements, unrelated to the Mishnah. There are Amoraic teachings about the Mishnah, some anonymous and some in the names of individual rabbis.

Certainly by the time of Rav Ashi we have evidence that the Mishnah and its Amoraic explanations and debates were taught together:

> R. Aḥa son of Rava said to R. Ashi: Shall we say that (in the *beraita* under discussion) we have a refutation of R. Yoḥanan's view? ... (Reply:)—Was it not also reported thereon that R. Zera said, etc.
>
> (b. Men. 48a)

> Said Ravina to Rav Ashi: Are the words '*In the morning, in the morning*, in connection with the wood (of the altar) at all superfluous? Surely they are really necessary for their text meaning, the Divine Law saying that they should precede the second pile for the incense? He replied: Have we not explained, etc.
>
> (b. Yoma 33b)

The recurring phrases, "Was it not reported (*velav 'itmar 'alah*)?" and "Have we not explained (*velav mai 'oqimna' 'alei*)?" indicate that these explanations of the Mishnah had achieved a definite form by then.

At Sura and Nehardea, the teachings of Rav had been discussed by Samuel, and vice versa. The teachings of both academies were thus taught to the students of each: these formed the Talmudic nucleus. Rava and Abaye taught similarly. But nevertheless the growing collections of Amoraic teachings were not comprehensive, and were still "primitive" in their arrangement.

First to attempt some kind of comprehensive collection were the sages of Pumbedita.[1] A number of passages (b. Pes. 104a, b. A.Z. 38a, b. B.B. 86a) refer to the differences in versions of of the same teaching reported by Sura and Pumbedita. But the following passage indicates that the latter sages made an attempt to collect the teachings of Sura in addition to their own:

[1] *Ibid.*, p. 29.

> It has been stated: The School of Rav said in the name of Rav: (The number of processes is) two and three; but Samuel maintained that it is three and four. Thus they taught in Sura, but in Pumbedita they taught: the school of Rav said in the name of Rav, etc.
>
> (b. A.Z. 75a)

As the corpus of knowledge grew, it became necessary to arrange a conference of representatives of all the academic traditions, in order to cut down the conflicting variants, in traditions and in terminologies, of the many academies.

The great principles underlying the Mishnah had been worked out by the School of Rav. Now the situation required the work of careful analysis to bring order into the textual confusion. And so Rav Ashi assembled scholars at the academy at Sura to settle on the correct texts and to order them. He had been interested in this even while a student of Rav Kahana:

> Said R. Ashi: I repeated this discussion before R. Kahana, whereupon he observed to me: Let this apply where (the debtor) believes (the creditor that the pledge has been lost).
>
> (b. B.M. 35a, and similarly b. Shev. 4a, b. Suk. 19a)

Zuri credits Rav Ashi with this single purpose throughout his career as student and scholar. He notes evidence of similar activity in Pumbedita during the office of the last Rav Kahana (385-414), and asks whether the latter might have actually competed with Rav Ashi (whose office lasted from 372-427) in this respect.[1] Because of Rav Ashi's lengthy life, he was able to revise all the tractates during the yearly *Kallah* months, the time when his academic conference was in session. Zuri agrees with Weiss on the meaning of the "two editions" of Rav Ashi, mentioned on b. B.B. 157b.

Whereas Weiss only briefly indicates the prior development up to Rav Ashi, and goes into great detail about the additions made to the Talmud by the following generations, Zuri, who gives a more extensive discussion of the teachings of the schools before Rav Ashi, mentions later developments hardly at all.

In Zuri's view, Rav Ashi's work as editor is characterized by:

1. The attempt to attribute names correctly to Amoraic teachings:

> Mar Qashisha, son of R. Ḥisda, said to R. Ashi: It has been expressly stated in the name of R. Yoḥanan that ... He said to him: Did I not say

[1] *Ibid.*, p. 32.

to you that you should not transpose the names of scholars? That statement was made in the name of R. ʾElai.
(b. B.Q. 96b)

2. The bringing together and joining of relevant passages: Zuri stresses the sensitivity of Rav Ashi to the proper arrangement of material, and quotes the following as an illustration:

> Our Rabbis taught: *And it came to pass when the Ark set forward that Moses said*, etc.: for this section the Holy One, blessed be He, provided signs above and below, to teach that this is not its proper place. ... And where is its proper place?—In (the chapter on) the banners.
> (b. Shab. 155b-156a)

But the Amoraic answer here is anonymous. The author has assigned it to Rav Ashi for stylistic reasons. Zuri mentions that he will discuss this aspect of Rav Ashi's abilities in a later chapter, but does not resume the discussion, though he emphasizes this "sensitivity" again.

Indications of Rav Ashi's editorial work can be found in:

1. Statements indicating that certain explanations of the Mishnah were incorporated by him in a specific place: "Was it not reported (*velav ʾitmar ʿalah*)", e.g., b. Men. 48a and b. Yoma 33b, above.

2. The many questions left unresolved, with the term *teiqu*, "the question stands".

Thus Rav Ashi set the Amoraic discussions into fixed texts, woven into the order of the Mishnaic discussions. In fact, it is to him that we owe the descriptive term for a tractate of the Talmud: a weaving (*messekhtaʾ*):

> But Rav Ashi says: Will you weave all these things (*meḥitaʾ meḥitinhu*) into one web? Where it was stated it was stated; and where it was not stated, it was not stated.
> (b. Pes. 42a)

A central part of Zuri's argument assigns "very many, if not most" of the anonymous portions of the Talmud to Rav Ashi. Here are examples of his method:

1. A passage in b. Git. 65a-b uses Mata Meḥasia, a suburb of Sura, as an example in a discussion of a divorce document. Zuri points out that the place of editing of the passage must be the Sura academy.

2. The following anonymous passage turns out, later in the tractate, to be the view of Rav Ashi:

> Has not one authority taught: 'If a man assigns in writing his property to two of his slaves, they acquire ownership and emancipate one another', while it has been taught by another. If a man says, 'All my

> property is made over to my slaves So-and-so and So-and-so', they do not acquire ownership even of themselves? ... When do we say this? (When he makes out) only one deed. If, however, (he makes out) two deeds, they do acquire ownership.
>
> (b. Git. 42a)

> Ravina thereupon said to Rav Ashi: How does this differ from the case regarding which it has been taught: 'If a man makes over all his property in writing to two of his slaves, they acquire possession and emancipate each other?' (He replied:) Have we not explained this to apply only where he writes two deeds?
>
> (b. Git. 87a)

3. Zuri assigns all anonymous answers to statements by colleagues of Rav Ashi, *to* Rav Ashi.

4. Zuri assigns to Rav Ashi passages which reflect his "special language and style". As a representative of the specificity of Northern thinking, Rav Ashi's ideas are couched in phrases which analyze the nuances of Mishnaic language, such as *Dayyqa' nami*, "There is evidence by implication", or phrases which draw distinctions between various cases, such as *Sha'ni hatam*, "The case is different there", or *'Afilu teima*, "One might even say", *'Iba'it 'eima*, "If you wish I might answer otherwise".

Another aspect of his style of thought is found in phrases like the following:

> Rather, said Rav Ashi: It is the same with the messenger of the congregation who consults. Now that you have come to this answer, say: etc.
>
> (b. 'Arakh. 11b)

> Said Rav Ashi: Now that Amemar has said that the law is in agreement with Samuel, etc.
>
> (b. Yev. 92b)

This, says Zuri, reflects the method of an editor surveying all his past decisions, and altering or revising previous material in the light of more recent decisions.

In reviewing the points presented by Zuri, it is apparent that no individual fact (e.g., Rav Ashi's reference to the categorization of an Amoraic interpretation of the Mishnah as a "weaving") can bear the full weight of his thesis. It is a large step, too, from the identification of certain anonymous passages with the known statements of Rav Ashi, to the assumption that the bulk of anonymous passages belong to him.

Zuri has added support to the accepted view of the editing of the Talmud through his closer analysis of the Talmudic texts. He has called attention to a characteristic method of Rav Ashi's thought: the careful analysis of Mishnaic language and the distinctions drawn between individual cases. In many of the passages under study, Rav Ashi does indeed seem to work this way. Yet Zuri's assignment of characteristic terms and phrases to Rav Ashi, and his attribution of anonymous passages on the basis of these key phrases, edges over into a kind of literary analysis which rests upon one's sensitivity to style. This raises a whole host of problems, among them the question of subjectivity.

Further, since Zuri has related Rav Ashi to the more comprehensive tradition of "Northern" thought-patterns, it is fair to ask why an anonymous passage with these characteristics cannot come from some other representative of the same school in Nehardea or Pumbedita. Attribution of specific texts on the basis of a general approach, in turn ostensibly derived from the texts, creates a kind of circularity which again throws us back on our own evaluation of the style of the texts. The reliability of Zuri's literary analysis might be determined by a kind of statistical study which was unavailable to him, but which is within our capability. Yet even then, we would derive support for his general thesis of the existence of the schools of thought, rather than the style of a particular individual.

Zuri has enriched the bare outline of the Geonic tradition. But once again we are referred back to that tradition. It is in order to point out that the Geonim were not archaeologists, attempting to interpret the famous passage on b. B.M. 86a. They were the recipients of a continuous tradition. Yet the Geonim were not literary historians, either. They were interested in "*hora'ah*", authentic teaching, and their tradition pointed to Rav Ashi as a key transitional figure in that chain of teaching. It is clear that a great portion of the Talmud comes to us from the work done in Rav Ashi's school. Yet the question of the final form, and the part played in it by the last generation of the Amoraim, and by the *Rabbanan Saborai*, must still remain open.

III

Y. I. HALEVY

BY

DAVID GOODBLATT

i

The work of Y. I. Halevy is a curious blend of rigorous analysis and traditionalist apologetic. On the one hand, it is clear that the whole mass of rabbinic literature has been carefully searched through and brought to bear on each question, with parallels examined and discrepancies noted. That shoddiness in the use of sources which Halevy exposes so unmercifully in the work of his predecessors is not to be found in his own researches. On the other hand, many of Halevy's conclusions derive more from his acceptance of the traditional rabbinic account of the development of the *halakhah* than from the data he has examined. Of course, he sincerely believed that he was showing how the sources themselves yield the same conclusions as the tradition. However, as I will show with regard to the question of the formation of the Talmud, the evidence Halevy offers rarely bears the full weight of his theories.

Yet Halevy cannot be dismissed. First, the traditional version of things is very sketchy and thus leaves room for conjecture. Once one assents to certain basic, but general, propositions, he is free to make of the data what he will. Second, Halevy is so faithful to the material that he is often unable facilely to impose the traditional account on the data. In such cases the implications of the evidence he adduces are evident despite his preconceptions. As a result of these two factors Halevy's work can still offer valuable insights. In the issue at hand he has made some important and, as usual, highly original contributions. Most striking is his breaking of the "log-jam" around the figure of R. Ashi (d. 427).[1] Some vague statements in the Talmud and in Geonic

---

[1] The dates given throughout this paper for the deaths of various Amoraim are the traditional ones, generally based on Geonic sources. There is no way to verify them.

sources had led to the widely held notion that the latter had "compiled" the Talmud. Most scholarly examination of the question in the nineteenth century was fixated on R. Ashi. Halevy called attention to the fact that the Talmud was in the process of formation throughout the Amoraic period, thus opening up the whole question of who compiled what. His own theory, for example, placed the decisive stage in the literary history of the Talmud almost a century before R. Ashi, though the latter still plays a major role. However, only a detailed examination can do justice to Halevy's theory and his approach to the material. Before embarking on such an effort I would like to offer some biographical background.

ii

Yiẓḥaq Isaac Halevy was born in Iwenec, a small town near Vilna, in 1847.[1] He grew up in Vilna and pursued the usual traditional disciplines, studying as a teenager at the renowned Yeshivah of Volozhin. Married at the age of eighteen, Halevy was offered a rabbinical post in a nearby town. On the advice of his mother, however, he declined the offer and went into business in Vilna. A few years later he was appointed to be one of the *gabba'im* of the Volozhin Yeshivah. This position, roughly analogous to that of a university trustee, became a springboard for further communal activity. Soon he was involved in Jewish affairs on a national level, including dealings with the lower echelons of the Russian government. Meanwhile, Halevy began to publish articles attacking the work of various religiously liberal and reform minded Jewish scholars. Among these articles were some on the relation of the Babylonian to the Palestinian Talmud. The latter were to provide the nucleus of his first book.

In 1895 Halevy's business failed, and he left Russia. He was to spend most of the next two years traveling, although he did settle in Pressburg, Hungary, a few months after leaving his homeland. At that time he tried to publish some of his novellae on the Talmud, but he had to abandon the project because of lack of funds. Shortly thereafter Halevy began work on an extensive history of the Jewish people in antiquity: *Dorot HaRishonim*. That same year he resumed his travels,

[1] All the biographical information which follows is taken from the memoir "My Father of Blessed Memory" [in Hebrew], by Halevy's son Samuel, in *Memorial Volume for Rabbi Yiẓḥaq Isaac Halevy*, ed. Moshe Auerbach (Bné Braq, 1964), pp. 13-63. See also O. Asher Reichel, *Isaac Halevy* (N.Y., 1969).

going as far as London. On the return trip he spent almost a year in Paris where he arranged for the Alliance Israelite to underwrite publication of his books. In due course, Volume III, covering the Saboraic and Geonic periods, was published in Pressburg in 1897. Echoes of his wanderings and economic hardship can be heard in his introduction to this volume. He writes there that he had wished to commence publication of *Dorot HaRishonim* with the volume on the Tannaitic and Amoraic eras, but the trying conditions and lack of books attendant on his incessent travels made this impossible.[1]

The unfavorable reaction to this highly polemical book caused the Alliance to renege on its promise to underwrite the next volume. Halevy, who was to spend the rest of his life trying to pay off his business debts, was now forced to seek new financial backing. Despite these problems he continued both to work full time on his opus and to devote himself to communal affairs. In 1906 he helped found Agudath Israel, an international organization of orthodox Jews. Some years earlier he had moved to Hamburg, and it was there that he died in 1914. In addition to Volume III, Halevy saw the publication of his volumes on the Amoraic period (Frankfurt A.M., 1901), and the Hasmonean-Herodian era (Frankfurt A.M., 1906). Three further volumes have appeared posthumously: on the Tannaitic period (Frankfurt A.M., 1918), the Biblical era (Jerusalem, 1929), and the end of the Second Commonwealth (Bné Braq, 1954). The first four volumes were reprinted in Berlin and Vienna in 1922-23. In 1967 an edition of all six volumes came out in Jerusalem. Besides his magnum opus Halevy published articles and reviews in a variety of journals.[2]

The difficult conditions under which Halevy worked make one tolerant of a certain lack of organization and logical sequence in his books. One should also note that the publication dates of the various volumes would indicate that he did not work in chronological order. His account of the formation of the Talmud, which I am about to summarize, is scattered through Volumes II and III. In any event, when the pieces are assembled, a relatively clear account emerges. For the sake of clarity I will first state Halevy's position without comment. In the following parts of this paper I will review it section by section in order to examine his evidence and methodology.

---

[1] Y. I. Halevy, *Dorot HaRishonim*, Volume III (Pressburg, 1897) Introduction.

[2] My information for this section is based on the partial bibliography compiled by Y. Shavit in the *Halevy Memorial Volume*, p. 80. See Reichel, *op. cit.*, pp. 160-170.

iii

According to Halevy the formation of the Talmud was an extended process comprised of four movements, each of which culminated in an important turning point. That process began more or less simultaneously with the promulgation of the Mishnah of Rabbi Judah the Prince. The latter's contemporaries, the last generation of Tannaim, began to assemble various materials relevant to the explanation of the Mishnah. Among these materials were Tannaitic traditions which had not been included in the Mishnah, as well as anonymous (i.e., not attributed to any named sage) comments and explanations (*setama degemara*). These sources were arranged[1] together with the section of the Mishnah to which they were relevant. The first two generations of Amoraim continued this work. They added the Tannaitic traditions which they had received as well as their own comments and explanations. This first stage reached its conclusion with the third and especially the fourth generation of Amoraim, for it was Abaye (d. 338), Rava (d. 352), and their colleagues who completed the arrangement (*siddur*) of the Talmudic materials which had accumulated up to that time. As their predecessors had done, they engaged in a critical sifting through and clarification (*bērur*) of the material. They fixed the final verbal formulation of the traditions, determined their authors, decided whether or not given sources were contradictory, and passed on the traditional explanations of the circumstances of certain cases in the Mishnah (*'oqimta*). In addition, the dialectics involved in deciding the above issues were now included in the materials assembled.[2] Halevy asserts categorically that the generation of Abaye and Rava saw the definitive and conclusive arrangement of the Talmud.[3] I take him to mean that by this time the basic structure of most of the pericopae (*sugyot*) in the Talmud as we have it was already fixed.

The second stage in the formation of the Talmud was set by the activity of the generation of R. Ashi (d. 427). This activity consisted of adding the material which had accumulated since the time of Abaye

---

[1] Halevy uses derivatives of the root SDR throughout. I noticed only one instance of the word which means "edit" or "redact" (ʿRK) in his account of the formation of the Talmud. I have therefore used the latter phrase, avoided the former two terms, and have employed terms like "assemble", "arrange", and the like. My attempt to reflect Halevy's usage has resulted in a certain awkwardness.

[2] Halevy, *Dorot HaRishonim*, Volume IIa (Frankfurt A.M., 1901), pp. 481-82, 490-91, 522; Volume III, pp. 117, 119. On the last point v. II, pp. 591-93. [Henceforth I will use simply the Roman numeral and page numbers to cite Halevy.]

[3] II, p. 480, and cf. pp. 490, 496, 552.

and Rava, fixing the final verbal form of traditions for which this had not been done earlier, and deciding between variants in the sources which had been assembled earlier.[1] In all this R. Ashi and his colleagues were carrying on the work of previous generations. The unique contribution of these Amoraim—and the second turning point in the formation process—was the "conclusion" (*ḥatimah*) of the Talmud, or more precisely, the "arrangement [of Talmudic materials] for conclusion".[2] By this last phrase Halevy meant two things. First, all outstanding questions regarding the form, content, and provenance of the traditions were settled. Second, the materials were so arranged that the final outcome of each discussion and its legal implication would be indicated by the order of the pericope (*sugya*). That is, the Talmud itself could now be used to decide the *halakhah*.[3] What had been a commentary on a law code (viz., the Mishnah) now became a law code in its own right. This "conclusion" of the Talmud coincided with the end of the Amoraic period as marked by the deaths of Rabbah Tosfa'ah (474) and Ravina b. R. Huna (475 according to Halevy, v. below) the last of the generation of R. Ashi.[4]

The third and fourth steps in the formation of the Talmud thus occur in the Saboraic era. Halevy distinguishes the first generation of Saboraim, who were responsible for that third step, from the later Saboraim who accomplished the fourth. The distinctive activity of the earlier group concerned certain *sugyot* where questions had been left open by the last Amoraim. The latter actually had solutions to these questions. However, since those solutions were not based on Tannaitic sources, they were not inserted in the Talmud by the last Amoraim. The first generation of Saboraim now went ahead and added those solutions to the text, apparently motivated by a desire to preserve all the traditions they had received from their illustrious predecessors.[5] This third stage probably saw the writing down of the Talmud,[6] and also its termination (*siyyum*, on the meaning v. below).[7] Both the early and the later Saboraim added glosses (SBRY) where the Talmudic discussion was overly concise. The explanations yielded by these glosses were based on traditions received from the last Amoraim.

---

[1] II, pp. 560-62.
[2] III, pp. 116, 120.
[3] II, pp. 524, 591-92; III, pp. 116-17, 120.
[4] III, p. 19.
[5] III, p. 11, n. 3 and p. 50.
[6] III, pp. 25, 26.
[7] III, pp. 26, 36, 50.

The later generation also added to the Talmudic discussions of given sections of the Mishnah short quotes from the relevant section of the Mishnah as an introduction.[1] After the Saboraic period, Halevy maintains, nothing was consciously added to the Talmud.[2]

iv

Halevy's theory, particularly the large role he assigns to Abaye and Rava, is at variance with the usual view that R. Ashi "compiled" the Talmud. With various minor modifications this view was shared by most of the rabbinic scholars of his time. It is not surprising, therefore, to find that Halevy devotes a lot of space to proving the existence and extent of what I may call a "proto-Talmud" before the time of R. Ashi. Most of the evidence he marshalls is internal, i.e., based on an analysis of the text of the Talmud as we have it. His method is to show that certain *sugyot* or parts of *sugyot* date back to early Amoraic times, while others presuppose the existence of early *sugyot*. These ancient pericopes are the result of the assembling and arranging of Talmudic materials which took place in the early stages of the formation process.

One of Halevy's methods for uncovering traces of such early *sugyot* depends on observing those comments and discussions in the Talmud which are anonymous, as opposed to those attributed to some specific Tanna or Amora. These anonymous sections (*setama degemara* or *detalmuda*) often serve as a framework for a number of attributed sources. In such cases, Halevy believes, the anonymous sections are unassailable evidence of the assembling and arranging process. Moreover, a relative date can be established for many of these sections, beyond noting that they are later than the sources which they encase. For example, if a fourth generation Amora quotes an anonymous comment and treats it as authoritative, perhaps by using an inference from it to settle a question, then it may be assumed that the comment dates from the third generation at the latest. Halevy cites numerous instances of this kind and is able to trace some of the anonymous frameworks as far back as the generation of Rav (d. 247).[3]

One example of this approach concerns b. *Yev.* 115a-b where a

[1] III, pp. 21, 36-37, 50, 145.

[2] III, pp. 32, 138.

[3] II, pp. 551-556; III, pp. 117-8. For a critique of Halevy's treatment, see Abraham Weiss, *Studies in the Literature of the Amoraim* (1962), pp. 295-307; for Weiss' own treatment, pp. 24-58; and his *Leḥeqer HaTalmud* (New York 1954), pp. 408ff.

Tannaitic precedent is quoted and then discussed in an anonymous section. Immediately following this the Talmud relates that R. Ḥisda (d. 309) attempted to apply this precedent in a case which came before him. However, Rava (d. 352) pointed out to him that the circumstances of the two cases were different, relying apparently on the anonymous explanation of the Tannaitic precedent. Thus, Halevy claims, the precedent and its framework must have already existed as a unit, a *sugya*, in the early fourth century.[1] Of course, what we have here is the old problem of the chicken and the egg. One could argue that the anonymous explanation is later than Rava, and, in fact, is based on his comment. One would point out that R. Ḥisda was obviously unaware of that explanation, for he would not otherwise have attempted to apply the precedent to the case before him. If the explanation had already been joined to the precedent to form a unit, then one wonders how R. Ḥisda could have known the latter without the former. Moreover, R. Ḥisda predeceased Rava by 43 years according to the traditional dates. It is not impossible that a young Rava had contact with the elderly R. Ḥisda (who is supposed to have lived past ninety). But it is most improbable that he would have corrected a sage so many years his senior in this way. This makes it more likely that Rava's comment is a reaction to a report of what R. Ḥisda had done some time earlier.[2] This comment then became the basis for the anonymous explanation. Finally, it is interesting to note that the latter is introduced by the term *vetisbera* (WTSBR') which some scholars, though not Halevy, take to be a sign of Saboraic origin. The fact that the explanation comes before Rava's comment poses no difficulty to this alternate pre-history of the *sugya*, for Halevy himself cites numerous cases of interpolations into early sections.

Such is the case in another example of Halevy's attempts to uncover early strata of the Talmud. On b. B.Q. 101a we find an involved question posed anonymously, introduced by the formula "it was asked of them" ('YBB'Y' LHW). After some discussion Ravina, a contemporary of R. Ashi, explains the circumstances of the question. This is followed by the solution of the latter by means of a Tannaitic source and then a comment by Rava. Rava lived almost a century before Ravina, so the latter's comment must be a late interpolation. By removing it we can see the earlier form of the *sugya*, viz., the question, the answer, and Rava's comment. It was this form of the *sugya* which

[1] II, pp. 554f.

[2] I owe this point to Professor Jacob Neusner.

was known to Ravina and which prompted his explanation—an explanation later inserted into the text.[1] So Halevy. Once again, however, an alternative to his reconstruction of the *sugya* could be suggested. One could argue that the question and solution, both of which are cited anonymously, were combined with the comment of Rava to form the *sugya* in the time of Ravina (i.e., the time of R. Ashi) or even later. It does *not* have to be assumed that such a unit existed before Ravina.

Halevy's attempt to uncover strata in the Talmud which predate R. Ashi is thus not convincing. His underlying assumption, that many of the anonymous sections are early, remains only an assumption. It can be maintained with equal reasonableness that they are *all* late. Evidence of the kind represented by the above examples is subject to contradictory, or at least alternate, interpretation. Perhaps the other type of internal evidence which Halevy offers is less equivocal. It is based on showing that late Amoraic discussions presuppose a certain arrangement and order in the early materials.[2] A complex example is cited from b. Men. 30b-31a where the Talmud reports that Rava b. Ḥinena quoted ʿUlla who quoted R. Ḥanina (all are Amoraim) who stated that the law follows R. Simeon Shizuri (a Tanna). A long discussion follows seeking to identify which dictum of R. Simeon's is referred to by R. Ḥanina. Various dicta are suggested and rejected. The reason for rejection in each case is that some other Amoraic tradition is cited which declares the suggested dictum of R. Simeon to be the law. Had R. Ḥanina referred to the suggested dictum, then his endorsement would have been combined with, or included in, that other Amoraic tradition. The *sugya* then concludes with the suggestions of R. Papa (d. 376) and R. Naḥman b. Isaac (d. 356) as to which dictum of R. Simeon is meant. Halevy argues that this whole discussion makes no sense unless we assume that those other Amoraic traditions had already been combined with the dicta of R. Simeon which they endorsed. Otherwise there would be no basis for the assumption that had R. Ḥanina referred to one of the latter, then necessarily his statement would have been combined with the other tradition which does so. After all, different Amoraim could refer to one and the same Tannaitic saying. Hence we must assume the existence of proto-*sugyot*—in this case, dicta of R. Simeon Shizuri combined with Amoraic endorsements of them—prior to the time of R. Naḥman

[1] II, p. 556.
[2] II, pp. 557-562. The two examples below are from pp. 557-58 and 560-61 respectively.

b. Isaac and R. Papa. Thus Halevy. However, the *sugya* in b. Men. is patently later than the last two sages, for their own comments are encased in the anonymous framework of this section. So while Halevy may be right that this pericope does presuppose some assembling and arranging of Talmudic material into units, it cannot prove anything about the state of the Talmud in the late fourth century, nor—in the absence of any way to date the framework—about its state prior to the generation of R. Ashi.

Another example of this approach is based on b. Ḥul. 11a. After a discussion about the origin of a certain principle relevant to the laws of ritual slaughter, the Talmud asks whence is derived the principle of following the majority, i.e., relying on probability in cases of unknown circumstance. A number of Amoraim answer, suggesting various laws, which have nothing to do with ritual slaughter, as the basis. The last answer is that of R. Ashi who asserts that the principle of following the majority derives "from [the law of] ritual slaughter itself". Halevy points out that R. Ashi's statement implies other attempts to ascertain the origin of this principle in the context of a discussion of ritual slaughter laws. In other words, his statement makes sense only if we assume this *sugya* existed before him in its present form and place, viz., a discussion of the origin of the majority principle arranged in this section of the tractate *Ḥullin* which deals with ritual slaughter. Since many of the Amoraim who appear in the discussion are early, it cannot be argued that the whole *sugya* is based on a session in R. Ashi's academy. One could say that this section is the creation of R. Ashi, though, or one of his disciples.

V

Halevy has thus tried to exhume some remains of the early stages of the formation of the Talmud, with questionable success. He also adduces a few statements in the Talmud which he believes refer directly to those early stages. He cites the well-known statement of R. Naḥman (d. 324) about "fixing" (QBʿ) an explanation in the *gemara*.[1] He also notes the activities ascribed to R. Naḥman b. Isaac (d. 356), such as commenting on variants in the Mishnah, giving mnemonics for Amoraic discussions, and correcting Amoraic traditions.[2] How-

[1] b. ʿEruv. 32b, cited III, p. 117.

[2] II, pp. 500-502. Halevy understands this rabbi's cryptic description of himself on b. Pes. 105a as referring to these activities.

ever, Halevy's main case is based on the evidence yielded by the analysis of individual *sugyot*. I have tried to show that the methodology and assumptions involved in these analyses are somewhat doubtful. Yet it must be recalled that all Halevy claims for the early stage of the formation process is that Tannaitic and Amoraic sources were assembled and arranged in connection with sections of the Mishnah to which they were relevant. In addition those sources were critically examined and explained. Put in this way, I do not see how his assertion can be rejected. I cannot imagine how sessions at the Amoraic academies took place without assuming the existence of such units of traditional material. That such units were assembled and studied in connection with the Mishnah from earliest Amoraic times can be granted. Thus what Halevy asserts about the first stage of the formation of the Talmud is not the aspect of his theory which most requires demonstration. Rather it is his frequent and categorical assertion that this assembling and arranging (*siddur*) of Talmudic materials reached its definitive conclusion in the time of Abaye and Rava, which must be proved.[1]

The generation of Abaye and Rava marked the first turning point in the formation of the Talmud, and perhaps the most significant from the literary point of view. This assertion of Halevy's is the most original and striking part of his theory. Oddly enough, he offers little literary evidence for it. The analysis of *sugyot* discussed above proved, *at most*, that many units of Talmudic material had been arranged before the time of R. Ashi. Only in some of those cases was a date in the first half of the fourth century, the period of Abaye and Rava, indicated. Moreover, explicit connections between these two sages and the arrangement of such early strata are still fewer. Halevy does cite two instances where anonymous comments—the tell-tale sign of "editorial" activity—in earlier strata are later, in the time of R. Ashi, attributed to Abaye.[2] Further, he notes four cases where statements given in the Babylonian Talmud in the name of Abaye or Rava are cited in the Palestinian Talmud in the name of "the rabbis from there" (= from Babylonia, *rabbanin detaman*). Given Halevy's understanding of the significance of anonymous sections, this means that the Palestinian sages knew these statements of Abaye and Rava in the form of "edi-

---

[1] For this assertion v. II, pp. 480, 490, 496, 552, 567. Cf. III, pp. 117, 119 where no generation is singled out.

[2] II, pp. 566-67.

torial comment".[1] Granting his evaluation of these phenomena, one may wonder whether these six instances are sufficient to establish his claim for the role of Abaye and Rava. I suspect that the underlying basis, never really made explicit, of this aspect of his theory is the great frequency with which these two authorities appear in the Talmud. But I doubt that even this fact—which would first have to be set forth in an exact and statistical way—could support his thesis.

vi

Halevy does offer more evidence—evidence which is more historical than literary. To begin with, he cites the following passage from the Epistle of Sherira Gaon (ESG):

> ... and after this [viz., Rabbah and R. Joseph, were] Abaye, and Rava. And there was a great persecution [ŠMD'] in Palestine and authoritative instruction [*hora'ah*] diminished greatly there, and those Babylonians who were there—like Ravin, R. Dimi, and the *Naḥōtē* [those who traveled back and forth between Palestine and Babylonia]—emigrated to here [= Babylonia]. ...[2]

Sherira thus reports a persecution which occurred during the careers of Abaye and Rava. Since the former died in 338 and the latter in 352, this persecution cannot be identified with the troubles under Gallus and Ursicinus in 351. Hence, Halevy concludes, there must have been persecutions in Palestine in the first half of the fourth century which may be assumed to have followed upon the conversion of Constantine to Christianity.[3] As a result there was a great influx of the major Palestinian authorities as well as the permanent return of the Babylonian *Naḥōtē* around 325.[4] Further evidence of this influx is derived from passages in the Talmud which refer to Palestinian authorities being present in Babylonia. In particular Halevy notes the report that Ifra Hormizd, mother of Shapur II, sent a cash gift to R. Ammi, who had been a major Palestinian Amora. He believes that this shows how

[1] II, p. 567. The phrase is my own.

[2] *'Iggeret Rav Sherira Ga'on*, ed. B. M. Lewin (Haifa, 1921), cited and discussed in II, pp. 367, 455-56; III, pp. 121, 126.

[3] II, pp. 366-67, 555-56; III, p. 124. On the events of 351 v. Saul Lieberman, "Palestine in the Third and Fourth Centuries", JQR, n.s. 36, 4, pp. 329-370 and cf. M. Avi-Yonah, *Bime Roma uBizantiyon* (Jerusalem, 1952), pp. 124-130. V. also Jacob Neusner, *A History of the Jews in Babylonia, IV. The Age of Shapur II* (Leiden, 1969), pp. 28-29, and p. 31, n. 3. On the probable absence of any persecutions of the Jews after Constantine's conversion, Neusner, pp. 27-28.

[4] II, pp. 456, 467, 469, 473, 481; III, pp. 11-22, 124, 145.

well received the Palestinian emigres were by their Babylonian colleagues—so well that even the Queen Mother heard of their advent and honored them![1] At this point it must be asked whether the story about Ifra Hormizd can be accepted without further ado as fact. The lack of Iranian attestation of this name (the second element is common) and the improbability of the mother of a Sassanian emperor having direct dealing with an emigré member of a small minority group make it highly unlikely.[2] The uncritical credence which Halevy gives to this story is typical of his method, and it seriously vitiates the strength of his case in so far as it purports to rest on historical evidence. Indeed, modern scholarship has found little basis for assuming any major (or even minor) persecutions in the second quarter of the fourth century in Palestine.[3] The proof offered by Halevy—the presence of some Palestinian sages in Babylonia and a statement in the late tenth century ESG—is not very convincing in the absence of other evidence.

The effect of this supposed influx of scholars must be understood in the light of another of Halevy's theories. He asserts that during most of the Amoraic period one particular school was recognized as supreme and authoritative, as the "general academy" (*metivta kollelet*), to use his term. This construct is based on a few vague passages in the ESG.[4] Halevy does not deny that other schools existed, a fact for which there is abundant evidence, but asserts that from the death of Rav (247) to that of Rava (352), and again under R. Ashi, there was one particular school which was acknowledged as supremely authoritative. During the first half of the fourth century, the academy so acknowledged was that of Pumbedita. It was to this school, then, that the mass of Palestinian scholars came when they arrived in Babylonia. Thus when Abaye became principal of the general academy, he presided over a consistory which included all the major authorities of his generation, both Babylonian and Palestinian. The latter brought with them their own Talmudic materials, viz., the Palestinian Talmud in the state it was in at the beginning of the fourth century. This new material augmented the mass of Babylonian traditions from the first three generations of Amoraim. The accumulation of materials had thus reached a point where it was felt to be both desirable and necessary to submit it all to a critical sifting through and clarification (*bērur*).

[1] III, p. 122 cited from b. Bava Batra 10b.

[2] Neusner, *op. cit.*, pp. 35-39.

[3] V. p. 36, n. 3.

[4] V. the passage cited III, pp. 481, 495 and the discussion pp. 480-81, 490, 494-96. For the passages v. ESG, ed. Lewin, pp. 84-90.

The presence of all the Amoraim in one consistory made such an operation eminently feasible.[1]

Except for the evidence Halevy cites for his theory of a general academy, he offers no proof for the existence of the consistory and its work. He does find some allusions to their work, though. He claims that the phrase *havayot dAbaye vRava* (HWYWT D'BYY WRB') refers to the critical sifting-through mentioned above. While earlier generations also engaged in this activity—for we find the same phrase used with regard to Rav and Samuel—it was the generation of Abaye and Rava which brought this work to its definitive completion.[2] Aside from some slender internal evidence, then, Halevy's case for the role of the last named sages in the formation of the Talmud is based on the nature and work of the consistory over which they presided. In effect, his assertion rests on circumstantial evidence. And those circumstances —the presence of all the Jewish legal authorities of the age in one place—depend on historical constructs which are, at best, questionable.

vii

As mentioned earlier, the generation of R. Ashi marks the second great turning point in the formation of the Talmud.

Indeed, Jewish tradition had always assigned to R. Ashi the central role in the compilation of the Talmud, as Halevy notes.[3] He adds that while "it is true that the tradition [*qabbalah*] of all Israel does not require proof, the matter is quite evident from the words of the *gemara*".[4] In other words, Halevy believes that there is literary evidence of this fact, i.e., evidence based on the analysis of sections of the Talmud. The literary or internal proof which he finds is of two kinds. First, he notes that many *sugyot* end with concluding statements or decisions by a sage of the generation of R. Ashi. The latter himself does not reply to that statement, or enter into the discussion, or appear in the *sugya* in any way. Nonetheless that sage's statement is introduced by the formula "R.N. said to R. Ashi". According to Halevy these statements were made at sessions of the consistory meeting at Mata Meḥasya, the general academy at that time. R. Ashi is addressed as head of the consistory which was engaged in critically sifting through

[1] II, pp. 490-494.
[2] II, p. 490.
[3] III, p. 29, and cf. pp. 17, 81.
[4] Cf. II, p. 589.

and arranging Talmudic materials.[1] A similar phenomenon is to be observed with Ravina and is similarly explained by the fact that the latter sometimes substituted for R. Ashi as head of the consistory.[2]

A second kind of internal evidence comes from passages where Halevy claims that we actually find R. Ashi explaining his intention in arranging a given *sugya* in a certain way. For example, in b. *Ket.* 7a we read:

> R. Papa said in the name of Rava that it is permitted [to have intercourse for the first time] on a festival, but forbidden on the Sabbath. R. Papi said to R. Papa, "What is your opinion? [Is it that] since a wound which is necessary [for eating=slaughtering an animal] is permitted [on a festival], a wound which is not necessary [for eating, as here, puncturing the hymen] is also permitted? If so then it would be permitted to burn incense on a festival—for since burning which is necessary [for eating=cooking] is permitted, burning which is not necessary [for eating, as here with the incense] would also be permitted". He [R. Papa] replied, "For your sake does Scripture say 'only that which is eaten by *every* man...' [which indicates] something which is the same for everyone." [Rashi explains that incense is only indulged in by those used to luxury.] R. Aḥa b. Rava said to R. Ashi, "If so, then one must be forbidden to slaughter a deer which crosses one's path on a festival since this is not the same for every one". He [R. Ashi] said to him, "I said that which is *necessary* [not the same] for everyone. A deer is not necessary for everyone."

Halevy points out that in response to a question about the conversation between R. Papi and R. Papa, R. Ashi replied, "I said ..." He can only be referring to his activity in arranging the sources. A second example from page 69a of the same tractate shows R. Ashi replying "I said ..." to a question about an anonymous discussion of the view of R. Yoḥanan.[3]

The above internal evidence has a good deal of *prima facie* plausibility. My acceptance of it is qualified by a lack of refinement in Halevy's methods of analysis. To begin with the last example, the word I have translated "said" (from the root 'MR) can also mean "explain". Thus R. Ashi might merely be stating how he understood a difficult passage. In the absence of any investigation of the use of this word, which in some of its forms is clearly a technical term, Halevy's proof cannot be accepted without reservation. As for the first kind of evidence, here too one must hold back—though for

---

[1] II, pp. 562-70; III, 82-83.

[2] II, pp. 589-91.

[3] III, p. 81 and v. p. 82 for further examples.

different reasons. Halevy's argument assumes that the text of the Talmud found in our standard printed editions is reliable. But some kind of reference to the testimony of manuscripts is necessary before one can dismiss the possibility that the phenomenon he has noticed is the result of scribal error. That is, a scribe used to writing "R.N. said to R. Ashi" might let his pen run on and add the last three words even where they do not belong. Beyond this, one would like to see a statistical report on the occurrence of this phenomenon including all the sages involved. A few examples are illustrative, not probative. I do not mean to be overly picayune in reviewing Halevy's arguments. I only wish to show that this kind of analysis of *sugyot* requires more in the way of external control and refinement before it can be completely convincing.

The internal evidence is supplemented by historical considerations analogous to those Halevy noted in connection with Abaye and Rava. Like the consistory presided over by the latter, the one which met at the general academy of Mata Meḥasya under the principalship of R. Ashi included all the sages of Babylonia and many of the chief authorities of Palestine.[1] At least part of the basis for this assertion is Sherira's testimony to the pre-eminence of R. Ashi and his academy.[2] As for the presence of Palestinians, Halevy uses Geonic traditions to identify two sages, mentioned together with R. Ashi on several occasions, as Palestinian—and possibly one or two others.[3] Since the Talmud only rarely records a sage's place of origin, Halevy feels that one may reasonably extrapolate from these few and assume that there were many others who emigrated to Babylonia in the wake of persecutions—which apparently continued for several decades after the troubles under Gallus and Ursicinus. These emigres brought with them the Palestinian Talmud now in its final, i.e., present, form. Halevy spends several pages trying to prove that the consistory of R. Ashi both knew and used the Palestinian Talmud. These proofs are instances where the Babylonian Talmud either quotes or seems to depend on passages in the Palestinian.[4] This is the traditional explanation for the superior authority of the Babylonian Talmud—a view which was seriously challenged in Halevy's times by Z. Frankel and others. However, this dispute is too complex to be dealt with here.

---

[1] II, p. 562; III, p. 27.
[2] V. II, p. 598.
[3] II, pp. 573-79.
[4] III, pp. 126-30.

It is sufficient to observe that Halevy's case for the "international" character of the consistory of R. Ashi is no stronger than his case for the similar nature of the sessions of Abaye and Rava.

viii

In one sense the strength of the evidence which Halevy offers for the role of R. Ashi in the formation of the Talmud is not important. After all, there was never any doubt about the *fact* of his involvement in the process. Rather the issue is the *nature* of his involvement. Since Halevy believes that Abaye and Rava were responsible for the "conclusive arrangement" (*siddur*) of the Talmudic materials, it is not surprising that he understands the contribution of R. Ashi and his colleagues as having more of a legal than a literary nature. He uses the term "conclusion" or, more literally, "sealing" (*ḥatimah*) to denominate the second turning point in the formation of the Talmud, for which they were responsible. It involved arranging the materials in such a way as to enable the Talmud to serve as a law code.

The basis for this understanding of the second turning point is the well-know statement from b. B. M. 86a to the effect that Ravina and R. Ashi are the end of authoritative instruction (*sof hora'ah*).[1] Since this statement is paralleled by one about Rabbi [Judah the Prince] and R. Nathan being the "end of Mishnah" (*sof mishnah*), Jewish tradition always assumed that *sof hora'ah* must have something to do with the compilation of the Talmud. Halevy accepts this assumption and follows through on the parallelism. He argues that just as *sof mishnah* evidently refers to the promulgation of the Mishnah and the end of the Tannaitic period, so *sof hora'ah* refers to the "conclusion" of the Talmud and the end of the Amoraic period. In both instances the termination of the era was a conscious, as well as a divinely-inspired, decision—in Halevy's words, "It was the voice of God and the consensus of all the sages of the generation, with the consent of all Israel..."[2] The consequences of the termination of each are explained by Halevy as follows: Whereas the Tannaim could adopt an independent position vis-a-vis Tannaitic legal traditions, the Amoraim could not. Similarly with the end of the Amoraic period, subsequent generations accepted the Amoraic traditions as authoritative and bind-

[1] V. ESG, ed. Lewin, pp. 69, 95, as well as Halevy's extended discussion of the date of the death of Ravina b.R. Huna at III, pp. 7-9.

[2] III, p. 22.

ing. They no longer felt free to to change even the literary form in which the legal views of the Amoraim were handed down. Thus literary as well as legal consequences ensued on the end of the period. These consequences were the same ones entailed by the conclusion of the Talmud, which was the main expression of the end of the Amoraic period. As Halevy puts it,

> Therefore, while until those days [viz., of the conclusion of the Talmud], the authority of *hora'ah* possessed by the sages of each generation was based on the principles of the oral tradition which they had received ... now, with the conclusion of the Talmud, since all this [i.e., literary and legal questions *re* Talmudic sources] had been clarified, determined, and fixed ... by this very fact in itself 'there was no longer any *hora'ah* [a quote from the ESG]', i.e., *hora'ah* by individual decision, but rather [there was] *hora'ah* based on what was already explicit in the *gemara*—just as we do today.[1]

It turns out, then, that Halevy's understanding of R. Ashi's contribution to the formation of the Talmud arises not from the internal evidence as much as from his interpretation of the phrase from b. B. M. and its elaboration in the ESG, as well as by indirection from the role he had assigned to earlier generations. His equating of *sof* wi*hora'ah* th the end of the Amoraic period and the conclusion of the Talmud does leave one loose end: the fifty years which elapsed between the death of R. Ashi and Halevy's date for the end of the era. Halevy deals with this, casting a polemic eye on I. H. Weiss, by repeatedly minimizing both the quantity and originality of the materials added to the Talmud in this half century. He asserts that the last Amoraim merely added precedents and traditions of the older members of the generation of R. Ashi plus some very brief and necessary glosses. The few cases where these additions seem of a more substantive nature turn out on closer examination to be no different. Halevy stresses that none of these additions involve the creation of new *sugyot*, and that "the Talmud as a whole as it is before us is according to the arrangement (*siddur*) of R. Ashi and his colleagues in his days. ..."[2]

ix

Because of the paucity of sources from this period, anyone who deals with the Saboraic age must depend on Geonic traditions. The

[1] II, pp. 591-92 and cf. p. 524.
[2] III, p. 20 and v. pp. 19-21.

latter identify certain sages mentioned in the Talmud as Saboraim, and certain passages as of Saboraic provenance. It is not surprising, then, that Halevy's discernment of two different phases of Saboraic activity, corresponding to the last two stages of the formation of the Talmud, is based primarily on an extremely close reading of the following passage from the ESG:

> And thus *hora'ah* was added generation after generation until Ravina, and after Ravina it ceased... and after this although there certainly was no more *hora'ah*, there were Saboraim who interpret who are close to *hora'ah*, and they are called the Saboraic rabbis, and they explained all that was still undecided—for example, R. Reḥumi, R. Joseph, R. Aḥai of Be Hatim, and R. Revai of Rov (who some say was a Gaon and very long lived). And they fixed many explanations [SBRY] in the *gemara*, they and the rabbis who were after them also, like R. ʿEna and R. Simonai....[1]

Halevy understands Sherira as clearly separating a first generation of Saboraim "who interpret who are close to *hora'ah*" from the later generations, "the rabbis who were after them". While both are responsible for glosses which were inserted in the Talmud, the early group also "explained all that was still undecided". Halevy claims to be able to discern this distinction not only in other passages in the ESG, but also in the Talmud itself.[2] I shall return to this below. Here I would like to mention that he uses this distinction, together with another of his close, contextual readings of Sherira, to explain the latter's statement that "most of the Saboraic rabbis died in [the space of] a few years".[3] He asserts that this line refers only to the first generation, and he belabors Graetz and Weiss for not seeing it in context and as a result limiting the whole Saboraic era to fifty years.[4]

Before illustrating the two different Saboraic contributions to the formation of the Talmud, Halevy explains the phrase about the early Saboraim explaining "all that was still undecided". He points out that the phrase cannot be taken literally, for unanswered questions and unresolved problems can be found on almost every page of the Talmud. Rather the meaning of Sherira's statement is this. The generation of R. Ashi found themselves unable to supply solutions based on Tannaitic sources to a number of problems. They did possess answers to these problems, but ones based only on their own reason-

---

[1] ESG, ed. Lewin, p. 69, cited III, p. 24.
[2] III, p. 24.
[3] ESG, ed. Lewin, pp. 97-98, cited III, p. 24.
[4] III, p. 2 and *passim*.

ings and decisions. Since their solutions lacked a Tannaitic support, the last Amoraim did not insert them in the Talmud, but left these questions open. The early Saboraim, however, went ahead and added those solutions to the text.[1] With the addition of these last remnants of the literary legacy of the Amoraim, the Talmud was considered "terminated" ('YSTYYM), to use the phrase from ESG.[2]

Halevy cites several examples of this activity, including the following from b. Yev. 37a:[3]

> If one marries [a widow or divorcée] within three [months of the dissolution of her previous marriage] and then flees—R. Aḥa and Rafram disagree on this. One says that we excommunicate him; the other says that his flight is sufficient for him. There was a case like this, and Rafram said to them, "His flight is sufficient for him".

On the basis of other evidence, Halevy identifies the two sages named in this passage as from the last Amoraim. He then points out that the last line must have been added later, or else the first part of the passage would have specified which sage said what. In fact, Halevy claims, it was added by the early Saboraim. The fact that they left the original wording (i.e., up to the last line) intact shows that the Saboraim did not tamper with the Talmud text which they had received. If this is true of the earlier generation, it is *a fortiori* true of the later Saboraim. Examples of their activity are also cited by Halevy, though in some cases it is hard to see how he decides that a given passage is Saboraic.[4] On the basis of all these examples he maintains that with the exception of the phenomenon discussed above which was limited to "those who interpret who are close to *hora'ah*", the contribution of the Saboraim to the formation of the Talmud was limited to the insertion of glosses and introductory quotes from the Mishnah.[5]

Actually, all of the above sources serve Halevy more as illustration than as evidence. Given the uncertainty involved in designating sages and passages as Saboraic, one cannot fault Halevy if most of his case rests on his understanding of the relevant sections of the ESG. Certainly his insistence on the full utilization of Gaonic sources and,

---

[1] III, p. 11, n. 3 and p. 50.

[2] V. III, pp. 26, 36. This is how Halevy explains the term.

[3] V. III, p. 89. For the other examples v. pp. 56-60, 89, 98-99.

[4] E.g., the case from b. Ḥul. 66a, cited III, p. 36, as against the more obvious one on p. 38.

[5] On the last point v. III, p. 36 and cf. pp. 21, 50, 145.

more importantly, on a careful and thorough reading of them seem to be prerequisites for any serious research on the issue under discussion. However, Halevy's extremely close reading of the ESG sometimes strikes me as more of a reading *into*. It reminds me of nothing so much as the way the Amoraim read the Mishnah, in that an absolute precision of expression as well as total reliability is assumed for the document dealt with. I would submit that neither assumption is justified with respect to the Geonic sources. In any event, Halevy's description of the activity of the Saboraim and his frequent insistence that they neither added to nor subtracted from the essential structure of R. Ashi's Talmud—a description almost indistinguishable from what he says about the last Amoraim[1]—is contraverted by evidence which he himself adduces. This evidence demonstrates that entire *sugyot* and many legal decisions are products of the Saboraim[2].

X

My lengthy discussion of the evidence Halevy offers for each discrete element in his theory has disclosed some serious weaknesses in his methodology. The analysis of *sugyot*, which yielded the internal or literary evidence, was often not convincing. It suffered from a lack of refinement and external control. Halevy's historical constructions, so important in providing circumstantial evidence for aspects of his theory, revealed an uncritical acceptance of Talmudic statements as historic facts. Finally, and most generally, the evidence often appeared insufficient to support Halevy's conclusions. Looking at it from another perspective, one gets the feeling that much of his account is based on something other than the data he has assembled. In fact, the latter are schematized to a great degree—a fact which becomes apparent when we consider Halevy's theory as a whole. Thus Halevy draws explicit and detailed parallels between the redaction of the Mishnah, the arrangement of the Talmud (*siddur*) by Abaye and Rava, the conclusion thereof (*ḥatimah*) by R. Ashi, and the end of the Saboraic period. At all four of these occasions, according to Halevy, we find all the sages of the generation assembled in one place, in a time of peace and good conditions, thoroughly acquainted with all that had gone before in the development of the *halakhah*, handing on

[1] Cf. III, pp. 21, 37.

[2] V. e.g., Sherira's attribution of the opening *sugya* of b. Qid. to the Saboraim, cited III, p. 32, and the case from b. Ḥul. 59b, cited III, p. 60.

and augmenting the legal traditions of Israel.[1] What we have here is part of the rabbinic myth of the uniform and orderly development of the *halakhah* overseen by a central, universally recognized authority, heir to the Great Assembly and the Sanhedrin.

It is this myth which provides most of those conclusions which the evidence could not support. Yet it is a tribute, albeit a left-handed one, to Halevy's thoroughness and faithfulness to the material that the data are not successfully schematized. The tension between the data and the myth is evident at many points in his theory. It is this tension which explains his inability to distinguish clearly between the contribution of Abaye and Rava and that of R. Ashi. While the latter's special activity was supposed to have been *ḥatimah*, it is sometimes referred to as *siddur*,[2] and sometimes as a combination of both.[3] When Halevy tried to differentiate between these two terms, he used the same distinction employed earlier to distinguish the work of Abaye and Rava from that of earlier Amoraim.[4] As might be expected, he has difficulty drawing a clear difference between the contributions of the latter two groups.[5] Similarly, the difficulty met with in understanding the Palestinian Talmud is sometimes attributed to its lack of *siddur*, sometimes to its lack of *siddur* for *ḥatimah*, and sometimes to its lack of Saboraic overlay.[6] The myth of the uniform development of the *halakhah* was probably what prevented Halevy from paying attention to the evidence which indicates that certain tractates come from different academies or periods than others.[7]

Despite the weaknesses in Halevy's approach and despite his subservience to myth of the *halakhah*, I do not think that Halevy can be ignored. He has assembled too much material, sifted through it too thoroughly, and critically reviewed the opinions of too many scholars not to be taken into account. We may disagree with Halevy—I think we must—but we cannot dismiss him. Moreover, I believe that some aspects of his theory are valid and important. Foremost is his conception of the formation of the Talmud as a continuous process of

---

[1] Explicit parallels are drawn at II, pp. 481, 500, 600; III, pp. 23, 27, 37, 126. Of course, one or more of these elements may have true at any of the occasions.

[2] V. e.g., III, pp. 19, 20, 21.

[3] E.g. II, p. 536; III, pp. 20, 26, 116-7.

[4] Contrast II, pp. 591-92 with pp. 481-82, 484.

[5] V.e.g., II, pp. 482, 490, 494.

[6] Cf. II, pp. 526, 529 with p. 536 and III, p. 36.

[7] V. his treatment of the peculiarities of b. Ned. and Naz. at II, pp. 48-49 and cf. J.N. Epstein, *A Grammer of Babylonian Aramaic* (Jerusalem and Tel-Aviv, 1960), pp. 14-16.

assembling, arranging, and evaluating traditions—a process carried on at all the academies in all the generations. This conception and his (perhaps unconscious) avoidance of the term "edit" or "redact" (I mean the root ʿRK and derivatives) force one to raise the question whether it is proper to use a phrase like the "redaction of the Talmud", and, if so, then in what sense. Secondly, Halevy's attempt to uncover early strata of the Talmud and reconstruct its evolution through the analysis of *sugyot* appears to represent a fruitful approach. As I have already mentioned, this method must become much more sophisticated than it was in Halevy's hands. Refinements and controls, like the ones promised by current work on text criticism based on manuscripts[1] unavailable in his time, should accomplish this. Finally I do not think it patronizing to point out that Halevy's work is over fifty years old. Few scholarly works in this century can expect to endure much longer.

---

[1] I refer to David Weiss Halivni, *Meqorot uMesorot*, below, part iv.

II

LITERARY CRITICS

IV

B. M. LEWIN AND THE SABORAIC ELEMENT

BY

ROBERT GOLDENBERG

Scholars have generally assumed that the entity which we call the Babylonian Talmud has a history which can be traced and accounted for. Certain of the main periods of that history have also been the subject of general agreement, ever since the time of the Geonim. It has been agreed that in the closing years of the Amoraic period there was a concerted effort, led principally by R. Ashi, to resolve all outstanding difficulties and ambiguities and to produce a finished product. This would embody all the authoritative decisions of past generations, and also provide a firm basis for the development of new decisions as future conditions might require them. The Amoraim, it was considered, were succeeded by the Saboraim, who polished up the text, added glosses where they thought them necessary, and left the text in a condition which would guarantee its proper transmission to the coming generations.

More recently, literary criticism of the Talmud has produced a few conclusions which make the picture seem rather more complicated. The tendency to summarize and organize earlier materials turns out not to have been peculiarly characteristic of the final Amoraic generations, but rather a function of the Amoraic academies throughout the period of their existence, from the time of Rav Judah and R. Nahman. Secondly, we find much evidence that the people who lived after the time of R. Ashi and his generation, Saboraim, continued to do the kinds of things which were presumably no longer necessary. In short, the history of the Talmud can only with difficulty be thought of as linear; it was, if anything, cyclical, but it was actually a process of accretion. The production of new materials and the organization (and reorganization) of old materials went on continuously, and literary evidence indicates that what we call the Talmud is actually an accumulation, whose various parts show highly varying degrees of organization and editorial complexity; the passage quoted below from

J. N. Epstein[1] is an example. Under the circumstances, how all these materials came together in the shape in which we find them is a question we cannot even begin to answer.

In B. M. Lewin's *Rabbanan Savora'ei VeTalmudam* (*The Saboraic Rabbis and their Talmud*)[2], we find much literary observation of great perceptivity, but acceptance of the old historical schema. The result is that the literary observations are interesting and useful, while the historical comments are unoriginal, disconnected, and of negligible value.

Review of Lewin's life and work provides the start of an explanation for this curious phenomenon. Benjamin Menasseh Lewin was born on May 10, 1879, near Horodetz, in Russia. He received his education in various *yeshivot*, where he also became acquainted with medieval Jewish philosophy and the writings of the nineteenth-century Jewish historians Graetz and Jawitz. After receiving rabbinical ordination from R. Abraham Isaac haKohen Kook, later Chief Rabbi of the Holy Land, he went at first to Berlin, and then, in 1907, he entered the University of Berne. While there he was active in the new organization of Orthodox Jewish students. He also published several articles in which he argued against the legitimacy of the textual criticism of the Bible. He emigrated to Palestine in 1920, and died there, in Jerusalem, on April 1, 1944. His *magnum opus* is *Oẓar HaGeonim*, a collection of Geonic responsa and commentaries, arranged according to the tractates of the Talmud. Thirteen volumes, going through Bava Meẓi'a', appeared during the years from 1928 to 1943.[3]

Two facts are relevant to our present interest: Lewin's militant Orthodoxy and his great interest in Geonic literature. Lewin's main work was the publication of Geonic texts, often with extensive introductions. His edition of the Letter of R. Sherira Gaon appeared in 1921; his biographical essay on R. Sherira had appeared five years earlier. Lewin must be considered a philologian and student of Geonica, rather than a historian.

The above evaluation of RST was to be expected. Lewin wrote a series of unconnected chapters, and while literary notes may successfully take this form, systematic history can not.

Because of the structure of RST, it will be necessary to repeat

---

[1] Below, p. 77.

[2] Jerusalem, 5697 = 1936/37.

[3] This information is taken from a brief autobiographical sketch Lewin published in *Sinai* 14, pp. 195-97.

Lewin's findings in schematic form, under three headings: (a) historical observations concerning the transition from Amoraim to Saboraim, (b) comments concerning characteristic Saboraic activities, and (c) efforts to identify Saboraic material either in Talmudic or Geonic literature.

i

Lewin's historical investigations are primarily concerned with the expression *sof hora'ah*. He defines *hora'ah* as the "final conclusion (*masqanah*) of the *sugyot* and fixing (ḥtm) of the discussions of the Amoraim in the Gemara." In this context he alludes to R. Naḥman's question on 'Eruv. 32b ("Have you fixed [qv'] the discussion in the Gemara?"), which he understands as referring to a "fixed formulation, so that the conclusion might be a firm basis for *hora'ah*, and so that further discussion might rest firmly on it. In every generation, official concluders (*rabbanan desiyuma*)[1] added new decisions and traditions on the Mishnah to every *sugya*, and fixed (qv') them in the Gemara" (p. 1). Lewin also quotes R. Sherira to the same effect: "And as uncertainties arose, those interpretations of earlier teachers which had not been fixed in their own day were now fixed and studied, and the things which those earlier masters did were now recited in the Gemara" (ESG 64).

A *setama digemara*, in other words, had existed before the time of R. Ashi and his colleagues. He and his companions "compared all the traditions ... and sifted them at the academy ... and resolved all uncertainties [on the basis of] the Mishnah and Baraita and anonymous Gemara which were before them, and determined the conclusions and transmitted everything to the following generations" (p. 1). Lewin emphasizes that R. Ashi's younger contemporaries, his successors at Sura, had a part in finishing his work. The latter Ravina (b. R. Huna), whom R. Sherira twice called *sof hora'ah*, was the last of that generation, and he left the final stamp on the Talmud at Sura (p. 1; cf. ESG 69, 95).[2]

Lewin claims that this interpretation of the phrase *sof hora'ah* is also

[1] Cf. Lewin's *Ozar HaGeonim*, Berakhot, section on responsa, p. 128, n. 6. There, *rabbanan desiyuma* are defined as Rabbis who "fixed (ḥtm) the legal determination of the *gemara*".

[2] The younger Ravina was the nephew of the older. When the Talmud said that "R. Ashi and Ravina were the end of *hora'ah*" (B.M. 86a), it did not specify its reference. See further below, p. 54, n. 1.

that of Halevy, who wrote that the Ravina to whom the Talmud referred was not the contemporary of R. Ashi but the younger man of that name.[1] R. Sherira's intention must therefore have been to signify a certain interval of time when he said that R. Ashi and Ravina were *sof hora'ah*. Lewin then quotes S. J. Fein, who, he says, had anticipated even Halevy:

> The Talmudic expression ... [mentions both] R. Ashi and Ravina; it seems to mean the Ravina who was R. Ashi's colleague and who died during his lifetime. But R. Sherira Gaon in his letter extends the end of *hora'ah* and with it the conclusion (*sym*) of the Talmud to Ravina who presided at Sura after Rabbah Tosfa'ah ... It seems that he thinks the Talmud meant to indicate the beginning and the end [of the period]...[2]

He then discusses Halevy's emendation of the text of R. Sherira's letter, which had moved up the date of Ravina's death from 811 Sel. (= 500 C.E.) to 786 (= 475), and rejects it (pp. 4-6), adducing much evidence in his own support. He thus concludes that the period of *hora'ah* ended at Sura with the death of Ravina b. R. Huna, in the year 500 C.E.

With regard to Pumbedita, R. Sherira says (p. 97) that the period of *hora'ah* ended there during the time of R. Yosi, who assumed the presidency of the academy in 787 (= 476 C.E.). R. Sherira mentions him elsewhere (770) together with R. Aḥai of Bé Ḥatim, who was one of the Saboraim; they are found together as well in Ta'anit 18b. R. Yosi, who is thus seen to have been a transitional figure at Pumbedita, outlived Ravina b.R. Huna by fourteen years (p. 7).

This précis indicates why Lewin's historical findings are unoriginal and disconnected. They depend both for organization and for content on R. Sherira's letter, as Lewin thought it had been understood by Halevy, whose huge influence on Lewin is duly acknowledged.[3] The

[1] I do not understand Halevy in this way. In *Dorot HaRishonim*, III, p. 22, he writes explicitly that the Talmud meant the older Ravina when it said "R. Ashi and Ravina are the end of *hora'ah*," and that its intention was to include them and their generation. Halevy adds that R. Sherira understood the Talmud in this way, and that his *other* statement, that Ravina bar R. Huna was the end of *hora'ah*, was designed to fix more precisely the end of the period, which the Talmud had defined rather loosely. His two uses of the phrase *sof hora'ah* do not apply it to the same person. In a rather obscure comment, Halevy seems to admit that R. Sherira had thereby caused great trouble to his readers and had led many of them astray.

[2] S. J. Fein, *Nidḥei Yisra'el* (Vilna, 5611 = 1850/i), p. 35, n. 1, as quoted in RST, p. 4.

[3] Moshe Beer writes that "in all matters of history and chronology, [Lewin]

outlines of R. Sherira's narration, however, are presupposed, not presented, and the present reader may find it helpful to consult the summary and critique of Halevy's theories found elsewhere in this volume.[1] Lewin, like Halevy, uncritically accepts the historical reliability of R. Sherira's letter, and like him assumes the validity of the "halakhic myth," the myth that imposes on our sources a literary and legal coherence they themselves hardly exhibit.

R. Sherira wrote in his letter that after the deaths of the last members of R. Ashi's generation "even though there was no more *hora'ah*, there were Saboraim who provided interpretations which were close to *hora'ah*; ... and whatever was still an issue, they interpreted" (pp. 69-70). Lewin himself comments on this as follows:

> The first generation of Amoraim, whose days extended from the last generation of Tannaim, and of whom it could be said, "Rav is a Tanna and can dispute [their words]," [is directly analogous] to the first generation of "our Rabbis the Saboraim," whose days extended from the last generation of "our Rabbis of *hora'ah*," and of whom it was said that they "came close to *hora'ah*." (p. 11)

Lewin, still following the lead of R. Sherira, sees the Saboraim as having continued and brought to completion the work of the Amoraim, although without their freedom of innovation. He shows that the Saboraim continued to use Amoraic terminology, and that even the long *sugya* at the beginning of Qiddushin, which had long been recognized as Saboraic, exhibits modes of argument which were characteristic of the earliest Amoraic periods, and even of the Tannaitic *midrashim* (p. 17).[2] He documents the familiar assertion that the Saboraim were concerned with questions of accurate ascription (pp. 12-13). He shows that summary introductions like "now that we see that the law has not been decided ..." are characteristically Saboraic, although one such statement is attributed on b. Shev. 48b to the Amora R. Ḥama (p. 12). The Saboraim represent no discontinuous development after the Amoraic period, but rather a further step in the labors the Amoraim themselves had begun.

Lewin seems uncertain, however, that this is really how to understand the phrase "close to *hora'ah*." We have just seen that Saboraic methods were in many respects very close indeed to the old Amoraic

follows Halevy, without any independent critical approach." *Bar-Ilan Annual* 4-5, p. 189, n. 25. The discussion of Ravina's death is the only exception I could find.

[1] Pp. 29-47.

[2] Lewin takes these observations, with acknowledgement, from Jawitz, *Toldot*, ix, 219.

modes of study. At one point, Lewin says explicitly that the "interpretations which are close to *hora'ah* are interpretations which are designed as *hora'ah* and which constitute *hora'ah*" (p. 42). On the same page, however, he quotes R. Sherira (pp. 17-18) to the effect that that the Tannaim and Amoraim added nothing to the teachings of the Men of the Great Assembly, but rather clarified them and put them in order. He then says that the Saboraim likewise innovated nothing, and did not create *hora'ah* of their own. In keeping with this estimate of their work, he describes them as having created a "talmud to the Talmud" (p. 43), and says that this new "talmud" kept developing throughout the Geonic period.

Lewin, while espousing the traditional view that the work of the Amoraim and that of the Saboraim were in fact radically different, seems to have sensed that the Saboraim and even the Geonim did many things just as the Amoraim themselves had done them. It seems to me that the Saboraim are different from the later Amoraim in a similar way to that in which the later Amoraim had differed from their predecessors. That is, all three groups represent stages in one and the same process. It may be that Lewin would have said that the Saboraim preserved certain Amoraic methods of procedure, but had different, less ambitious purposes. This distinction, however, does not appear in Lewin's book.

ii

Most of RST is devoted to Lewin's search for traces of Saboraic material in the literature which has survived to our own day. We possess no books called Saboraic. All our literature is either earlier, that is, Talmudic, or later, that is, Geonic. Lewin tries to find later additions to the first of these bodies of material, and older survivals in the second. I here review some of his findings, in particular those instructive of his methods and germane to broader historical issues.

Lewin's most striking claim is with regard to the word *perush*. He contends that the word is often equivalent in meaning to the word *parush* (= separate) and indicates a comment separate from the main body of text, although somehow related to it. After the period of *hora'ah* ended, the text of the Talmud became fixed, and all further Amoraic or later materials were *perushim* in this manner. The Saboraim created a *perush* or *sevara* for any Talmudic passage which they thought was in need of it; these were fixed and transmitted along with the Talmud itself (p. 26).[1] These *perushim* were often written into the margin of Talmudic texts. From there, they were occasionally moved into the body of the text, and preceded by the key word *perush* to distinguish them from the *hora'ah* itself. In support of this theory, Lewin quotes from the introduction to the eleventh-century Commentary on the Mishnah of R. Nathan Av haYeshivah:

> Those who came after R. Ashi interpreted the difficult and unclear passages in the Talmud; [these were] the Saboraim and those like them [*vezulatam*] among the heads of the Academies. This [material] was inserted into the Talmud in the form of *perush*, since it is not from the *Gemara*. Thus you will find "*perush*" marked on it, so that it be kept separate from R. Ashi's *Gemara*.[2]

Lewin then gives dozens of examples of cases where our printed texts of the Talmud have lost the key word, but where various manuscripts preserve it (pp. 27-40). He shows that *perushim* were often quoted in Geonic literature as well. Sometimes the word was there attached, used in this technical sense, to a passage which was not in fact an explication of what preceded it, that is, where the word could not be given its more common interpretation. This led the editor of the Spanish Recension of *Halakhot Gedolot* to emend it to *psaq*, an emendation which Lewin now shows to be unnecessary (p. 41). From Geonic literature, Lewin draws his final bit of evidence from the Geonic Commentary on Tahorot, where it is stated that "an unclean *perush* ought not to eat together with an unclean *'am ha'areṣ*" (p. 41, n. a). Here we find an interesting corroboration of his claim that the two words *perush* and *parush* were occasionally interchanged.

Lewin was in general very sensitive to key words. He takes care to point out that *perushim* were often introduced with the word *talya* (p. 41), and elsewhere he suggests that *qushya* and *peruqa* were also used in this manner, particularly by the early Geonim (p. 19). Geonic literature exhibits certain stock phrases which Lewin claims are indicative of Saboraic materials; among these are *tarbiṣa'ei*, and *nusḥa dimetivta* (p. 33). The word *mistabra*, or the phrase *hakhi nami mistabra*, often signifies Saboraic interpolations (pp. 15-16). Quoting a manuscript in

[1] Elsewhere, Lewin quotes and apparently endorses Jawitz's opinion that *sevara* was not transmitted, each scholar rather creating his own rationale. *Cf.* Jawitz, *Toldot*, IX, 219, and RST, p. 18. I do not know how to resolve this tension, except by suggesting that Lewin had not wanted to endorse Jawitz's theory. There is no indication, however, that this was the case.

[2] As quoted from *Kiryat Sefer*, X. 385; *cf.* RST, p. 26.

the British Museum, Lewin says that "all these things were in the margin of the manuscript, and were moved into the text and became part of it" (p. 18).[1]

Finally, even where no key word was used, Saboraic statements were often inserted into the Talmud in such a way as to distinguish them from Amoraic statements. Thus, we find "R. Aḥai said" only twice in the Talmud; elsewhere some other, less common verb is used (p. 14).[2]

Lewin heavily depends on the comparison of many texts and manuscripts. His way of showing that *perush* is often a technical indication of a late insertion, for example, was to take parallel occurrences of the same extended discussion, and to show that some versions used the word, while others had an explicit ascription to Saboraic authority, and still others named no particular source at all. This method is generally dependable, as long as it is kept under control. In the case of *perush*, this control was provided by the presence of two kinds of corroborating material. First, Lewin could quote an early authority. Second, he could show examples where the word *perush* was obviously not used in its more familiar sense. These, together with much evidence of a cumulative rather than a probative nature, added up to a convincing proof. Elsewhere, however, Lewin tries to show that *sevira lan* was systematically used by the Geonim to indicate reference to earlier materials. The proof here is much weaker, because the corroboration mentioned above is not provided. Lewin can show parallel texts where *sevira lan* seems equivalent to ascription to "the great successors to the Savoraim" (*ravwata divetar rabbanan savora'ei*). He does not, however, quote anyone else who interpreted the phrase as he does. Of all his examples only one uses *sevira lan* in such a way that it could not be assigned its customary meaning (cf. pp. 56ff.). That one example, on p. 59, compares the two versions of *Halakhot Gedolot*, as follows:

Warsaw edition, p. 114c—

sevira lan de'amar R. Naḥman halakhah keRabbi.

Spanish Recension 474—

sevira lan keR. Naḥman de'amar halakhah keRabbi.

Lewin says that the latter version "is certainly a correction of our version, which [uses] uncommon phraseology, but more original if we examine it. It is certainly meant to indicate that this is a tradition

[1] No further identification of the MS. is supplied.

[2] This too is acknowledged as coming from Jawitz, *Toldot*, IX, 220.

from 'the great successors of the Savoraim'." This is the only unequivocal example, however, so the cumulative force of the proof is limited. "Our" version could rather to be taken as a corruption of the other, and the other be taken as the more original—the rule of *lectio difficilior* notwithstanding.

Lewin's theory is dependent in several places on the assumptions that the Talmud was written down very soon after the Amoraim had done their work, and that present texts spring from a rather small number of original manuscripts. It is unlikely that the oral tradition would have become so stratified had it continued to develop without interruption, or that independent written recensions were so few in number. Halevy, on whom Lewin depends, does claim that the Talmud was quickly written down[1], but Lewin never gives any indication that he considers the matter worth discussing.

iii

Nothing in RST indicates that Lewin wanted to deny the traditional conception of the formation of the Babylonian Talmud. He does not discuss the matter as an abstract question, but he understood the Talmud—as had Halevy—as the result of a long-term project, executed chiefly by the later Amoraim, but brought to completion by their Saboraic successors. This conclusion is vexing in Lewin's case because of his ability to locate Saboraic materials through the careful use of the methods of literary analysis. The evidence he uncovers points clearly to general conclusions which vary from the traditional conception of the Talmud. His interest remains throughout in details. He offers no discussion of the general nature of the whole, and certainly no consideration of historical, non-literary issues. The result is that Lewin's own contribution—much like most of the passages which he discusses—is largely small and parenthetical. He points out an unrecognized key word here, an unnoticed Saboraic usage there. That entity called the Babylonian Talmud, however, is never the subject of discussion.

I see little value in trying to trace the "redaction" of the Babylonian Talmud. That word connotes a coherent supervised process, but literary analysis of the document provides more and more evidence that no such process can be detected. Even the "formation" of the Talmud

---

[1] *Dorot haRishonim*, III, 23 f.

cannot be fruitfully pursued at this time. The whole seems far too loose in its construction, too much the product of an untraceable sequence of events. We do not yet know the extent to which various tractates or even chapters form coherent wholes. How are we to discuss that huge quantity called the Talmud?

The Talmud, then, taken as a whole, should be at the end of the current scholarly agenda. While the literary analysts—and I do think the job is chiefly theirs—are working on this first problem, historians of religion can direct their attention to another. The belief which has prevented the realization of the true literary nature of the Babylonian Talmud is that the "Talmudic age" came to an end with the completion of its literary product and was succeeded by the "post-Talmudic age," which left a literary corpus of its own, called "Geonic." The Geonim themselves held that belief; R. Sherira makes that clear. The innumerable Geonic references to "the Talmud" reinforce the impression. Only after presupposing that they lived in a subsequent, inferior age did the Geonim lose sight of their own influence on Talmudic literature. They then concluded that it had really been "finished" during the earlier period. Why did the Geonim form such a judgment of themselves? Is it another example of the habit of thinking that past ages were superior to the current one? Did particular events help bring it into existence? We cannot avoid these questions much longer.

V

JULIUS KAPLAN, HYMAN KLEIN, AND THE SABORAIC ELEMENT

BY

TERRY R. BARD

i

The shortage of evidence about the redactors of the Babylonian Talmud poses problems for the contemporary scholar. With the exception of two allusions (b. B. M. 86a, B. B. 157b), the Talmud remains mute regarding its own formation. Julius Kaplan, *The Redaction of the Babylonian Talmud*, re-evaluates earlier assumptions. It is difficult to discern a precise methodology in Kaplan's rather "bulky" exposition.[1] Yet, as Boaz Cohen rightly suggests, Kaplan brings "to the surface numerous passages hitherto not considered" in the investigation of this problem.[2]

Initially, Kaplan presents resumés of the opinions held by Graetz, Frankel, Rapoport, N. Brüll, I. H. Weiss, Y. I. Halevy, and Z. Jawitz. It is not within the scope of this paper to weigh the opinions of these scholars. Their respective views on the editing of the Talmud will be stated concisely to indicate what Kaplan accepts and rejects. Graetz accepts entirely R. Sherira's statements:

1. And after Ravina had properly superseded Samuel Yarhina'ah in the book of Adam [genealogy of the whole human race] where it was written, Ashi and Ravina conclude the *hora'ah*.
2. And fourth, in the seventh month was the 13th of Kislev of the year 491, Rabana Avina the son of Rav Huna, who was Ravina, died and he concluded *hora'ah*.[3]

---

[1] Cohen, Boaz, "The Redaction of the Babylonian Talmud" (review), *JQR*, 24, 1933–1934, p. 265.

[2] *Ibid.*, p. 263.

[3] *Epistle of R. Sherira Gaon*, pp. 95. Four explanations of *hora'ah* are: (1) a transmission of oral law; (2) insertion by scholars of halakhic material; (3) the right to change the Talmud whether in substance or form; and (4) legislative activity. Kaplan is concerned essentially with explanations 1 and 4.

He thus ascribes the initial editing of the Talmud to R. Ashi (d. 427, Sherira). Ravina bar R. Huna and R. Yosi, respective heads of the academies at Sura and Pumbedita, completed R. Ashi's work. Frankel minimizes the role taken by R. Ashi and the Saboraim in the editing of the Talmud. Moreover, he claims that the Talmud was complete before the death of Ravina bar R. Huna, and that the Saboraim merely added marginal notes. Rapoport, however, contends that it was indeed R. Ashi who compiled the Talmud; it was committed to writing between his death and the death of Ravina bar R. Huna. Brüll also asserts that following Judah the Prince's example, R. Ashi was the first editor of the Talmud, i.e., the *halakhah*. The Saboraim merely introduced notes and not *halakhah*. Weiss is the only scholar to credit R. Ashi with reducing the Talmud to writing. Halevy presents a rather unconventional view: R. Ashi and his "associates" (Kaplan) composed thirty-seven treatises containing the entire Talmud. The Talmud, however, remained open for some time after that. According to Kaplan, Jawitz represents only a minor deviation from Halevy. Halevy divided up the redacting of the Talmud into three successive stages: R. Ashi, Ravina bar R. Huna, and Rabbah Tosfa'ah. Jawitz transfers Ravina bar R. Huna's role assigned by Halevy to Rabbah Tosfa'ah. Jawitz also adds that the Saboraim are to be regarded merely as disciples of the Amoraim. It is to these conclusions that Kaplan directs his arguments.

Though Kaplan considers all the above possibilities, his position is clearly linked to Brüll's. In addition to amplifying Brüll's findings, Kaplan differs from Brüll in two respects. First, Kaplan considers the *structure* of the Talmud; second, Kaplan credits the Saboraim with the redaction of the *Talmud*.

The chapters "Internal Evidence" (IV) and "Anonymous Parts" (V) are nothing more than lengthy strings of essentially unanalyzed quotations. Kaplan admits that neither of these considerations provides any real formative information concerning the compilation or the redaction of the Talmud. Internal evidence leaves no doubt as to the prominence of R. Ashi and his school:

> The school of R. Ashi stands out conspicuously by virtue of its great productivity and of the number of scholars associated with it. With very few exceptions, no other name is as frequently mentioned and as centrally placed in the Talmud as that of R. Ashi. A careful examination will show about fourteen hundred Talmudic passages in which R. Ashi is mentioned nearly seventeen hundred times in the center of a group of almost a hundred illustrious names. (Page 71)

Despite *this* statistical approach, the *prominence* of the school of R. Ashi is well attested. R. Ashi's *editing* cannot be proved on the basis of such internal evidence.

Anonymous passages provide no more of a link. Kaplan concludes that the "order of talmudic records" can contribute little to an understanding of the compilation and redaction of the Talmud. Kaplan presents five major rules for ordering of names in the Talmud; we will consider three. These rules are mostly extra-Talmudic attempts to explain the ordering of names in Talmudic texts. In "chronological" ordering, R. Ashi's name often would appear last. Accordingly, "in the few instances where discussions by R. Ashi are continued by later Amoraim, his name ... precedes rather than follows the others" (pp. 80-81). "Academic" ordering usually places the more authoritative decision or opinion at the end of other opinions. This order was evident in the academy of R. Judah HaNasi, wherein "transactions ... proceeded from the lower ranks toward the higher. In order to insure free and independent judgment, matters which had been decided by the great academic council were first voted upon by members of inferior scholastic rank (b. Git. 58b-59a)" (p. 81). Indications in the Talmud suggest that this ordering "prevailed in all the academies in the Amoraic period" (p. 81). R. Ashi's name appears last in lists of his contemporaries. Ordering by "quotations" is suggested by the Tosafists (b. Shav. 5b): "A statement taken out of its original connection and applied to the discussion of another subject will be placed at the end of the discussion" (p. 85).[1] These "rules" of ordering are not hard and fast. Many variations occur, and it is doubtful whether they help appreciably in determining the compiler or redactor(s) of the Talmud. They are of greater help in dating texts and people than in solving our problem.

Alternatively, Kaplan suggests that problems of the editing and redacting of the Talmud can be resolved if the *structure* of the texts is considered. This is his major thesis, which assumes the authenticity of b. B. M. 86a,

> Ravina and R. Nathan concluded the Mishnah, R. Ashi and Ravina concluded *hora'ah* and a sign thereof is the verse, "Until I went to the sanctuary of God; then I understood their end (Psalm 78)."

Kaplan accepts Brüll's view that *hora'ah* = *gemara*. Kaplan shows that

[1] Fourth is the rule of "logical order" (R. Akiva Eger 1761-1783), and fifth, the rule of "dependent order".

there are literary and structural differences between *gemara* and *talmud*. *Gemara* is "a statement put in simple and concise language, in order to record the final conclusion resulting from a previous, sometimes lengthy and complex, discussion." *Talmud* is broader, embracing "practically all the elements which enter the various discussions recorded in the Talmud" (pp. 196-97). Consequently, *talmud* precedes *gemara*. (This distinction applies to *halakhah* alone). Kaplan suggests that *Talmud* must have been "reduced" to writing last of all the legal material. It was not written down until people feared its destruction or loss. Kaplan contends that the Saboraim evinced such fears, and, as such, are "the designers and the real builders of the *talmud*" (p. 312):

> In the deserted halls of the academies, among the wreckage of the old system of oral instruction [i. e., under the Amoraim], the Saboraim came face to face with the danger of losing contact with posterity (p. 297).

Hence, it became necessary to compose a *talmud* for the elucidation of Mishnah and *gemara* (cf. b. Git. 60a [p. 298]).

The implications of "*talmud* as an elaboration of *gemara*" for the editing of the Talmud, in its traditional sense, are far reaching: *talmud*, being of later date than *gemara*, was recorded later than *gemara*. But the time of redaction is more complex. In addition to the difficulty in distinguishing between *talmud* and *gemara*, the problem in differentiating between originally oral and originally written transmission emerges. While laws did exist orally,

> The prohibition against the writing down of *halakhah* never applied to Mishnah or gemara. The results of long discussions and sanctions by the great assemblies of the academies, these were collections that were intended for everlasting use. Accordingly, they were recorded in writing to be kept in the archives of centers of learning, while armies of students kept them alive by oral study and special divisions of "tannaim" doing lip service perpetuated them by constant repetition. At the same time, the prohibition applied to the other and vaster branch of study, namely to that of talmud. Intrinsically inexhaustible, largely hypothetical, and in its sound parts, always discoverable by suitable methods of analysis and research, talmud was the proper subject of the prohibition. Any writing of it was strictly interdicted. Its preservation was not sought, nor much desired (p. 274).

This last statement, appears to be the inference of a scholar in the seclusion of his study, inventing ways to simplify an otherwise complex problem. The textual proofs—convincing in themselves—with which he supports his theory indicate the major faults of his exposition: he provides no historical analysis of the texts he uses; he cites passages out of context; and he sees little or no relationship between texts.

Kaplan finds in *haggadah* a dichotomy similar in structure to *gemara/talmud*. Kaplan defines *haggadah* as a "valuable extended talk" (p. 282), easily broken down into brief propositions and elaborate discourses on the propositions (cf. p. 280). Such a casual generalization of *haggadah* is suspect. The structure of *haggadah* as a literary form cannot be viewed in isolation, especially when the literature covers vast periods of time and areas of concern.

Kaplan disagrees with his contemporaries about the link connecting the Amoraic and the Saboraic periods. He contends that the line between them is somewhat vague because many Amoraim were active in the Saboraic period (p. 309). The beginning of the Saboraic period may be dated most reasonably with the death of Ravina bar R. Huna, and with the ascent of R. ʿEna and R. Simona. This is based on an acceptance of the information given by R. Sherira. Both of these events are subsequent to the death of R. Ashi. The Amoraim edited *gemara*. R. Ashi, composer of the parts of *gemara* ascribed to him, was also the compiler of other *gemara*. His disciples continued this process until the beginning of the Saboraic period. Then the Saboraim redacted *talmud*. They rearranged and transposed much of the material of R. Ashi—which accounts for the fact that the *gemara* for twenty-three tractates of Mishnah is missing.[1] No additions were made after the Saboriac period.[2]

The Geonim, who viewed the Talmud as absolutely closed, became mere interpreters (p. 318). In a single attempt to introduce history into his study, Kaplan distinguishes between the Saboraic and Geonic periods as follows:

> The really distinctive fact about the Saboraic period is that it represented an interregnum (p. 318) ... the new Geonic schools were pattern-

[1] Cohen, *op. cit.*, p. 264.

[2] Peripheral to his argument, Kaplan notes a difference between *gemara* and *sebara* citing b. Yev. 25b as his source (p. 209). Hyman Klein has pursued this line of thought more thoroughly (cf. "Gemara and Sebara", *JQR*, Vol. 38, 1947-1948, pp. 67-91; "Gemara Quotations in Sebara", *JQR*, Vol. 43, 1952-1953, pp. 341-363; "Some Methods of Sebara", *JQR*, Vol. 50, 1959-1960, pp. 124-146). Kaplan notes the difference merely to support his point that there was a difference in activity between the Amoriam and the Saboraim (as well as the Tannaim). Klein elaborates on these differences; but he does not argue from a limited point of view trying to fit these distinctions into a preconceived scheme.

> ed after the Amoraic academies ... (though) the newly produced Talmud constituted the final authority for the Geonim. (p. 319)

He cites no evidence.

We turn now to a consideration of Kaplan's methodology. Kaplan's position is, in a way, a reaction to the studies of Graetz. Kaplan's hypothetical construct of *gemara/talmud* is an imposition upon the texts rather than a conclusion drawn from them. For example, Kaplan accepts Brull's analysis of b. B. B. 157b:

> Ravina said, "In the first version, R. Ashi told us [that] the first [creditor] acquired [the right over the land]; the second version of R. Ashi [however] told us [that the land was] to be divided. And the law is [that the land] is to be divided."

Two editions can be credited to R. Ashi (and his academy) and *gemara* = *hora'ah*. Kaplan develops his position from this point. Boaz Cohen suggests a difficulty:

> Assuming for the sake of argument that Dr. Kaplan's hypothesis concerning the meaning of the term Gemara is correct, we still cannot assent to his view that R. Ashi is the compiler only of the Gemara. There is no doubt that Brüll's ingenious theory that *hora'ah* is to be explained in the light of Ber. 5a is right. However, the original and correct reading is *lahoratom zo talmud*... (Kaplan, p. 289, n. 2, is inaccurate when it implies that only the Munich Ms. reads *talmud*. As a matter of fact all early uncensored editions preserve this reading—note 4). Hence the passage in B.M. 86a would contradict Kaplan's theory that R. Ashi is the compiler of Gemara.[1]

This fact makes Kaplan's structural hypothesis suspect. Convinced of the validity of Brüll's citation and scholarship, Kaplan assumes that R. Ashi took a definite part in the formation of the Talmud. Kaplan sees his task as one of defining what part of the Talmud can be credited to R. Ashi. This tacit acceptance of others' findings is characteristic of Kaplan's use of texts. Kaplan assumes that texts can be explained and understood properly in isolation from their context. He feels justified in making positive assertions about matters which texts suggest as tentative at best. For example, from a discussion between Ravina and Rav Naḥman (b. Pes. 105a-b) wherein Ravina states his function in the academy as follows:

> 'I am neither a self-pretended scholar nor a visionary [story-teller] nor unique [in this ruling], but I am a teacher and systematizer of traditions, and they rule thus in the Beth Hamidrash as I do ...'[2]

---

[1] Cohen, *op. cit.*, p. 264.
[2] *Ibid.*

Kaplan concludes:

> As president of the academy (Ravina) ... did not participate in its discussions... He used only to take note of the conclusions, to ratify them, or to put them to a vote, and stamp them with a *gemara* ... (and) to arrange new contributions by determining the texts. (p. 254)

Ravina says nothing about his position or his participation in discourses, except to show that he and the other members of his academy decided a certain case in the manner stated.

When Kaplan feels that history does play a role in his study, he relies on the conclusions of others and ignores the texts. B. Ber. 43a relates the following discussion:

> R. Ḥisda said to R. Isaac: What blessing is said over this balsam oil? He replied: Thus said Rav. Judah: "Who createst the oil of our land." He then said to him: "*Leaving out R. Judah, who dotes on the land of Israel, what do ordinary people say*?"—he replied: Thus said R. Yoḥanan: "who createst pleasant oil." R. Adda b. Aḥva said: "Over costum the blessing is, 'Who createst fragrant woods,' but not over oil in which it is steeped." R. Kahana, however, says, "Even over oil in which it is steeped, but not over oil in which it has been ground." The Nehardeans say, even over oil in which it has been ground. (Italics mine.)

On the limited basis of the italicized words, Kaplan concludes:

> There is no doubt ... that the new form of Zoroastrian persecutions which interfered greatly with study at night proved a source of great irritation for many of its victims. It seemed particularly serious to Palestinian scholars. (p. 256)

Even a cursory look at this text shows no mention of "Zoroastrian persecutions". We can only assume that Kaplan was inferring this from the statement that R. Judah dotes on *'ereẓ yisra'el* in the context of R. Sherira's Epistle. On both counts Kaplan's conclusions are unfounded and mistaken. The passage in b. Ber. indicates *only* the varieties of blessings said over "balsam oil". Kaplan shows little understanding of the history of the period. Though his distinctions between *gemara* and *talmud* are interesting constructs, their legitimacy remains questionable. R. Ashi's role in forming, compiling, and editing the *gemara* also remains questionable.

ii

Julius Kaplan and Hyman Klein approached the formation of Talmudic *sugyot* in similar ways. Kaplan invented structural categories of *gemara* and *talmud*; Klein isolated *gemara* and *sebara*. Both men were unconcerned with the historical context from which Talmudic literature emerged; they were interested with literary analysis. Kaplan was concerned with the redaction of the Babylonian Talmud, while Klein was involved more explicitly with the formation of *sugyot*. He discussed the redaction of the literature only peripherally.[1]

Data for a precise biographical sketch of Hyman Klein are unavailable. He was born around 1900. In 1945 Klein was teaching at Aria College in Winchester, England. He taught at the Liverpool Talmudical College (England) from 1947 until around 1953. By his late fifties, Klein had moved to Jerusalem where he died in 1958.

Although Klein never wrote a major work, one has the impression that he intended to so; his articles on the distinctions between *gemara* and *sebara* suggest that they were parts of a developing *magnum opus*. Klein described the development of the Talmud in purely literary terms. Although he was familiar with Weiss' work, Klein was most indebted to Kaplan's structural dichotomy.[2] Unlike Kaplan's, however, Klein's focus is more modest and thorough.

In "Mekhilta on the Pentateuch",[3] Klein paved the way for his eventual distinction between *gemara* and *sebara*. Here he argued for the initial unity of "core *midrashim*" scattered throughout the midrashic literature of Torah (specifically the *halakhic midrashim*).

Klein accepted Kaplan's definition of *gemara* as a short, concise statement, but he disagreed with Kaplan's process of formulation. Kaplan suggested that *gemara* was the conclusion of a "long and involved talmudical discussion";[4] *talmud* preceded *gemara*.[5] Klein placed *gemara* first in the process. *Gemara* is the simplest statement which is then amplified and interpreted by *sebara*. These two elements provide the "central core" for every *sugya* (i.e., Talmudic discussion).[6]

Klein proposed a variety of ways by which to distinguish between

---

[1] *GSBT*. I have used Klein's own abbreviations for "Gemara and Sebara" *(GS)* and "Gemara Quotations in Sebara" *(GQS)* and my own for "Some Methods of Sebara" *(SMS)* and "Some General Results on the Separation of Gemara from Sebara in the Babylonian Talmud" *(GSBT)*. Klein's exclusive concern with literary structures neglects all non-literary problems presented by the sources. Klein claims that non-literary questions may be asked only *after* he has explained the literary problems, method and development of the text, cf. *GS*, p. 70.

[2] Although he claims that he had been coming to his conclusions before Kaplan and Weiss had published their works.

[3] *JQR*, Vol. 35, 1944-45, pp. 421-434.

[4] J. Kaplan, *The Redaction of the Babylonian Talmud*, p. 233.

[5] Cf. above.

[6] *GS*, p. 69.

gemara and *sebara* in varying *sugyot*. First, an Amora can be credited only with the most concise statement which bears his name. Thus, for example, in the statement from b. Ḥul. 32b,

> ... R. Zera had put the following question: What is the law if the intestines were perforated after the first organ [i.e., the windpipe] but before the second organ [was out]? Is the first organ to be reckoned together with the second in order to render the animal clean, and not *nebelah*, or not?
>
> (Soncino translation)

only the first question can be credited to R. Zera. The last question must be regarded as a later addition. The Tosafists also saw this. This proposal assumes that (1) the individual Amoraim were incapable of inconsistency, and that (2) the original statement *(gemara)* is always found in *the* simplest form.

A second way to distinguish between *gemara* and *sebara* derives from linguistic study; it relies on the distinction between Hebrew and Aramaic statements in the Talmud. Klein suggested that wherever connected or semi-connected Hebrew phrases occur, all the original words were entirely in Hebrew[1]; the interpretations were in Aramaic. (Hebrew phrases thus isolated may also be composites of the original words and Hebrew interpretations[2]). Klein thus supposed that all Aramaic (save Hebrew quotations) was saboraic.

Klein also distinguished between *gemara* and *sebara* by the dichotomy of "question and response".[3] Here Klein noticed that the question is usually in Aramaic and the response in Hebrew. The response is usually direct. Therefore, Klein concluded, the statement or "response" preceded the question, which "was constructed afterwards to account for the Amora's interpretation".[4] Citing b. Mak. 4a, Klein also concluded that "the Aramaic framework of question and decussion in which a series of *Amoraic* comments on a Tannaitic text is embedded should be looked upon as a construction subsequent in date to that of the original statements".[5]

---

[1] *Ibid.*, p. 75.

[2] *Mishnah* and *gemara* on b. B.Q. 19a.

[3] *GS*, p. 77.

[4] *Ibid.*

[5] *Ibid.*, p. 80. The fourth category which Klein isolated is "quotation and rebuttal". The rebuttal may be either in Hebrew (e.g., b. B.Q. 32b) or in Aramaic (e.g. b. B.Q. 23b). If it is in Aramaic, it is easy to distinguish the *gemara*; if it is in Hebrew, greater care must be taken, but the result is the same. Alternative versions provide the fifth way to distinguish the Talmudic elements. Here Klein distinguished between two words found in the Babylonian Talmud which

Klein realized the limited scope of his discussion in *GS*; his distinction between *gemara* and *sebara* was found only in relatively clearly defined, simple cases where *sebara* is an explanation of or inference from *gemara*. Consequently, Klein published another article to account for the more complex cases of "*gemara* quotations in *sebara*". The title of this article suggests Klein's thesis, namely that the authors of the *sebara* knew *gemara* materials and frequently quoted from them in their excurses. This assertion raises several questions, of which Klein was quite aware: What is the nature of *gemara*? How is it to be distinguished from *sebara*? Why did the Saboraim quote *gemara*?

Klein claimed that the Amoraim, following the example of the Tannaim,[1] selected their material from a pool of "*gemaric*" materials; the same was true for the Saboraim. According to Klein, the Tannaim, Amoraim, and Saboraim made conscious efforts to select those materials necessary for the correct understanding of the "Oral Law" and for its preservation.[2] All three were actually compilers. *Sebara* made no substantive addition to a *sugya*; rather, it was designed to enhance the understanding or appreciation of *gemara*.[3] Klein's suggestion that the Amoraim and Saboraim were *consciously* involved in creating, selecting and compiling Talmudic material in an ongoing developmental manner is novel; it is equally problematic. If the major occupation of the Tannaim, Amoraim, and Saboraim was as Klein portrayed it, one must question what actually transpired in the various academies. It seems that creation and transmission of materials was at least as significant as selection.

The difficulty with Klein's proposal is not with his description of

are generally used to indicate alternative versions, *'mr* and *tene*. The same text is assumed for the expansions which follow either of these words, cf. *GS.*, p. 87. Klein's final method of distinction is the use of certain technical expressions such as *tene hd'*, *tene*, *tene rabnn*, *metyve*, etc. These phrases date earlier than expressions such as *'ykh' de'mre*, and *'ykh' demtne lh* ("some say" and "there are some who teach thus...") which introduce alternate versions, and thus, may be dated later than initial *sebara*. Klein hypothesized that technical phrases before any Talmudic passage are part of the sebaric interpretation and not of the original text, cf. *GS*, p. 87.

[1] Klein criticized what he called the traditional assumption that the Mishnah of R. Judah the Prince (c. 200 C.E.) became the "primary subject of study" in the Babylonian academies of Nehardea and Sura; leaving other materials (i.e., tannaitic *baraitot*, etc.) for further clarification, Klein contended that "not only the Mishnah but also Tosefta, Sifra, and Sifré were studied and commented upon as independent works," cf. *GQS*, p. 342. This position is accepted by modern scholarship.

[2] *GQS*, p. 343.

[3] *Ibid.*, p. 343, n. 6.

the compilers' methods or with the developmental theory of compilation: Kaplan, Halevy and others had already indicated this by showing that Amoraic and Saboraic periods overlapped.[1] Klein's hypothesis is questionable because he fails to include non-literary, and especially historical, evidence in his literary analysis. Klein did raise some historical questions and did offer answers in agreement with tradition and with earlier scholarship.[2] The Amoraim continued to annotate tannaitic compilations in Rabba's academy and probably up to and through R. Naḥman b. Isaac and R. Papa.[3] Klein also agreed with earlier findings that a single *gemara* corpus became attached to the Mishnah in the "generation of R. Ashi",[4] though he could accept the fact that *gemara* material continued to develop for some time after that: "It is still impossible to state with any degree of certainty when the *Gemara* was compiled or when the *Sebara* was added to it".[5]

Klein was not really interested in historical questions in *GQS*. Though he was skeptical of the validity of these traditional statements, Klein used them to date the processes he described. This uncritical use of earlier traditions, however, remains suspect. Despite this criticism, Klein's conclusion that the compilers of *sebara* were able to select from a pool of gemaric materials and choose those which best served their purposes deserves careful consideration. The material which the *sebara* selected from this "pool" was used in four ways: explanatory quotations, source quotations, anticipatory quotations, and uncompleted quotations.[6]

Klein limited his discussions to halakhic literature. By isolating (halakhic) *gemaric* materials, Klein noticed that, for example, the same *beraitot* often appear in different *sugyot* (e.g., b. A. Z. 62a and Tos. Sheb. 6.26; also y. Sheb. 8.6 [38b] = y. A. Z. 5.1 [44c]) are followed by the same groups of material irrelevant to at least one of the cases at hand. Thus Klein concluded that collections of "purely *halakhic* and *midrashic* baraitot" were studied and annotated systematically.[7] *Gemara* quotations, found in *sebara*, were made from these annotations.[8]

---

[1] Cf. elsewhere in this volume.
[2] Cf. *GQS*, pp. 344-345.
[3] Klein indicated here that he intended to do a study of this in the future.
[4] *GQS*, pp. 344-345.
[5] *SMS*, p. 125.
[6] Cf. *GQS*, pp. 347-349.
[7] Throughout this discussion, Klein made no distinction between aggadic *midrashim* and halakhic *midrashim*, nor did he discuss aggadic *baraitot*.
[8] *GQS*, pp. 350-351.

Although Klein's selection of sources in support of this hypothesis was limited, his conclusion that collections of material were available to the men of the academies and that they were transmitted from masters to disciples is convincing. Klein agreed with Kaplan and others that *gemara* and *sebara* overlapped and thus that the Saboraim were heirs to these collections too.[1]

Having established his major thesis, Klein then discussed some of the methods of the Saboraim.[2] Klein had already indicated some of these methods in *GS* and *GQS*;[3] he added three more to this list:

1. The authors of the Sebara assumed that the Gemara, like the Mishna, contained no redundant clauses, and that each new item of Gemara supplied information not contained in the preceding Gemara.
2. If an item of Gemara seemed redundant, the authors of the Sebara drew attention to the fact and added a note to make the information provided more explicit.[4]
3. The authors of the Sebara apply the same methods of interpretation to the Mishna and the Gemara.

The Sebaraim exposited *gemara* according to Amoraic precedent.[5] Thus, by extension, Amoraic phrases such as "here Rabbi taught an unnecessary *Mishnah*" which appear many times when referring to "unnecessary expositions" in *mishnayot*, are paralleled by *sebaric* terminology. Literary analysis can establish such arbitrary distinctions.

Klein examined the use of "it was not stated explicitly, but by inference" in the Talmud. Here Klein contended that we are dealing with a statement which the Talmud regards as inference, rather than direct words of an Amora.[6] Theoretically, this explanation is note-

---

[1] Cf. also *SMS*, p. 125.

[2] *SMS*.

[3] "1. Sebara employs Aramaic except when it is using familiar Hebrew technical words or phrases, or is quoting Hebrew sources. (2) The Amoraim wrote *scholia*, not merely on the *Mishnah*, but also on other tannaitic works, for example, on collections of *baraitot* and on *halakhic midrashim*. (3) The *gemara* of the Babylonian Talmud incorporates only a selection the of *gemara* that was available, just as the *Mishnah* incorporates only a selection of the tannaitic material that was available. (4) The authors of the Sebara knew of this omitted gemaric material and they frequently cited from it for their interpretations of, and discourses on the *gemara*." *SMS*, pp. 124-125.

[4] This assumes that it was already fixed and that they could not select from the gemaric material but had to account for the presence of a certain *gemara*. This assumption contradicts Klein's theory that the authors of the *sebara selected* material.

[5] *SMS*, pp. 126-127.

[6] *Ibid.*, p. 135. A. Weiss (*LeḤeqer HaTalmud*, New York, 1954, pp. 111 ff.) and Kaplan (*The Redaction of the Babylonian Talmud*, New York, 1933) provide the initial separation of these phrases which Klein analyzed.

worthy; practically, it becomes tendentious. Klein's example (B.M. 36a) suggests problems in his method.[1] b.B.M. 36a states

> "If you say a bailee who entrusted (an item) to (another) bailee (is culpable)"—Rav said that he is exempt and Rabbi Yoḥanan said that he is culpable (obligated).

The text continues:

> Rav Ḥisda said (*'mr*), "Rav's (position) was not stated explicitly, but was inferred,"

and then cites a case from which it is concluded:

> "Someone who saw Rav decide this case thought that Rav exempted the gardener-bailee whenever one bailee entrusts the bailment (i. e., bond) to another bailee, he is exempt. This is not so, however." (Klein's translation)

Rav Ḥisda claims that Rav never stated "a bailee who entrusted (an item) to (another) bailee is exempt"; this was incorrectly inferred from Rav's decision in one particular case (i.e., that of the "gardener-bailee").[2] Abaye intervened to explain this point "as if R. Ḥisda's assertion [*'mr Rav Ḥisda*] was nonexistent".[3] After presenting some reasons why Abaye ignored R. Ḥisda's assertion, Klein concluded that it is more likely that R. Ḥisda *never* actually said, "Rav's (position) was not stated explicitly, but was inferred". Since he had already established the fact that *'mr* represents *sebaric* interpretations, Klein found no difficulty. Some modern scholars concerned with the transmission of talmudic material through *schools* have suggested that where *'mr* appears in the Talmud, a sage's actual words are apt to be recorded. It is rather dubious to assert that R. Ḥisda did not make a statement when the text indicates that he did. Klein's distinctions are arbitrary; there is no systematic choice of the phrases which he selects to explain.

Implicit in Klein's hypothesis is the idea that the Talmud represents a continuous development. The *gemaric* and *sebaric* materials represent *sebaric* selections from a vast literature and interpretations of it. This selection-process probably took place around the time of R. Ashi, when there was a mixture of Amoraic and Saboraic activity. The

---

[1] Cf. *SMS*, pp. 135-141 for his discussion.

[2] *SMS*, p. 136.

[3] *Ibid.*

Saboraic period terminated by the sixth century.[1] Klein made no mention of *when* the material was reduced to writing, although he implied that after the time of R. Ashi, additional selections from the "gemaric material" began to diminish and the *gemara* began to take on a more stable form, though not yet fixed.[2] We do not know whether this form was oral or written.

It is quite reasonable to assume that a continuous "pool of materials" existed. The men in earlier academies selected or excluded materials. Where necessary, they elucidated them, perhaps by methods which Klein proposes. Rabbis in later academies received these materials and made their contributions where necessary. No distinction between Amoraic and Saboraic activity is possible except that the later sages received a more extensive *masora* (received tradition). It is likely that this was the manner in which the Talmud was formed. It is also probable that different schools handled the materials in different ways. Klein limited Talmudic materials to *gemara* and *sebara*. He might have further differentiated "strata" *in sebara* rather than treating it as a single and distinct systematic endeavor. He moderately changed the "traditional" historical distinction between *gemara* and *sebara* (b.B.M. 86a and *ESG*) and concluded that these indicate two distinct "periods" which overlapped; rabbinic activity in each was distinct.

---

[1] *Ibid.*, p. 127, n. 6.
[2] Cf. *GSBT*, pp. 370 f.

VI

JACOB N. EPSTEIN

BY

ROBERT GOLDENBERG

Jacob Naḥum ha-Levi Epstein was born in Brisk, Lithuania, on November 21, 1878, into an old rabbinical family. He received a standard *yeshivah* training until he was sixteen, at which point his formal education ceased until 1907, when he entered the University of Vienna to study Semitic philology. After transferring to Berne, he received the doctoral degree in 1913; he then settled in Berlin, where he stayed until 1925. In that year, he went to Jerusalem as a member of the original faculty of the Hebrew University. He remained there as professor of Talmudic Studies until his death on February 28, 1952.[1]

In 1950, *Tarbiẓ*, the publication of the University, which he edited, presented its twentieth volume to Epstein in honor of his seventieth birthday. Included in its contents was a list of Epstein's published works up until that time. The list breaks down as follows:

Bible (7 items)
Halakhic Midrashim (8 items)
Mishnah, Tosefta, and Talmud (19 items)
Palestinian Talmid (6 items)
Aggadah (1 item)
Geonim and their contemporaries (33 items)
Early medieval authorities (*Rishonim*)—(25 items)
Philology (29 items)
Archeology (4 items)
History (4 items)
Palestinian Geography (2 items)[2]

Despite the breadth of interest here reflected, the strong emphases on philology and on post-Talmudic literature are noteworthy. Both emphases are relevant to our current project.

---

[1] Simḥah Asaf, "His Life and Work," in *To the Memory of Professor Jacob Naḥum Epstein* (Magnes Press, Jerusalem, 1952), pp. 9ff.

[2] *Tarbiẓ* 29 (1949), p. xvi.

Most of Epstein's major published works appeared later than 1950, in fact posthumously; these major works include:

Introduction to the Text of the Mishnah (5708 = 1947/8) (=ITM)
Introductions to Tannaitic Literature (1957)
Introductions to Amoraic Literature (1962) (=IAL)
A Grammar of Babylonian Aramaic (1960)

He also edited texts, chiefly the *Mekhilta of R. Simeon b. Yoḥai* (1955). All the posthumous works were edited by his chief pupil and eventual colleague E. Ẓ. Melamed.

Our chief interest here is in Epstein's thoughts on the history and redaction, or formation, of the Babylonian Talmud. In addition to IAL, articles in various periodicals are germane to this theme. I shall limit my own illustrative materials to examples taken from IAL. Not all of the other materials are readily accessible, and they add little to IAL. IAL did not appear during its author's lifetime, and never received final editing at his hand. This accounts for the opacity of its style and thought. Its editor, Professor Melamed, by his own admission refrained from touching up the author's work or from improving its cogency even where the author had clearly made an error which he himself would have corrected had he had the opportunity.[1] The materials consist of notes Epstein used for his classroom lectures. They were never organized for publication. Epstein apparently did plan to produce a book, but he never accomplished it. Furthermore, since his course each year took the form of the study of a particular text, the book contains extended introductions to various tractates and even chapters of the Babylonian Talmud. But barely two pages treat that body of literature on any greater level of generality.

What are the questions Epstein asks? Can we determine the text's construction? How clearly can we distinguish its various segments? Where do they come from? How old are they? How are they related to each other? Did they know about each other? Do they react to each other? We shall study Epstein's answers to some of these questions, and look at some examples of his method in arriving at those answers.

The few places where Epstein does discuss the Babylonian Talmud (= BT) more generally come at the beginning of his introduction to a tractate.[2] Melamed has taken one such discussion from the introduction to Sukkah and has placed it at the beginning of the book:

---

[1] IAL, p. 7. Compare S. Lieberman, *Siphre Zuṭṭa* (N.Y. 1968), pp. 125-136.
[2] Cf. IAL, pp. 84, 103.

> The Babylonian Talmud is also (?)[1] not entirely of one piece:
> The early Amoraim began to order (sdr) it—they ordered the *Baraitot* next to the *Mishnayot*, they explained the Mishnah in short statements and decided the law...; they added laws that are not in the Mishnah, derivative laws (*halakhot-toladot*), and arranged them in a/the Talmud...
> We have remnants of the ordering of a Talmud from as early as the time of R. Naḥman (ʿEruv. 32), R. Joseph and their disciples Abaye and Rava...; the statements (*memrot*) multiplied and the discussions grew; they brought *sugyot* from Palestine to Babylonia and from Babylonia to Palestine; the academies became separated and each learned the Talmud in its own way (*derekh*) and manner (*shiṭṭah*) ..., and the "*sadranim*" (e.g., R. Naḥman b. Isaac...) "ordered" it, until the passage of time arrived at Ravina and R. Ashi "the end of *hora'ah*," "the orderers of the Talmud," who gathered all the earlier material, normally in the received form (as Rabbi had done with the Mishnah), explained it, filled it out (*hishlimuhu*), and "ordered" it. But its ordering was not completed in their time; two generations of Amoraim still came after them, who filled it out and added to it more explanations and *sugyot* until the Sevoraim came and "sealed" it (ḥtm)..., which is to say an external ordering generally without changing anything, aside from additions and connections between statements and *sugyot*, connections which to be sure do sometimes change the whole *sugya* and all its sources; they moved *sugyot* from place to place, filled one out with another, and tried to reconcile (*lehashvot*) them.
> But traces of the different sources were not obliterated; "inverted *sugyot*" (*sugyot hafukhot*) clearly give witness to them.
> These (?)[2] show that each tractate is a book to itself, which generally differs in its opinion and ordering [from the others], and they are not all from the same period... Furthermore, not every tractate is of one piece; there are contradictions and points of oppisition within a tractate from chapter and from matter (*ʿinyan*) to matter, and even duplications within one tractate.[3]

This excerpt is as clear a statement as can be found of Epstein's judgment of the Babylonian Talmud and how it came to be. His treatment of each tractate is a consequence of his conception of the whole, given his overriding interest in literary and philological questions. There was nothing general to say, because there was no generalized matter about which to speak.

The theory here propounded is never demonstrated except by all the details in all the introductions yet to come. It would have better been placed at the end of the book, rather than at its beginning. No

---

[1] The text gives no indication about what "also" refers to.

[2] The antecedent of "these" is not clear. It cannot be "*sugyot*," since the verb is masculine.

[3] P. 12.

evidence is offered for the claim that Abaye or R. Ashi played a role in the process of formation. We occasionally find, in the discussion of a particular tractate, a listing of the Amoraim who contributed to its final editing.[1] Generalizations like the one quoted, however, are never given detailed documentation. The crucial terms *sadran* and *sof hora'ah* are not explained; that is why I merely transliterated them above. Epstein uses the traditional epithets to indicate that these people did in fact do something, but he does not tell what he thinks they did, nor does he ever say what he thinks those terms mean, or how the traditional sources understood them. Nor can Melamed be faulted for placing the passage at the beginning of the book; Epstein had used it to begin his introduction to Sukkah.

IAL contains no statement of methodological principles. The reader must infer the principles from particular examples of their application. A good example can be found at the very beginning; there Epstein discusses the unity of Pesaḥim. Modern printed editions of BT print "*slika lah Pesaḥ rishon*" after ch. 4 of the tractate, "*slika lah Pesaḥ sheni*" after ch. 9 and "*slika lah Masekhet Pesaḥim*" after ch. 10. MS Munich, furthermore, has the ten chapters in the order 1-4, 10, 5-9, and gives similar concluding formulae. Epstein finds internal evidence that this traditional division of the tractate has a firm basis in reality. Among his arguments we find the following:

a. On Pes. 81b (M 7:8) we find a difficulty raised (rmy) on the basis of a Mishnah at the end of ch. 3. In the corresponding place (49b), however, the same difficulty is not raised. *General principle*: If a certain discussion is cited in one place, but not in another place where it is equally appropriate, the second must not know about it. It must therefore have a different origin.

b. On Pes. 70a (M 6:3) a Mishnah is cited from ch. 10 and a statement of R. Ḥisda is *quoted* (*v'amar*) to explicate it. In ch. 10, however, this statement is not repeated where we would expect it, in the gemara to that Mishnah itself (116a). This argument is based on the same *General principle*, but here Epstein adds the following: "This is normal in two tractates and is based on different arrangements ('rk) and different academies, but it is not normal in one tractate".

c. On 85a a Mishnah is cited (with the formula *tnan hatam*, which normally introduces a Mishnah from a different tractate) from the end of ch. 10, along with an Amoraic discussion (R. Huna, R. Ḥisda)

[1] See, for example, the discussion of Bekhorot on pp. 127ff., and see below, pp. 83-84.

about it. The entire discussion is repeated *ad locum* on 120b-121a; this is not normal in one tractate. *General principle*: Talmudic material from the same source will not repeat itself. Epstein cites the Tosafot in b.B.B. 29a who use the same principle; the reference is found on 159b.[1] This principle is not altogether consistent with the one adduced in cases (a) and (b) above.

d. On Pes. 64b (ch. 5) a certain opinion about the Paschal rite is attributed exclusively to R. Yosi the Galilean, while on 121a (ch. 10) it is implied that R. Ishmael might have had that opinion too. *General principle*: If different sources attribute different opinions to the same man, they cannot have a common origin. Epstein does not mention that the Talmud is aware of this principle; the man's various students might have transmitted his opinion differently.

e. On Pes. 14a we find *reference* to a dispute among Abaye, R. Adda b. Ahava in the name of Rava, and Ravina in the name of Rava. The dispute itself, however, is found nowhere in the BT. Here Epstein himself states the *principle*, although he calls it a conclusion from these places, and not a rule for understanding them: "The tractate in which the text appears has a different edition (ʿrk) from the tractate which is the appropriate place for the text, but from which it is missing".[2]

This partial selection indicates Epstein's method of operation. Using a variety of literary canons, he breaks down a text into a set of component parts, which were at one point independent of each other. He then discusses the way these independent units may be related to each other. He, or more often Melamed, divides the introductions to the tractates into sections, with such names as "the relationship of X to other tractates," or "inverted *sugyot*" (this very often), "different layers," "quotations from other tractates." These are essentially comparative rubrics, which are not designed to deepen the analysis of a particular entity.

One example of Epstein's analysis of "inverted *sugyot*" follows:

> M. Pes. 1; 5—R. Judah would further say, Two loaves of disqualified thank-bread [which was leavened] used to be left on top (*ʿal gav*) of the Temple Portico. As long as they were left there, the people could eat [leaven on the Eve of Passover]...

---

[1] P. 14, n. 8. Since "30a" would have been more appropriate than "29," I suspect that we may have a typographical error, and that the reading should be "159b." The problem with prefixes mentioned below, p. 84, n. 4 below may have a similar origin.

[2] All the above from IAL, pp. 13ff.

> [So the printed text in the Talmud. Albeck's edition of the Mishnah has "on the roof (*'al gag*) of the Temple Porico," and mentions no alternative versions.]
>
> BT Pes. 13b—The Tanna recited "*'al gav*" before Rav Judah. He said to him, Does he have to hide them? Recite "*'al gag*."
>
> BT Suk. 44b—The Tanna recited "'al gag" before Rav Judah (printed editions: R. Naḥman). He said to him, Does he have to dry them out? Rather say "*'al gav*."[1]

What we have here is two versions of the same "incident." Since neither makes any reference to the other, we can infer that each academy thought it was teaching the only known version of that incident. Such an inversion can have either a narrative context as here, or a legal context in which the opinions in a legal dispute are distributed differently among different people in different Talmudic sources. Pes. 64b attributed an opinion to R. Yosi the Galilean, while Pes. 121a attributed it to R. Ishmael as well. There, of course, the "inversion" was not complete, since 121a did not deny that opinion to R. Yosi. The nature of the phenomenon, however, can be seen quite clearly. It is not clear to me why Epstein isolates "inverted *sugyot*" from his other categories of analysis. Two possible reasons come to mind: (a) there are so many more of them that for convenience he treats them separately, and (b) this is a category of which traditional commentators have been aware; cf. Tosafot on Men. 58b.

Epstein claimed that ordering activity was going on as early as the time of R. Naḥman. I nowhere found what he thought the enigmatic conversation in 'Eruvin actually means. His assertion that "we have remnants of the ordering of a Talmud from as early as the time of R. Naḥman" is allowed to stand, elucidated only by the citation "'Eruv. 32b."

Epstein also shows that certain anonymous discussions in the BT are very early. The second chapter of Pes. begins thus:

> MISHNAH: As long as it is permitted for one to eat [leaven], one may feed [it] to ones' animals...
>
> GEMARA: As long as one may eat, one may feed, so when one may not eat, one may not feed... [Discussion ensues]... But then "as long as one may eat" should be "as long as one eats" (omitting the word *mutar*).
>
> (Pes. 21a)

At an earlier point, the following discussion is found:

---

[1] IAL, p. 48.

> Rava said to R. Naḥman, Let the Master say the Halakhah is according to R. Meir, since there is an anonymous Mishnah in accordance with his view [*setam lan Tanna kavateh*, referring to 21a]... That's not "anonymous," since *mutar* presents a problem.
>
> (Pes. 13a)

Epstein infers that R. Naḥman was familiar with the give-and-take which is presented anonymously on 21a. He does not discuss the possibility that the anonymous discussion on 21a developed *after* the time of R. Naḥman, in order to explicate his vague statement as preserved in the schools. But his observations provide a corrective to the tendency to date all anonymous materials late.[1]

As far as late materials are concerned, Epstein does occasionally generalize about the nature of Saboraic materials. Saboraim will assume familiarity with sources quoted elsewhere, especially in the same tractate, without quoting them.[2] *Sugyot* were worked over by the Saboraim; R. Huna, b. Beẓ. 6b, responds to R. Kahana on 6a[3], but the "anonymous Talmud" [*setam haBavli*] has moved his comments away.[4] Elsewhere, Epstein identifies the *sugya* in b. Pes. 9b-10a as Saboraic, and offers the following reasons: all *Mishnayot* and *Baraitot* (except one) are known from elsewhere in BT, and also the *sugya* on M. Ṭahorot 5:5 is found in full, with the names of its participants, in Ket. 27a, while here it is anonymous. These two facts indicate the Saboraic origin of the *sugya*.[5]

Epstein offers two proofs that Nedarim had a much later editing (sdr) than other tractates:

> a. Abaye could say to you (*'amar lak Abaye*), My comment is consistent even with R. Judah...
>
> (Ned. 5b)
>
> Abaye could say to you, This is R. Judah [and therefore I needn't accommodate my view to it]. But it is Abaye who said, My view is consistent even with R. Judah!...
>
> (Ned. 6a)

[1] IAL, p. 15.

[2] IAL, p. 37.

[3] *Ibid.*; cf. PT Bez. 1:1.

[4] In reference to the egg laid on a Holy Day, R. Kahana had asked of Rav, Why is this different from a calf born on a Holy Day? R. Huna eventually answered, also in the name of Rav, An egg is not finished until it emerges. The only trouble with Epstein's example is that all the intervening material may have been inserted *en bloc*; it is possible that nothing was "moved." Epstein quotes none of it in his text.

[5] *Tarbiẓ* 17 (1945), p. 23.

The phrase *'amar lak* is elsewhere never used with regard to the actual words of a person; it always introduces the answer which the academicians say he *might* have said.

b. Onions on which rain had descended and which had sprouted forth, are forbidden if their leaves had turned black; if they had become green they are permitted. R. Ḥanina b. Antigonus says: As long as they can be plucked out by their leaves, they are forbidden. In the year after the Sabbatical year, the like of these are permitted.
(M. Shev. 6:3—Soncino ed.,
London, 1948; S.M. Lehrman, tr.)

The prohibition in the Mishnah refers to additional [growth]. But then what did RaShBaG[1] mean to add, since it is taught, RaShBaG says, Whatever grew up under obligation is obligated, whatever grew up free is free. The first Tanna also said that! The whole Mishnah was taught by RaShBaG.
(Ned. 59b)

The problem here is that we find no other reference to such a statement by R. Simon b. Gamaliel in which he dealt with the Mishnah under discussion, and furthermore "obligated" is hardly the right terminology for discussing the prohibition of the Sabbatical Year. Epstein claims that "RaShBaG" is in fact a corruption of RaḤBaG, who is R. Ḥanina b. Antigonus (!), which exchange he finds elsewhere as well.[2] R. Ḥanina is in fact found in our Mishnah and does indeed disagree with the first Tanna there. Once the corruption had occurred, Epstein continues, someone imported a statement of R. Simon b. Gamaliel in order to explain what his name was doing in the *sugya*. That statement had originally dealt with tithes, in which context its terminology was appropriate (cf. Git. 22a). Given the strangeness of the language in Nedarim, I find the first proof of lateness unconvincing. The second is impressive.

On the question of the "strange language" of Nedarim, Epstein has the only major dispute with other writers. Isaac Halevy's theory was that this language reflects the Palestinian influence of the copyists through whose hands our copies of Nedarim have gone. Epstein replies that these words have "not even a shadow of truth."[3] The differences are too great. Furthermore, they were not then studying the BT in Palestine. And none of this "Palestinian" terminology is in

[1] RaShBaG is a traditional abbreviation for the name R. Simon B. Gamaliel. I reproduce it in the translation because it is crucial for Epstein's argument.
[2] IAL, p. 55f.
[3] IAL, p. 56.

the PT. He also attacks the theory of Levias that since these tractates were not studied, their terminology underwent less change than the others. Epstein replies that comparison with medieval citations and manuscripts shows that there *was* change. He states, "Levias would have us believe that since they were not studied they *kept* their Geonic vocabulary, while the others, because they were, *acquired* pre-Geonic vocabulary!" Epstein concludes that the reason must be "basic"—they had a different composition (ʾrk), at a different time and place, by a different editor (sdr).[1]

Epstein makes many references to standard medieval writers on Talmudic literature, but almost none to the scholarly writers of the nineteenth and twentieth centuries. His response to Halevy and Levias is the only one of its kind. He seems to assume the redactional activity of Abaye and R. Ashi without demonstrating it.

Let us now proceed to the identification of important personalities in the history of the BT. The earliest one whom Epstein mentions was R. Naḥman, as we have seen.[2] He also names the following:

Abaye—b. Shab. 36a, Abaye uses the phrase "We too say." Epstein apparently takes this as evidence of redactional activity, as if Abaye had been putting together a list of things, and added his own entry to it.[3] Actually, the context consists of just such a list. Epstein has little to say about Abaye's activity. He and R. Ashi are at one point called "builders of the Talmud."[4]

R. Ashi uses the same phrase in the same place. Epstein has little to say about the activity of R. Ashi, presumably because he takes it for granted. Most of his comments are in regard to R. Naḥman b. Isaac, who refers to himself on b. Pes. 105b as on "orderer" (*sadran*). He takes it in its simple literal sense: one who takes separate bits of tradition and puts them in order. Elsewhere, he calls R. Naḥman b. Isaac a redactor (ʿrk) and a fixer (ḥtm) of traditions, and refers to Taʿanit 15a, Ḥul. 56b, and Ket. 10b, where he, like Abaye and R. Ashi, uses the expression "we too say." In several places, R. Naḥman b. Isaac provides mnemonics (e.g., Shab. 60b, Nid. 45b, Qid. 44a, ʿArak. 11a). In two places, he is concerned to resolve ambiguity in Palestinian

---

[1] *Ibid.*

[2] Above, pp. 80-81.

[3] IAL, p. 178.

[4] *Ibid.* At the end of the introduction to several tractates, Epstein catalogues the appearances of various Amoraim in those tractates. He will often emphasize that Abaye and R. Ashi appear very often, but he does not discuss the significance of this frequency.

traditions (B.B. 135b, Ber. 38b). In particular, Epstein finds great evidence of such activity in chapters 1 and 10 of Pesaḥim, and draws the conclusion that the editor (sdr) used these chapters in R. Naḥman b. Isaac's edition (sdr).[1]

We turn lastly to Epstein's treatment of the question of the place of editing. One of his important working principles is that an anonymous Talmudic statement will never refer to its own place of origin by name. Thus on Pes. 42b, shortly after the word "here," we find a reference to "R. Shimi the Meḥozan." Epstein infers that "here" therefore cannot refer to Meḥoza.[2] Epstein first states on linguistic grounds that the tractate Nedarim could not have been edited (ʿrk) in a place which used the dialect[3] of Sura or Nedardea (or Pumbedita). Also, Rava the Meḥozan is mentioned far more frequently (*ca.* sixty-five times) than Abaye the Pumbeditan (twenty-seven times) or R. Naḥman b. Isaac the Pumbeditan (two times, one a quotation from Yev.), or R. Papa from Nersh (eight times), R. Ashi the Suran (ca. twenty times) or Ravina (*ca.* twenty times).

On 50b, there is a reference to "Rav Judah of (or in) Nedardea"—the evidence varies as to whether the prefix should be *d* or *b*.[4] In either case, however, the emphatic "Rav Judah of/in Nehardea" shows that the editing took place neither in Nehardea nor in Pumbedita, where he had been principal. Epstein holds that the reference must be to the famous Rav Judah b. Ezekiel, since he is called a student of Samuel. We do find in Nedarim the common phrase "Rav Judah quoted Samuel," but these are from the "early general Talmud"(*HaTalmud haqadum vehakelalli*);[5] the case-report here is different.

In a later period, Meḥoza belonged to the District of Pumbedita (ESG p. 88); its dialect was different from that of Nedardea (Ket. 54a: "He recognized from her voice that she was a Meḥozan"). The Meḥoza academy still existed in the time of R. Ashi. Its Talmud reached Sura and Pumbedita in small quantities only, and was not studied there; the

---

[1] IAL, pp. 21f., 178. Much of the above seems taken from Halevy, *Dorot HaRishonim*, II, 500.

[2] IAL, p. 22.

[3] Epstein, *Grammar*, p. 14. There he adduces Qid. 71b to support the claim that different dialects were spoken in various cities.

[4] Since Rav Judah was principal at Pumbedita and not at Nehardea, the text is difficult in any case. Epstein suggests two solutions to this problem, but we shall not stop to examine them here. Also, modern printed editions have the prefix *m*, of which Epstein makes no mention at all. See above, p. 79, n. 1.

[5] Another interesting term whose precise significance is apparently never spelled out.

Geonim therefore ignored it as well. On the basis of this evidence, Epstein suggests that Nedarim as we have it "possibly" came from the academy at Meḥoza.[1]

Conclusion: Epstein's power of literary analysis permitted him to isolate the component parts of materials that had always been considered unitary, and even to identify the origins of the separate sections. This kind of literary analysis is a necessary first step. As a guide to the literary analysis of the BT, however, Epstein's book is seriously flawed. It is full of references which are not spelled out, and which are not always clear. Subtleties of the kind Epstein performs are often inadequately explained. Even when he tells the section he is discussing, he will usually quote its first few words and then add "etc."

Epstein remains throughout the book strictly the philologist. He is interested only in understanding a text. So he asks where a certain tractate was edited, but he never asks what happened to the materials (if any) left out of it, and why. His conclusions imply that similar *Gemarot* were edited in other schools in addition to the ones whose work we have received. What happened to them? Why were they lost? Can we trace either the preservation or the loss of these various materials to particular historic events? Why did the whole process of development stop? Was there *ever* anyone who had all the material in front of him? Epstein implies that there was not. In that case, however, what we have represents the end-product of a series of random events. It just happened that a certain Tanna happened to remember a certain *sugya* in a certain way at a certain place, and that that Tanna's work is what happens to have survived to our own day.[2] ITM concludes that the Mishnah was in fact written down very soon after its completion.[3] We find no similar discussion in IAL, only an Appendix in which Epstein discusses the two recensions of the Letter of R. Sherira Gaon. He decides that the so-called French Recension, which denies that the

---

[1] IAL, pp. 69f. There are a few linguistic indications that Nedarim may be Suran, but they are based on Geonic language, and Epstein admits that they require us to ignore a time-span of 400 years. I have therefore not quoted them in the text.

[2] There is an analogy between the formation of the Hebrew Bible and that of the Talmud. In each case, someone had to decide to include certain things, and not to include others. The analogy to the formation of the New Testament seems even stronger, because we know that materials of exactly the same type as the accepted portions (i.e., gospels and epistles) were rejected. Who decided to accept certain Talmuds (or tractates or chapters) as "canonical "gemara, and to omit others?

[3] ITM, pp. 692-706.

Mishnah and the Talmud were written down, is the earlier version, despite the opposite conclusion of his predecessors.[1] This, however, is an exercise in Geonic philology; Epstein thought that the Mishnah was written, so we cannot try to infer his opinion about the Talmud from his preference of the French Recension of R. Sherira's letter. We receive no hint whatever of his opinion on this matter.

---

[1] IAL, pp. 610-615.

VII

ABRAHAM WEISS: SOURCE CRITICISM

BY

SHAMAI KANTER

Abraham Weiss was born in Podhajce, Galicia, in 1895.[1] He received a traditional Talmudic yeshivah education, paralleled in his early years by secular studies with a private tutor, in German. On a higher level, the Gymnasium of Storoznyetz provided both secular and religious studies. Weiss received his rabbinical ordination in 1916, and went on to study at the Rabbinical Seminary of Vienna, and at the University of Vienna, where he earned a Ph.D. in History and Classical Philology. Weiss later moved to Warsaw where he taught at several institutions, most notably serving as Docent for Talmud at the Institute for Jewish Science. During all of those years, Weiss was involved in Zionist activity, and in Jewish communal affairs in Warsaw. In 1939, he served as spokesman for the delegation which went before the commanding general of the German occupying forces to protest the enclosure of the Warsaw ghetto. In 1940 he traveled a long, circuitous route from Poland, through Italy, to the United States, where he was able to accept a previously-tendered offer of a position on the faculty of Yeshiva University. Abraham Weiss served as Professor of Talmud at Yeshiva University for over a quarter of a century. Subsequent to his retirement he went to live in the State of Israel.

Abraham Weiss' studies in rabbinical literature range from the Mishnah to the *She'iltot* and *Halakhot Gedolot* of the Geonim[2], representing so far seven major books and more than five times that number of scholarly articles.[3] In the main, Weiss deals with the Babylonian Talmud, applying his own method of higher criticism and form-

[1] Information on the life of Weiss derived from the article by "Jubilee Committee", "Prof. Abraham Weiss—A Biographical Sketch", *The Abraham Weiss Jubilee Volume*, English section, pp. 1-5.

[2] Meyer S. Feldblum, "Prof. Abraham Weiss: His Approach and Contribution to Talmudic Scholarship", *The Abraham Weiss Jubilee Volume*, English section p. 8.

[3] Benjamin Weiss, "Rabbi Abraham Weiss' Bibliography," *The Abraham Weiss Jubilee Volume*, Hebrew section, pp. 5-11, lists 37 major articles.

critical study to the Talmudic text. While at the University of Vienna, Weiss had originally planned to specialize in the economic history of the Talmud.[1] This led him to try to separate the various strata of historical material in the text; it became his life's work.

Meyer S. Feldblum's lengthy essay, in *The Abraham Weiss Jubilee Volume*[2], describes the scope and significance of Weiss' approach. Previous investigators of the development of the Talmud had sought their information in external factors; but Weiss was convinced that the only proper method of study lay in a combination of conceptual and textual analysis. Beginning with an analysis of the use of terms which indicate a quotation of sources, he moved on to more extensive research into the earlier and later elements within Talmudic discussions, and into their significance for chapters, tractates, and for the Talmud as a literary entity.

The building-block of the Talmud, Weiss points out, is the *sugya*, any independent Talmudic discussion-unit which uses the Torah or some other traditional source, plus logic, to clarify a problem.[3] Two kinds of materials can be identified as the earliest work of the Amoraim: (a) a short, explanatory note to the Mishnah or some other older source, and (b) an independent short statement, the *memra*. From these evolve two corresponding types of *sugyot*: (a) the explanatory *sugya* and (b) the independent *sugya*.

These *sugyot* develop either as "simple" or as "complex" in form. The simple S*ugya* (e.g., the bottom of b. Git. 32b) begins with a question ("How many witnesses must be present at the cancelling of a bill of divorce?") which is discussed by one or more contemporary rabbis. Or a question (e.g., b. Git. 15a-b) can be explained by a series of rabbis of successive generations, each one commenting on the previous strata.

The complex *sugya* makes use of other *sugyot* or fragments of *sugyot*. New material can be added at the end, or inserted into the body of the material. In some cases, the material will not follow chronology, showing that its conceptual development was not the same as the method of exposition.[4]

By following the presence of statements by individual rabbis within

---

[1] "Jubilee Committee", *Jubilee Volume*, p. 4.

[2] *Jubilee Volume*, English section, pp. 7-80, Hebrew section, pp. 13-72. Further references will be to English section only.

[3] Meyer S. Feldblum, *Jubilee Volume*, p. 13.

[4] *Ibid.*, p. 30.

the *sugyot*, as quoted or as quoting, Weiss arrives at his conception of the origins of the Talmud. He demonstrates the presence of *sugyot* of Palestinian rabbis R. Yoḥanan and Resh Laqish, and even some material by Rabbi Judah the Prince which is Amoraic in form.[1] On the other hand, there are no *sugyot* attributable to Rav and Samuel, and little from Rav Huna and Rav Judah. Weiss concludes that Palestine was the place of origin of the *sugya* in both content and form, and that students of Rav and Samuel organized the first Babylonian *sugyot* as a means of developing the material taught them by Rav and Samuel, on the model of the Palestinian *sugyot*.[2]

Based upon the work of these Pumbeditan scholars, the Talmud in our possesion was transmitted to Meḥoza after the death of Abaye, from there to Nersh by Rav Papa, and from there to Sura-Mata Meḥasia in the time of Rav Ashi.[3] There were, however, other Talmuds of other academies (as is indicated by various terms for indicating sources, e.g., *tenan hatam*, it was taught elsewhere).

Weiss' analysis of the *sugya* is highly detailed. In some *sugyot* the introductory section is anonymous, while in a later section, a later Amora is named. One can assume, in many cases, that the earlier, anonymous section was known to the later Amora, who comments upon it. But we have places where an early Amora seems to be commenting on the statement of a later Amora: this obviously reflects work of an editor. Therefore, there is no need to say that in all cases a later Amora knew early, anonymous material upon which he appears to be commenting.[4]

Further, Weiss asks,[5] can we say that a *sugya* was created in the presence of the author of the *memra* on which it is based, or was the discussion created later on the basis of his statement? Where the statement of one rabbi is quoted by another, and followed by discussion, did the transmitter of the *memra* also transmit the discussion, or was the discussion created later? Weiss shows that all of these possibilities occur.[6] In addition one *sugya* will seem to have knowledge of an extra-Mishnaic source (Tosefta, Midrashé Halakha) while another will not.[7] He concludes therefore that each *sugya* has its own

[1] *Ibid.*, p. 14.
[2] *Ibid.*, p. 15.
[3] *Ibid.*, p. 39..
[4] *Ibid.*, p. 15.
[5] *Ibid.*, p. 19.
[6] Abraham Weiss, *LeḤeqer HaTalmud*, pp. 164ff.
[7] Meyer S. Feldblum, *Jubilee Volume*, p. 34.

individual character and history (an important conclusion for his view of the development of the Talmud as a whole).

Weiss' analysis of the 7th chapter of the tractate Ketuvot is an example of his approach.[1] He notes that in this chapter there are ten statements of Samuel, quoted by Rav Judah, plus a number of other statements of Samuel from other sources. Compared to chapters 6 and 8 which have only one or two *memrot* of Samuel, this is significant: in fact, the quotations from Samuel form a full commentary on the Mishnah of that chapter. Weiss concludes that these statements originally formed a unit, that they represent Samuel's lecture on the Mishnah, as given to his students in the Academy of Pumbedita.

How, then, does this commentary come to be scattered through the Gemara, as we presently find it? Though Weiss does consider that possibly the framework of the discussion was worked out elsewhere, and that some editor later inserted these quotations from the Pumbeditan Talmud throughout the *sugya* in appropriate places, he rejects this in favor of a simpler explanation: Rav Judah's transmission of Samuel's lecture on the Mishnah represents the earliest stratum of the *sugya*, the basis of all later strata. It is reasonable to assume that similar material from Rav and Samuel existed for chapters 6 and 8 of the tractate; yet this material has been mainly lost to us.

A running commentary is not the only form found within the Talmud, however. There are various collections of *memrot*, organized topically or formally: collections on a particular subject, sayings of a single sage. One of the most striking examples of such collections is found in b. B. Q. 11a-b.[2] In the Babylonian Talmud, it exists as a series of statements of R. Elazar quoted by ʿUlla. But in y. Qid. 1.4 the same material occurs in a different form: it is a series of answers to questions which R. Judah sent to R. Elazar. The Babylonian schools did not preserve the questions which were the origin of the collection, though they preserved the collection of answers.

Thus, the Talmud is composed of various strata: an early one, from the students of R. Judah, a central, large, homogeneous stratum from Rava and Abaye, and later strata. Weiss asserts a significant contribution to the *sugyot* of the Talmud by the Saboraim: not only is the opening section of almost every tractate Saboraic, but much other material as well.[3] The Saboraic contribution, however, "disappears"

---

[1] Abraham Weiss, *LeḤeqer HaTalmud*, pp. 6-10.
[2] *Ibid.*, p. 97.
[3] Meyer S. Feldblum, *Jubilee Volume*, p. 53.

from view, since part of their work is absorbed into the Talmud, while their collections of halakhot were used by the Geonim as the basis of Geonic halakhic collections.

Weiss deals with the question of whether the Oral Tradition was written down, from the same standpoint of internal analysis. He demonstrates the reliance of the schools upon written texts, not from chance remarks (e.g., material cited by I.H. Weiss) but from the texts themselves. For example, in his discussion of tractate Baba Qamma, he notes stylistic variations between the strata of the *sugya* on b. B.Q. 2a-3b where the older discussion uses the phrase "*ma'i hi*', What is it?" while the later one uses the phrase "*ma'i nihu*" for the same purpose and meaning.[1] Such a stylistic difference would have been ironed out in an orally transmitted text, thus showing that the earlier stratum had attained fixed written form. Similarly on b. B.Q. 48a, a statement of Raba is understood as using the term "lies down" (rbẓ) by the colleagues of Rav Papa. Rav Papa explains the word as meaning *lays down*, which is a difference of pronunciation only, to resolve their difficulty. This teaching of Rava, the earliest stratum of this particular *sugya*, was thus in the possession of Rava's student, Rav Papa in written form. An orally-transmitted text could not be misunderstood in that way.

For Weiss there can be no question of the "final editing" of the Talmud: he sees the Talmud as a continuous process from the time of the Amoraim to the Geonim.[2] Under his analysis, the idea of a final redaction, and of Rav Ashi's role as editor, dissolves like a metaphysical problem in the hands of a linguistic analytical philosopher.

First, asks Weiss, what does the concept of an editor mean? What would his work have consisted of? He must either have reworked previous material into a form he wanted, or he must have arranged previous material, supplying completions or transitions. Further, for him indeed to be editor, his work should be apparent throughout the Talmud. But Weiss' investigation shows no such evidence. Though there are general developmental rules for Talmudic material, each *sugya* seems to have its own developmental history. There is no general principle governing the division of material, or how parallel material is copied from place to place (much parallel material need not have been transferred, given the idea of an over-all plan).[3] Quoted material

[1] Abraham Weiss, *LeḤeqer HaTalmud*, p. 99.
[2] Abraham Weiss, *Hithavut HaTalmud BiShelemuto*, p. 242.
[3] *Ibid.*

often contradicts its citation, showing that it had been introduced later, on the basis of a marginal note. And, finally, there are whole tractates, identical in earlier strata with the rest of the Talmud, which did not undergo the same post-Amoraic stylistic development (Nedarim, Nazir, Temurah, Keritot and Me'ilah) as the other tractates.[1]

If there is no editing, then no editor: *leit siddur*, *v'leit sadran*! Weiss disposes of the famous Talmudic passage long understood as referring to Rav Ashi's editorship quite briefly. The term "*sof hora'ah*, the end of (authentic) teaching" (b. B.M. 86a) refers to the teaching of *halakhah*, specifically to the end of the Amoraic period. The time of persecutions under Yazdagird, in 455 C.E., was a watershed in the Talmudic process: because of the years of upheaval and instability there was a break in the steady development of the Talmud. Scholars encountered many problems in understanding the material they had inherited, and a good deal of intellectual effort was expended in consolidating the knowledge of the tradition. Because of this, the period before the upheaval was looked upon as being especially authoritative.

As for the reference to two "editions" of Rav Ashi's teaching (b. B.B. 157b) Weiss shows parallel evidence that the term *mahadura'* means only the review of legal opinions by a scholar later in his life.[2]

Those passages which are adduced to show a redactional role by Rav Ashi fit easily into Weiss' over-all scheme. Every later stratum "edits" and re-forms the earlier material. For example, in b. Ket. 7a, Rav Ashi seems to refer to a view quoted in the name of R. Papa as his own.[3] Other scholars have understood this as pointing to R. Ashi having set the Talmud in its fixed form. For Weiss, such passages merely show that Rav Ashi taught the particular *sugya* in question. Parallels to this occur for other sages, but naturally there are more of them for Rav Ashi, when we consider his major role as head of his academy, and the length of time he was active.

Weiss then turns to the Epistle of Sherira Gaon, and submits it to a closer analysis than any of his predecessors.[4] He concludes that Sherira has been misunderstood, and that he too does not refer to the editing of the Talmud by Rav Ashi in any way. The ESG is divisible into two parts, which are different in content and character. The first part gives

---

[1] Meyer S. Feldblum, *Jubilee Volume*, p. 40.

[2] Abraham Weiss, *Hithavut HaTalmud BiShelemuto*, p. 245, n. 91; b. Git. 29b, b. B.M. 44a, b. A.Z. 52b.

[3] *Ibid.*, pp. 251-254.

[4] *Ibid.*, pp. 246-250.

a history of rabbinical tradition, based on Sherira's own analysis of Talmudic sources. The second part, beginning with his response to a question about the history of the Saboraim after Ravina (ESG, Lewin edition, p. 6) recounts the history of the *yeshivot* from the time of the Exile to the time of Sherira. It is based upon an old Geonic chronicle, which Sherira expanded by adding details drawn from the Talmud.

A) In part 1, the history of rabbinical tradition, Sherira mentions Rabbi Judah the Prince many times as the editor of the Mishnah; but he never once explicitly refers either to the redaction of the Talmud or to Rav Ashi as editor. He does mention the prediction of Ravina and Rav Ashi as *sof hora'ah*, and says that after them came explanation and interpretation that were "close to *hora'ah*". But while he speaks of Mishnah specifically, he speaks of the Talmud *generally*: as "*talmuda'*, learning" or "*hora'ah*, teaching" from generation to generation. When Sherira mentions that after Ravina *talmuda'* and *hora'ah* ceased, he quotes b. B.M. 86a, giving the distinct impression that he intended to describe Amoraic achievement ending with Ravina, and that Rav Ashi enters only by being included in the same source. At this point, we do not know *which* Ravina, or why the Rav Ashi in the quotation is not referred to by Sherira himself, similarly to Ravina, to say that after Rav Ashi *hora'ah* ceased.

B) In part 2, the history of the heads of the academies, Sherira mentions Rav Ashi in detail, including many details from the Talmud. At the end he quotes b. B.B. 157b, about the first and second "reviews" of Rav Ashi's teaching, but he does not quote the source mentioning *sof hora'ah*, as if it did not relate to Rav Ashi at all. Later in the list, when he mentions Ravina b. Huna, who died eighty years after Rav Ashi, Sherira declares *he* is the Ravina who is *sof hora'ah*, the last Amora. Further on, in the list of the heads of the Pumbeditan academy, Sherira mentions *R. Assi* (who acceded to his post fifty years after the death of Rav Ashi). R. Assi, he says, ended the Amoraic period in Pumbedita; *he* is *sof hora'ah* and the end of the Talmud. Then Sherira goes on to describe the Saboraim.

Weiss concludes, therefore, that Sherira understood b. B.M. 86a as referring not to Rav Ashi, but to Rav Assi, head of the Pumbeditan academy, who together with Ravina b. Huna marks the end of the Amoraic period. Weiss does not say whether the difference in spelling (Ashi = Assi) is a textual corruption, or just equally valid spellings for the same name.[1] But he does supply several references which show

[1] Abraham Weiss, *Hithavut TaHalmud BiShelemuto*, 251, n. 108a.

that the latter Rav Assi is mentioned, though the name is spelled *'ŠY* (b. Shab. 42b, b. Ket. 2b). There is therefore *no* mention of Rav Ashi as the editor of the Talmud, or for that matter as *sof hora'ah*, in the ESG.

True, later authorities mentioned Rav Ashi in the role of editor. Their misunderstanding was a simple one. It was only a question of identifying the R. Assi of *sof hora'ah* with the Rav Ashi of the first and second "reviews" or "editions", and drawing the all-important parallel to Rabbi Judah and his Mishnah. Their view maintained itself even with modern scholarship, which tried to approach the question through a search for external evidence. But such evidence is inadequate. Internal evidence, on the other hand, reveals the gradual literary growth of the Talmud through the process of study. Study and "editing" are really identical.

Having worked out his detailed studies on the development of the Talmud as a literary work, Weiss' task here was, as we have seen, only to show the inadequacies of those theories asserting a single editorial role for Rav Ashi. His reading of the ESG is convincing, as is his interpretation of the key Talmudic passages. To fault his conclusions, one would have to disprove the innumerable analyses indicating the varied histories of the tractates and *sugyot*, and to offer convincing evidence for the work and identity of an editor. It seems unlikely that this could be done.

VIII

ABRAHAM WEISS: THE SEARCH FOR LITERARY FORMS

BY

DAVID GOODBLATT

The contents of Abraham Weiss' book, *Studies in the Literature of the Amoraim*, are described more informatively by the Hebrew title, *'Al Hayeẓirah Hasifrutit Shel Ha'amora'im* [*On the Literary Creation of the Amoraim*]. The book examines the nature of the literary activity of the Amoraim. That is, Weiss seeks to identify and catalog the different kinds of literature produced by the Babylonian (and, to a lesser degree, the Palestinian) sages between the third and the fifth centuries. He points out that while several Tannaitic works by and large represent different *kinds* of literature, we have only the Talmud from the Amoraim.[1] The attempt to discern different kinds of literature produced by the latter, then, must be based on that one document.[2] Consequently this attempt must involve methods of analysis analogous to those of form criticism and source criticism—methods used so fruitfully in biblical studies.

In an important sense, much of Weiss' earlier work involves what I shall call, perhaps loosely, form criticism. I refer to his identification and description of what he considers to be the literary genres par excellence of the Amoraim, the *memra* and the *sugya*.[3] These two, he believes, are the main literary vehicles used by the Amoraim as well as the building blocks of the Talmud. Weiss defines the *memra* as "a short Amoraic statement which contains a complete idea, without any dialectics". The *sugya*, on the other hand, is basically a treatment of some aspect of a topic, generally in a dialectical form. The *memra*

---

[1] Abraham Weiss, *Studies in the Literature of the Amoraim* (New York, 1962), introduction, p. v.

[2] *Ibid.*, pp. 172, 251, n. 2, p. 264, n. 1.

[3] See the summary of Weiss' conclusions in Meyer S. Feldblum, "Professor Abraham Weiss—His Approach and Contribution to Talmudic Scholarship", in The *Abraham Weiss Jubilee Volume* (New York, 1964), pp. 7-80; on the *memra* and *sugya*, v. pp. 13-36 and the works cited in the footnotes.

—which can be in either Hebrew or Aramaic—may be "supplementary" or "independent". That is, it may explain or clarify some other source, or it may state a complete idea which stands by itself. Similarly, *sugyot* (plural of *sugya*) may be classified as either "explanatory" or "independent". In the former class some older source serves as a take-off point for the *sugya*. The latter are complete, self-contained discussions.[1]

In addition to characterizing the building blocks of the Talmud, Weiss also examines the literary form of the work as a whole. He concentrates on the Babylonian Talmud. Made up of *sugyot* and *memrot* (plural of *memra*) which originated at different times and places, the Talmud has had a complex literary history as, indeed, have many of the individual *sugyot*. Yet despite its composite and stratified nature, the Talmud, Weiss believes, may be viewed as a unified literary entity. Its organizational framework is provided by the Mishnah. "In general, not only because of its external form, but also because of its content and nature, the Talmud has the form of an extensive and wide-ranging commentary on the Mishnah. Not only the supplementary *memra* and *sugya* which are connected to the Mishnah, but even the independent *memra* and *sugya* are essentially only a kind of extension of the contents of the Mishnah".[2]

Thus the *memra*, the *sugya*, and the stringing together of the latter into a Mishnah-commentary constitute the primary kinds of literature created by the Amoraim. By primary, I mean that most Amoraic literature takes these forms. Moreover, these forms are the unique invention of the Amoraim, according to Weiss. The first half of *Studies in the Literature of the Amoraim* is devoted to a review of his researches and conclusions on these topics. Weiss then raises the question of whether other kinds of literature were created by the Amoraim. He sees this question in terms of both form- and source-criticism. Thus in the introduction he writes, "Here and there in the *sugya* material which is in it [the Talmud], there is Amoraic material which deviates from the *sugya* and *memra* in respect of its form. This material raises the question of the literary sources of the Talmud, that is, whether in this [the Amoraic] period other kinds of literature were also created which served as a source for the creators of the Talmud".[3] This formulation is somewhat confusing, for it blurs certain conceptual and

[1] Weiss, *Studies*, pp. 1-4.
[2] *Ibid.*, p. 5 and cf. p. v.
[3] *Ibid.*, pp. v-vi.

procedural distinctions. Two different issues are raised here. The first is form criticism. It is the question of whether we can identify in the Talmud forms of Amoraic literature other than the *memra* and *sugya*. If this can be done, then it is possible to ask whether or not those other forms also represent different sources which have been incorporated into our Talmud. The other issue is source criticism. Of concern here is the isolation of the sources of our Talmud. Having isolated them, one may then examine what literary form or forms these sources exhibit. Obviously, these issues may overlap, especially if one takes the second steps I have mentioned. Nonetheless the two inquiries clearly differ both in object and in procedure. Yet despite the confusion, this quote indicates that Weiss' main interest is form-critical. And it is the order of procedure required by this kind of inquiry that is followed in the researches in the second half of his book.

Weiss does devote one chapter to an investigation of the sources of the Talmud. Since my concern is with the Amoraim, I shall pass over his discussion of the Tannaitic sources.[1] He himself narrows down the topic, by eliminating from consideration what he calls traditional, as opposed to literary, sources. By the former Weiss means material "from a living tradition the content of which is transmitted orally" without a fixed literary form.[2] He is interested, rather, in material which was before the creators of the Talmud as finished units with a fixed form, whether handed down in writing or not. The quest for the Amoraic literary sources of our Talmud is further limited by Weiss' assertion that most *sugyot* had their origin as literary units in the Mishnah study-sessions of the academy which created the former work (primarily the academy of Pumbedita).[3] He states as a general principle that "it stands to reason that *sugya* material which is found in only one place was created in its present place as part of the Talmud and within the framework of the Mishnah where it is found and to which it is connected in some way." Such material is "not only the foundation and cornerstone, but also the major part of our Talmud."[4]

Having delineated the question in this way, Weiss then lists four categories of Amoraic material which the creators of the Talmud had before them and drew upon as finished literary sources. For this list he relies heavily on his previous studies which are cited in the foot-

[1] *Ibid.*, pp. 167-72.
[2] *Ibid.*, p. 167.
[3] *Ibid.*, p. 172.
[4] *Ibid.*, p. 6.

notes.[1] The first category contains certain Palestinian *sugyot* which have parallels in the Palestinian Talmud. On the basis of verbal agreement between the parallels, it appears that many of these *sugyot* came to Babylonia in the form of finished literary units. The second category is that of *sugyot* which originated at academies other than the one(s) which created our Talmud. Third, many *sugyot* or parts thereof appear in several places in the Talmud. In only one of these places are they original. In many cases, according to Weiss, these parallels are the result of the post-Amoraic polishing up of the Talmud's form and style (*shikhlul*, literally "completion"). That is, *sugyot* alluded to in a discussion were later quoted in full by being transcribed from their original location. However, in at least some cases the parallels originated in the Amoraic period. In such cases we can speak of the use of literary sources. The fourth category includes sources which apparently were created as independent literary entities. As Weiss points out, the first three categories all share the primary and usual form of *memra* and *sugya*. The fourth category, however, includes sources which may or may not have such a form. In this category, then, form criticism may overlap with source criticism, and at this point Weiss begins his form-critical inquiries.

The second half of Weiss' book is taken up with the cataloging and examination of Amoraic literary genres which differ from the *memra* and *sugya*. He also raises the question of whether or not these genres represent independent literary units or sources. I shall deal with this last issue separately. First I shall list and describe briefly the different forms. Weiss groups the latter into three broad categories: collections (*Qobeṣ*), *midrashim* and *aggadot*, and "tractates" or "treatises" (*massekhet* sg.).

The first category, that of collections, is by far the most extensive and variegated. Weiss cites over 125 instances of this form, and he asserts that his citations are by no means exhaustive.[2] He defines a collection as an assemblage of traditional material which has its own organizational framework. The latter may be topical or formal.[3] In general, a unit must contain at least three components before he considers it to be a collection. The commonest type is the collection of *memrot* all attributed to one sage.[4] For example, at b. *Shab*. 141a we

---

[1] *Ibid.*, v, pp. 172-73, notes 18, 19, 20.
[2] *Ibid.*, p. 189.
[3] *Ibid.*, p. 176.
[4] *Ibid.*, pp. 176-208.

find three statements of Rava cited one after the other in the form: "Rava said ... and Rava said ... and Rava said ..." Occasionally the collection form is obscured by the fact that discussions intervene between the components. That is, one or more of the elements in the collection may have led to the development of a *sugya*. Moreover, faulty manuscript transmission may have corrupted and changed the name of the sage whose *memrot* are collected in one place, thus obliterating the form. For example, if in the instance cited above the name "Rava" had been corrupted to "Rabbah" (RB' to RBH) in the second saying, then we could not recognize the genre.[1] Generally, however, the *collection form* is as easy to recognize as it is widespread.

Some collections include questions, usually introduced by the formula B'Y, as well as declarative statements. Indeed, some collections are composed entirely of questions. These latter may all be attributed to one sage, to several different sages, or they may all be anonymous.[2] A related phenomenon is a collection of questions constituted by the juxtaposition of apparently contradictory sources, introduced by the formula RMY.[3] In a number of collections the components share another formal feature in addition to that of attribution to one sage.[4] Thus the *memrot* in some collections are all transmitted, as well as uttered, by one sage.[5] Or, alternatively, the *memrot* may all be introduced by the same formula. For exemple, at b. Shab. 134a we find six statements of Abaye one after the other, and each one is introduced by the phrase "My mother told me".[6] Finally, the *memrot* in certain collections are actually legal decisions(*pisqe halakhah*, *pesaqim*), and there are several instances of collections of anonymous *pesaqim*.[7]

The second category, *midrashim* and *aggadot*, includes sections of the Talmud which constitute either explanatory *midrashim* of Biblical books (or parts thereof), or more general assemblages of aggadic material on a given theme. Weiss lists three instances of the former variety. The most extensive is a nine part midrash on the Book of Esther at b. Meg. 10b-17a.[8] The other two instances cover sections

---

[1] *Ibid.*, pp. 218-19.
[2] *Ibid.*, pp. 238-46.
[3] *Ibid.*, pp. 222-24.
[4] *Ibid.*, pp. 209-220.
[5] *Ibid.*, p. 220.
[6] *Ibid.*, pp. 210-11.
[7] *Ibid.*, pp. 247-50.
[8] *Ibid.*, pp. 276-92, esp. 281-92.

of Ruth, at b. Shab. 113b-114b,[1] and parts of Job, at b. B.B. 13b-17a.[2] In the latter category he includes a four part midrash on prayer at b. Ber. 31a-32b,[3] a three part one on the giving of the Torah at b. Shab. 86b-89b,[4] and one on the "works of the chariot" (*maʿasé merkavah*) at b. Ḥag. 13a-16a.[5] Finally, there is the well known unit which contains legends about the destruction of the temple at b. Git. 55b-58a.[6]

Related to the above category is that of "tractates" or treatises, i.e., a collection of material on a specific topic. Weiss cites a four part treatise on dreams at b. Ber. 54a-57b,[7] one on Ḥannukah at b. Shab. 21b-24a,[8] and one on "wonders and visions" at b. B.B. 73a-75b.[9] Also to be noted are shorter units on demons (*shedim*) at b. Ber. 6a and b. Pes. 110a, and on medicine at b. Shab. 110a-b, b. Git. 67b and b. A. Z. 28a.[10]

Identifying units of material which have forms other than that of *memra* and *sugya* is not the same thing as isolating literary sources of the Talmud. Weiss is quite aware of this distinction. Thus, for each unit of material which exhibits one of these other forms he poses the following question: Was the unit composed independently of our Talmud, and then inserted into the latter as a finished source at some later time? Or, alternatively, does it represent an excursus which grew by accretion in its present place, built up layer by layer like many complex *sugyot*?[11] As I shall note below in detail, Weiss concedes that in many instances this material did originate in the latter way, rather than having been inserted as a ready-made product. On the other hand, he argues, there is material whose "very nature" indicates that it was an independent literary source.[12] The category of collections will provide the clearest examples of the process by which Weiss tries to identify the latter phenomenon.

In the case of a collection of *memrot*, Weiss offers the following

---

[1] *Ibid.*, pp. 256-58.
[2] *Ibid.*, pp. 258-59.
[3] *Ibid.*, pp. 251-56.
[4] *Ibid.*, p. 260.
[5] *Ibid.*, pp. 260-61.
[6] *Ibid.*, pp. 261-63.
[7] *Ibid.*, pp. 264-70.
[8] *Ibid.*, pp. 270-73.
[9] *Ibid.*, pp. 273-75.
[10] *Ibid* ., pp. 264, n. 2.
[11] *Ibid.*, v, p. 174. Cf. re collections, pp. 176, 220, 231, and re *midrashim* and *masskhetot*, p. 294.
[12] *Ibid.*, p. 174.

methodological principle. "When they [the *memrot* in a collection] deal with different issues and are found in their present place only because one or some of them deal with the same topic as the framework, the most reasonable assumption is that we are dealing with a ready-made source." However, he immediately qualifies this by noting that "even in this kind of material, there is sometimes room to say that the whole collection or at least part of it came into being in its present place, or that in its present framework its literary form was fixed for the first time. However, one should not entertain such a possibility unless there is some specific reason [to do so] ..."[1] In any event, the principle is clear enough. When only one of a group of *memrot* is relevant to the framework, the best explanation for the presence of the others is that the creator of the *sugya* found the sayings grouped together in a source, and that he then cited the whole source.

At the end of the passage cited above, Weiss alludes to certain factors which could lead one not to apply the principle he has enunciated, which limit the latter's general application. One such factor is the appearance of the non-relevant *memrot* of a collection elsewhere in the Talmud. If it can be determined that the *memrot* in question are original in that other place, then the collection must have grown by accretion. That is, originally only the relevant *memra* appeared in the present context of the collection. At some later time someone copied *memrot* of the same sage from elsewhere and appended them to the relevant one. Thus was created the collection before us. The scarcity of a sage's utterances or the rarity of his name could provide a reason for citing all his *memrot* whenever his name appeared. In any event, broader application of Weiss' methodological principle will often require the determination of the original context of a *memra*. This is a rather complicated task. Relevance to a context is not necessarily an indication of originality in that context. For example, a *memra* whose original location was in a collection, where it had no relevance to its context, might then be copied in a section of the Talmud where it was relevant.[2] On the whole there seem to be few, if any, guidelines for deciding which occurrence of parallel passages is the original one. Each case must be examined and decided on its own.

Even in the absence of parallels to any of the components of a collection, Weiss' principle still may not be applied indiscriminately. If all of the *memrot* in a collection are attributed to one of the leading

---

1 *Ibid.*, p. 188.

2 *Ibid.*, v, pp. 181-82 on all the above.

sages of the academy which produced our Talmud, it is doubtful that the collection ever existed as an independent literary source. It is more likely that these sayings circulated in the form of living tradition and then were all given literary form (viz., that of *memrot*) together at the same time.[1] Conversely, if the *memrot* in a collection are attributed to a Palestinian, or to a Babylonian sage who was not among the personnel of the academy responsible for our Talmud, then it is more probable that the creators of the latter knew this collection as a finished literary source.[2]

Given the various qualifications and limitations which Weiss himself imposes on his general principle, it is not surprising that his conclusions are rather cautious and that they are couched in terms of probability and likelihood.[3] Nevertheless, general guidelines, however tentative, are offered for deciding whether a given collection represents an independent source or the product of accretion. In the case of the other forms Weiss provides no guidelines at all. This too is not surprising, given the results of his analysis of instances of these forms. Thus he concludes, concerning all three of the "tractates" which he cites, that they took shape in their present framework.[4] As regards the *midrashim* and *aggadot*, he concludes that only "sometimes" do we have an independent source before us.[5] Of the seven examples he gives for this category, only in three cases—one as a whole and two in part—is Weiss ready to say that the unit in question was inserted into the Talmud as a finished source. Interestingly, all three cases are Palestinian material.[6]

Weiss rounds off his treatment of the collection with an examination of two related topics. First is the issue of whether certain passages may not represent remnants of a more encompassing unit or collection. For example, Weiss notes that two different *memrot*, one at b. Git. 86b and the other at b. B. Q. 21a, are introduced by the same account: "R. Abba b. Zavda sent to Mari b. Mar, 'Inquire of R. Huna [the following matter]....' Meanwhile R. Huna died. R. Huna's son Rabbah said to him [Mari], 'Thus did my father say,...'" Since R. Huna died only once, both questions must have been asked and answered at the same time. It would thus appear that there existed a

[1] V. e.g., *ibid.*, p. 190 re Abaye.
[2] *Ibid.*, pp. 184-85, 202, 220.
[3] V. e.g., *ibid.*, pp. 198, 202, 203, 246.
[4] V. *ibid.*, pp. 270, 272-73, 275.
[5] *Ibid.*, p. 251.
[6] V. *ibid.*, pp. 255, 259, 262-63.

literary unit—posthumous responsa of R. Huna—parts of which are cited at two different places.[1] Such a conclusion is reasonable enough. A further question is whether these citations represent the whole unit. That is, was there more to the source which has been lost? Of course there is no way to prove this, but Weiss feels the possibility is very high in a number of instances.[2]

A second related topic is that of the *Sitz-im-Leben* of collections. Weiss cites four cases where a collection of *memrot* is preceded by an account of what appears to have been the circumstances in which the collection was formed. Included are the collection of a sage's utterances by his disciples immediately after his death, the sending of responsa, and a sage's eagerness to hear traditions of an important authority.[3] Needless to say, a plausible account of a possible *Sitz-im-Leben* for the collection form is very important. It gives added weight to Weiss' assertion that at least some collections represent independent literary sources.

[1] *Ibid.*, pp. 229-30.
[2] *Ibid.*, pp. 226-31. Cf., re Pesaḥim p. 250, and re responsa, pp. 234, 237.
[3] *Ibid.*, pp. 221-25.

III

BY WAY OF COMPARISON

IX

SAUL LIEBERMAN ON THE TALMUD OF CAESAREA AND LOUIS GINZBERG ON MISHNAH TAMID

BY

Herman J. Blumberg

i

The lives of Louis Ginzberg (1873-1953) and Saul Lieberman (b. 1898) touched in significant ways. Each received a traditional Eastern European Jewish education; they both studied at the same Yeshiva at Slobodka near Kovno. (Lieberman was ordained there.) In 1928-1929 they were both at the Hebrew University. Ginzberg, faculty member at the Jewish Theological Seminary as Professor of Talmud from 1902, was instrumental in bringing his younger colleague to JTS in 1940. Both scholars served as leaders of the American Academy for Jewish Research. Each enjoyed the respect of the Jewish academic community and a reputation for breadth of general knowledge and depth of understanding of Rabbinic Literature.[1]

Ginzberg and Lieberman approach Talmudic Literature and the history of the redaction of the Talmud as literary critics who seek to understand the history of the text's development through detailed analysis of its structure and content, its component parts, its language and the authorities named, its geographic and historic context. Here we will examine their analysis of single tractates of Mishnah and Talmud. Their studies are instructive as examples of the close scrutiny to which the text must be subjected and of the difficulties inherent in moving from literary analysis to conclusions in history. We will find that where Ginzberg's analysis of the text is narrow, limited primarily to language and structure, his conclusions are broad, often unsupported by his method. Where Lieberman's method is varied and thorough, his conclusions appear limited to that which analysis of the text can sustain.

[1] Ginzberg, Eli, *Keeper of the Law: Louis Ginzberg.* "Saul Lieberman", *The Universal Jewish Encyclopedia*, Vol. 7, p. 52.

In "The Mishnah Tamid"[1] Ginzberg sets out to prove: (1) that Tamid is not part of Judah's Mishnah; its method suggests a different editor, its contents were not disturbed by late editing; (2) that the editor of Tamid must have lived several generations before R. Judah the Prince; (3) that this tractate is the oldest Tannaitic work, compiled shortly after 70 C.E.

To prove the first two conclusions he analyzes Tamid, discerning its distinct structure and content, its linguistic peculiarities. He employs Tannaitic sources to support his dating of the tractate.

ii

Mishnah Tamid Does Not Form Part of the Mishnah of Rabbi Judah the Prince

Ginzberg begins by calling attention to a distinct characteristic of Tamid: the absence of references to authorities in support of, or in contradiction to, views given in the tractate. He makes a quantitative analysis: "Our" Mishnah includes a total of 508 chapters[2]; only six list no authorities. The tractate Sheqalim, approximately the same length as Tamid, refers to more than fifty authorities. The three references in Tamid that do quote authorities (Tamid 3:8, 5:2, 7:2) can be seen, through critical study, to be very late additions. By way of example we will examine one such "critical study".

Tamid 3:8 discusses the distance from which activity in the Temple could be heard:

> From Jericho they could hear the noise of the opening of the great gate; from Jericho they could hear the sound of the *Magrefah* (musical instrument?)...
> From Jericho they could smell the smell of the compounding of the incense. R. Eleazer b. Daglai said: There were goats at my father's house in the mountain of *Miḥvar* (east of the Dead Sea) and they used to sneeze from the smell of the compounding of the incense.

Ginzberg suggests that the statement is post-Talmudic. The entire Mishnah is taken over from a *beraita* or *memra* found in y. Suk. V, 55b. He cites two statements in b. Yoma 20b and 39b, which discuss how far the "sounds" produced at the Temple could be heard. Both indicate a much shorter distance! Neither Amoraic discussion takes

[1] *Journal of Jewish Lore and Philosophy*, 1919, p. 33ff.
[2] Ginzberg makes use of a Genizah fragment for this number.

cognizance of the statement in our Mishnah. Ginzberg concludes: "[This] shows that such a Mishnic statement did not exist at all at the time of the Amoraim."[1] Furthermore, in b. Yoma 39b when it is quoted, it is given as an Amoraic tradition and *not* as a Mishnah.[2]

Ginzberg disposes of other references to authorities in equally convincing fashion. He then considers two alternative explanations for the total absence of authorities: (1) "The Halakhot in Tamid were accepted by all the Tannaim... there was not need to quote any authority in support... no occasion for noting differences... or (2) this tractate was not edited by the same redactor as the rest of the Mishnah."[3]

In that many of the *halakhot* in Tamid were contradicted by other Tannaim and by Judah the Prince who, in other parts of his work made decisions contrary to laws described in Tamid,[4] Ginzberg concludes:

> ...the complete absence of references to authority in our tractate and the consistently carried out principle of ignoring these views with which the author (Rabbi) does not agree, can only be explained by the assumption that Tamid does not belong to the Mishnah of Rabbi who follows an entirely different principle in his work.[5]

Here Ginzberg rests on firm ground. He subjects the text of Tamid to close scrutiny and convinces us that the absence of authorities distinguishes it in method from Judah the Prince's work and was not considered in the editing of his Mishnah.

iii

The Mishnah Tamid is Older Than The Mishnah of Judah the Prince by Several Generations

Ginzberg relies exclusively on the same type of close literary analysis to establish the age of Tamid. He begins with a self-conscious evalu ation of the limitations of his first conclusions:

[1] *Mishnah Tamid* (hereafter *M.T.)*, p. 270.

[2] *M.T.*, p. 40.

[3] *Ibid.*, p. 42.

[4] For example, in Tamid 1:l the priest who had defiled himself at night immerses himself and returns to his fellow priests until the morning when the gates were opened, whereupon he left the Temple. R. Eliezer b. Jacob in Mid. 1:9 has the young priest leave immediately by the North Gate. Ginzberg brings more such contradictions and indicates that investigation would yield many more.

[5] *M.T.*, p. 44.

> The absence of references to authorities and the ignoring of opposing views are in themselves not sufficient proofs of antiquity, A disciple of Rabbi... may have chosen for his compilation a method different from that of his celebrated master.[1]

He proceeds to an investigation of the linguistic peculiarities of this tractate in which he finds:

> ...archaic words and expressions some of which never occur in Rabbi's Mishnah and other Tannaitic sources and some of which are only rarely found there.[2]

He concludes that these linguistic peculiarities "point to an age much earlier than that of the rest of the Mishnah."[3] While the exposition of words and phrases adds support to his suggestion of the uniqueness of the work, the conclusion that this reflects the antiquity of the tractate ("at least several generations before Rabbi"[4]) appears unwarranted.

Twenty-nine examples of words or phrases considered peculiar to Tamid are described. A sampling follows:

(a) *Pirḥé Kehuna* (1:1) The use of this term, "Young Priests "is peculiar to Tamid. Ginzberg maintains that all other passages where this phrase occurs are located in tractates such as Yoma and Middot whose dependency on Tamid is well established, or in other related texts.[5]
(b) *Bet Kisé Shel Kavod* (1:1) "The place of stool for easing oneself": Ginzberg suggests that we probably have here a contraction of *Bet Kisé* and *Bayit Shel Kavod*; "it is hardly conceivable", he says, that an almost identical expression (to *Kisé Hakavod*, Throne of Glory) should have been used to designate a privy!" In all events, the term appears here exclusively; elsewhere *Bet Hakisé*.[6]
(c) As to *Sonkin* (2:1) Ginzberg comments that the meaning is not clear and the etymology obscure. It occurs only here.[7]
(d) *Heḥalu* (2:2, 3:4:1) "they began" is the archiac (biblical) form of *Hitḥilu* which is used exclusively in Tannaitic and Amoraic sources.[8]

While Ginzberg proves the obscurity and the uniqueness of certain words and phrases in Tamid, he adds little information to the history

---

[1] *Ibid.*, p. 197.
[2] *Ibid.*
[3] *Ibid.*
[4] *Ibid.*, p. 205.
[5] *Ibid.*, p. 199.
[6] *Ibid.*, p. 200, n. 36; 201.
[7] *Ibid.*, p. 201.
[8] *Ibid.*

of the origin of the Tractate. We must enquire what level of obsolete or obscure words is found in other texts. Are these usages dependent upon parallel texts? Furthermore, Ginzberg's conclusion that "by the time of Rabbi such words were already obsolete and that the text must be dated very early"—at least four or five generations before Rabbi—does not necessarily follow.

Absence of these expressions in other Tannaitic works does not necessarily mean that they had become obsolete. Ginzberg himself argues that Tamid was well-known to Judah the Prince and his predecessors, but not used because it was a different kind of literature. Certainly, a definitive proof for this imaginative suggestion is not supplied.

Two problems remain: (1) the elimination of glosses and additional material for which the original editor is not responsible; (2) the dating of the compilation. Ginzberg believes that most of the glosses are of a different character from those which Rabbi Judah has added to the material taken over from the Mishnah collections of his predecessors. Hence, he finds it relatively easy to reduce the present text to its "original form." Having performed this task, he concludes:

> *After eliminating these additions, explanations and glosses found in the present text of Tamid we have in this tractate the oldest Tannaitic work, which though in the Mishnic form is distinguished from the Mishnah of Rabbi by method and language.*[1] (original italics)

It is beyond our purpose to evaluate Ginzberg's identification of glosses or additional material. The references are accurate (exception: p. 265, read "I,2" for "II,2") and the explanations reasonable. More problematic is the conclusion that we now have the "oldest Tannaitic work... distinguished from the Mishnah of Rabbi by method and language". The text is *different*: the dating remains unproven.

iv

Mishnah Tamid Was Composed Shortly After the Destruction of the Temple

Ginzberg offers one final proof of the early composition of Tamid. In fact, he is willing to suggest the approximate decade of composition. Here he moves from close literary analysis to conclusion in history. As students of methodology in historical research, it is im-

---

[1] *Ibid.*, p. 285.

portant to reconstruct the steps in his argument in some detail. Ginzberg proceeds in the following manner:[1]

The Tosefta (Yoma 1:13 and Zev. 6:13) gives two *halakhot* from Tamid (3:1 and last part of 4:1) as statements of R. Simeon of Miẓpah. A Tanna by this name is mentioned in one other passage, Peah 2:6:

> It once happened that R. Simeon of Miẓpah (thus) sowed (his field and came) before Rabban Gamaliel; and they went up to the Chamber of Hewnstone to inquire. Naḥum the Scribe said: I have received a tradition from R. Measha, who received it from his father, who received it from the Zugot, who received it from the Prophets as a Halakhah given to Moses from Sinai, that if a man sowed his field...

We might suppose that the incident described in Peah 2:6 took place before 70 C.E. because the "Chamber of Hewnstone" was located in one of the Temple buildings. In fact, if we follow the tradition that the Sanhedrin left the "chamber" in 30 C.E. (cf. b. Shab. 15a) then we must assume that Tamid was composed before the destruction of the Temple. Ginzberg rejects this suggestion, and, by identifying Rabban Gamaliel as Rabban Gamaliel II, he suggests that the incident occurred shortly before 70 C.E.[2] So far, little has been proven except to associate R. Simeon with Gamaliel II. Ginzberg now demonstrates that R. Simeon's *halakhot*, quoted in the Tosefta from Tamid, are in fact from the Tractate Tamid before us.

Tosefta Zev. 6:13 proves only the existence of a compilation describing the daily Temple service known as Tamid. A Palestinian Amora, R. Yoḥanan, draws the inference from that Tosefta and says that our Tamid and that of Simeon of Miẓpah are the same:

"...said R. Yoḥanan: who is the authority for the order (given) in (the Tractate) Yoma? R. Simeon of Miẓpah." (b. Yoma 14b; also y. Yoma II, 39d).

Ginzberg acknowledges that this may be the wrong inference, but calls upon his *own earlier conclusions* to support R. Yoḥanan's identification of R. Simeon with "our" Tamid, locating it after 70 C.E.:

> The statement of the Tosefta and the inference drawn from it by R. Johannan appear, however, in a different light, if we take them in combination with the conclusions we have reached in our critical study of Tamid. *We have seen that this tractate is of a very archiac character; that it does not form a part of Rabbi's Mishnah, that it did not go through the hands of a redactor; and, finally, that abstractis-abstrahendis, it came down to us in its original form.* (original italics) There is ,therefore, no reason whatsoever to

[1] *Ibid.*, pp. 285ff.

[2] *Ibid.*, p. 289.

> doubt R. Johannan's statement that our tractate of Tamid is the same as made use of by R. Simeon of Miẓpah, the contemporary of R. Gamaliel II. [1]

Again circular reasoning. The archaic character of Tamid is based upon his own, still unproven theory. He has not shown conclusively that the tractate is very old or that it has come down to us in its original form. And even if these conclusions seem justified, the proof that R. Yoḥanan's inference is correct is not evident.

Ginzberg now identifies the Temple officers mentioned in Tamid, Mattathiah b. Samuel (3:2) and Ben Arza (7:3) [Note correction in text: p. 290 last line, read "VIII:3"] as having occupied these positions in the last days of the Temple,[2] he suggests that "the probability is very great that Tamid was composed after the destruction of the Temple... To this conclusion we are urged by all that we have found about the peculiar character of Tamid which distinguishes it from the rest of the Mishnah."[3] In a footnote he explains that "the probability is very slight that Tamid was composed in the very last years of the Temple... the reference in Tamid to the officers instead of to the offices is best explained by the assumption that it was composed shortly after the destruction of the Temple."[4] In this same final paragraph of the essay, in which the first possible date for the compilation of Tamid is established, Ginzberg now reconstructs the history of the tractate.

Tamid was composed after 70 C.E. The foundation of the Mishnah of Rabbi was already set, including the division into 58 tractates. The *halakhot* dealing with the Temple services were set down in the order Qedoshim while the Temple was still in existence. After the destruction of the Temple, in an attempt to retain a "vivid picture" of what had been going on daily in the Temple, Tamid was compiled. The Tannaim from Rabbi Simeon of Miẓpah to R. Judah the Prince studied Tamid with great care, but did not incorporate it in their Mishnah collection. If it was studied with such great care, how could its language become obsolete in four or five generations? "The Mishnah is a Code of Law, Tamid an archeological study."[5] This last conclusion is ingenious and may be true, but Ginzberg's method

[1] *Ibid.*, p. 290.

[2] He relies upon Lerner, Gadetz and Büchler who "have proved the impossibility of Hoffmann's view" (that the Temple offices listed in Sheqalim 5:1 date from the time of Agrippa I, *M.T.*, p. 291, n. 113).

[3] *M.T.*, p. 291.

[4] *Ibid.*, n. 114.

[5] *Ibid.*, pp. 292-93.

has not yielded sufficient evidence that it is more than a good guess. Ginzberg's close comparative analysis of the Mishnah Tamid remains valuable for the student of Mishnah, but adds little to our firm knowledge of the development of the Oral Law.

V

S. Lieberman, *The Talmud of Caesarea*

Significant differences between the three tractates of Neziqin—Bava Qamma, Bava Meẓia'h, Bava Batra (hereafter *Baba'ot*)—and the other tractates in the Talmud Yerushalmi have long been recognized.[1] Lieberman notes that late commentators were aware of these differences, but attempted to reconcile them by forced and far-fetched *pilpul*. Halevy alone was willing to conclude that the variations between a *sugya* in Neziqin and parallels in other tractates are the results of separate editing. Lieberman acknowledges Halevy's contributions, but criticizes him for not attempting to explain the differences by references to conditions of history (time, place, local circumstances), and for not paying attention to the differences in style, language and content which flow naturally from these conditions.[2]

Lieberman performs the task Halevy ignores: to prove that the differences in *editorship* (Halevy's conclusion) are expressed not only by variation in occurrence of the same *sugya* in different places, but more specifically, by significant differences in style, terminology and the Amoraim associated with the text. These distinctions lead him to establish the location for the editing of Neziqin, not in Tiberias (I) (as is traditionally assumed), but in Caesarea (II), about 50 years before the completion of the rest of the Yerushalmi, in the 4th century C.E. (III). This method and these conclusions will also permit more general comments on the redaction of the Palestinian Talmud (IV).

For Lieberman, the analysis of the text permits us to understand the peculiarities of each academy, their common characteristics and methods. By discerning the nature of the separate schools, by dating them and locating them (where possible), we can begin to reconstruct

[1] "The Talmud of Caesarea", Supplement to *Tarbiẓ* II, 4. Jerusalem, 1931. In Hebrew (hereafter *TC*).

[2] Lieberman concedes that Halevy does compare style and terminology of Neziqin and other tractates. But he does not move to the logical conclusion: the literary differences are due not to errors in transmission, copying, but to the circumstances of their separate redactions.

the formation of the Talmud and understand how the law was transmitted. The discrepancies between the Babylonian and Palestinian Talmuds, and within each Talmud, can best be resolved by means of an understanding of the separate academies.

vi

Neziqin Was Not Edited in Tiberias

Lieberman shares with Ginzberg the task of establishing the distinctiveness of the tractate under discussion. Both depend upon an analysis of literary form and structure. However, where Ginzberg rests with an examination of form and vocabulary, which illuminate the text, but add little to the historian's use of it, Lieberman is more thorough. He acknowledges that most students of Neziqin recognize that its style is unique, different from other parts of the Yerushalmi, but concludes: "... it occurs to me that it is not worthwhile to linger upon such details; differences of this type are found, at times, in other tractates."[1] Accordingly, he proceeds to present three "hard proofs" that Neziqin was not redacted with the rest of the Talmud at Tiberias.

vii

Fundamental Differences in Construction or Content of Sugyot

Lieberman lists all the passages in Neziqin with parallels in other parts of Yerushalmi, 138 in number.[2] He then counts those *sugyot* which differ in construction or content from their parallels. He counts 50 such passages. Differences are expressed in these varied ways: (1) different conclusions for parallel passages; (2) totally different solutions to one difficult argument; (3) a matter left indefinite in one *sugya* is described with certainty in a parallel text, (4) a difficulty which remains unresolved in one *sugya* is answered in a parallel passage; (5) contradictions between passages in Neziqin and other passages in

---

[1] *TC*, p. 2.

[2] Fully three-quarters of this study is given over to the reproduction of these parallels. Unfortunately, he does not analyze and explain them. It is an understatement to suggest that Lieberman assumes his reader's knowledge of all that Lieberman takes for granted.

Yerushalmi in addition to those expected from transposed *sugyot* (*Sugyot Muḥlafot*).[1]

An example of different conclusions for parallel passages is seen in a comparison of B.Q. IX, 1,6d. and Git. V, 5, 7a. In the B.Q. passage the prohibition against demolishing a building in order to retrieve a stolen beam is limited to the land of Israel. In the parallel passage in b. Git. the same authority, R. Ya'aqov b. Aḥa in the name of R. Joshua ben Levi, would prohibit demolition be it in Israel or outside of Israel.

An example of parallel passages in which a matter is left indefinite in one and specified in the other is seen in the comparison of B.Q. VIII, 8; 6c and Ket. IV, 8; 8d. In the former passage we read that a certain matter of litigation was brought before Resh Laqish and the offender fined a litre of gold, a specific amount. In the latter passage neither the amount of the fine nor the judicial procedure is specified.

Lieberman also points to *sugyot* in Neziqin whose arguments clearly depend upon parallel passages the reader would expect to find in other tractates but does not; and conversely, *sugyot* in other tractates of Yerushalmi which should be paralleled in Neziqin, but are not.[2] Lieberman concludes that the editor of *Baba'ot* made use of a "talmud" which included these missing *sugyot* in their primary context.

viii

The Names of the Amoraim[3]

Lieberman's first "hard proof" might be compared to Ginzberg's analysis of the distinctive form of Tamid, namely the absence of authorities. However, where Ginzberg moves on to the problem of dating, Lieberman present two additional proofs for the uniqueness of Neziqin and the conclusion that it was edited outside of the academy at Tiberias.

He scrutinizes the roster of Amoraim included in Neziqin and observes:

---

[1] Lieberman dismisses this last group: "They do not add much to our proof."

[2] *TC*, pp. 4ff. Epstein makes a similar point. Lieberman admits that in and of itself this does not prove the uniqueness of Neziqin. It happens elsewhere in the Yerushalmi. However, what is unusual here and distinctive is that the Mishnah Neziqin makes references to *sugyot* which are not found in the gemara of the same tractate.

[3] *TC*, pp. 6-7.

(1) Amoraim mentioned frequently in Neziqin are less often listed in other parts of the Talmud. For example, *Devet Levi* is mentioned four times in Neziqin, not at all elsewhere in Yerushalmi; *Devet R. Yanai* is listed eighteen times; R. Nas'a fourteen times. These Amoraim are not mentioned with such frequency in any other single tractate in the Talmud.

(2) Late Amoraim mentioned regularly in the Yerushalmi are seldom found in Neziqin, viz. R. Yonah (three references), R. Huna, (2), R. Ḥanina (4), R. Bon (3), R. Man'a (18).

(3) The names of the Amoraim in Neziqin have forms distinct from these same names quoted in other parts of the Yerushalmi, for example:

Baba'ot	*Yerushalmi*
R. Ba b. Mina	R. Ba b. Binah
Resh Laqish	R. Shim'on ben Laqish
R. Zera	R. Zeira

ix

Terminology[1]

For his third proof Lierbeman points to the use unique in *Baba'ot* of three technical terms:

The term *Hekh 'avida* (How can it happen? i.e., name a case to which this rule will apply), which occurs quite frequently in Yerushalmi, does not appear at all in *Baba'ot*, despite the fact that Neziqin is filled with questions and problems. On the other hand, the expression *Hakhi dami* (How shall we imagine this case) is a new term, appearing in Neziqin and *nowhere* else.

Finally, the expression *'Inun de'amrin kan* (here they say) and variations of it are found in *Baba'ot* to introduce a point made in the Babylonian Talmud where we would expect *Taman 'amrin.*

Lieberman uses three separate measures to prove that the text is distinctive; he concludes the same editor could not have redacted Neziqin and the rest of the Talmud. While the uniqueness of *sugya*-construction in Neziqin is convincing, and the variation in names of Amoraim presents a real problem, the presence of a separate editor is not necessary. Traditions could have been handed down in slightly different forms, thereby explaining the variations.

[1] *Ibid.*, pp. 7ff.

X

Neziqin Was Edited at Caesarea

Lieberman now proceeds to locate the editing of Neziqin at Caesarea. He establishes the hypothesis by process of elimination: three major academies were located at Tiberias, Caesarea and Sepphoris. Lieberman accepts the widespread conclusion that Yerushalmi was edited at Tiberias.[1] Since it is clear that Neziqin was edited elsewhere we are left with a choice of Sepphoris or Caesarea. Sepphoris, Lieberman continues, must be discounted for two reasons: (1) it was situated only 18 miles from Tiberias; the ties between the two schools were constant and strong. It is difficult to conceive of significant differences between them. (2) The Amoraim identified with Sepphoris are seldom mentioned in Neziqin. Hence, by elimination, our tractate must have been edited at Caesarea.

Lieberman now turns to confirm his hypothesis. Here he combines the analysis of internal evidence of the text itself with a wider knowledge of fourth century Palestine to offer most convincing arguments. He first establishes the importance of the Academy at Caesarea. Noting that Caesarea was the political and commercial center in the land of Israel, he conjectures that almost all of the Tiberian scholars visited the coastal city frequently. He lists the Amoraim, beginning with the first generation, who are identified with Caesarea, having studied or taken up permanent residence there.[2]

He recalls frequent references to the group of Rabbis called *Rabbanan Dekisarin* and one reference which parallels *Rabbanan Dehakha*, meaning Tiberias, with *Rabbanan DeKisarin* (y. Shab. 13:1). Lieberman concludes: "From this we see that the Academy at Caesarea did not cease from the time of R. Hoshy'a Hagadol... until the days of R. Yosi b. Bon, and during this entire period, three Torah centers were maintained: Tiberias, Sepphoris and Ceasarea."[3] Lieberman finds that anonymous statements in Neziqin are attributed to the *Ḥakhmé Kisarin* in parallel passages. Thus we have hints (*remazim*) that Neziqin was edited in Ceasarea. He brings ten such examples, an impressive number.

The proposition that Neziqin was edited in Caesarea permits us to explain anonymous statements in the tractate by reference to localisms.

---

[1] *Ibid.*, p. 9.
[2] *Ibid.*, pp. 10-11.
[3] *Ibid.*, p. 10.

Lieberman also reminds us that the majority of the cases and practical decisions in Neziqin make reference to Caesarea. Finally, by locating Neziqin at Caesarea we have logical explanations for the unusual usage in Neziqin of many Greek words and for the special meaning of Greek terms found elsewhere in Talmudic literature. Lieberman admits the influence throughout Palestine of Hellenism. He suggests that the influence was more pervasive Caesarea. Even the *Shema* was recited in Greek there.[1] For example, in B.M. VI, 3; 11a we read:

> R. ʾAbahu said in the name of Rabbi Yosi Ben Ḥanina: One is not obligated to replace a (borrowed) ass (killed) on a side road. However one is so obligated if the ass is killed on a *Basileqi.*

Lieberman points out that all of our lexicons explain *basileqi* as a known type of buildings. But this makes no sense here for it parallels *kapandarya*, a "short cut" or "path". An early commentator unwittingly identified *basileqi* as *derech hamelekh* (i.e., an open, presumably guarded, street). Lieberman links the *derech hamelekh* with the Greek word designating the public (and guarded) roads which run from the seacoast to Lydda. By identifying the local usage of *basileqi* an unclear passage is explained.[2]

The final proof that Neziqin was edited in Caesarea is the link Lieberman perceives between Neziqin and the Talmud of the South, namely the Talmud of the Academy at Lydda. Lieberman says that the Caesarean and Lyddian academies were linked in manner similar to that of Sepphoris and Tiberias. We cite one example of many Lieberman brings to show the link between the two academies of the "south". In y. B.B. III, 5; 14a, we read:

> *Aval* a man who guards his wife's possessions (has) (does not have) Ḥazaqah for it is customary for husbands to watch over their wives' possessions.

In this passage it makes no sense to read *aval* as "but". The *Pené Moshe* reads *aval* as "in truth" or "indeed", citing interpretation of Genesis 42:21 in *Genesis Rabbah* 91:8.

> "And they said to each other: '*Aval* we are guilty!' R. Aba ben Kahana said—it is an expression used in the south: *aval* means "indeed" "in truth".

[1] *Ibid.*, pp. 12-13; p. 13, n. 4.
[2] *Ibid.*, p. 14.

Thus Lieberman brings considerable and varied evidence to locate the editing of Neziqin at Ceasarea. Particularly impressive is his resolution of textual difficulties by drawing upon usages characteristic of that seacoast center.[1]

xi

The Tractate Neziqin and Its Redaction Are Earlier Than the Rest of the Talmud

Lieberman confronts a problem similar to that faced by Ginzberg when, having established the distinct form and method of Tamid, Ginzberg moved to explain the origin of the differences. Of course, Lieberman has a greater working surface for further conclusions. He has pointed to the uniqueness of Neziqin and located it at the Academy of Caesarea. Nevertheless, like Ginzberg, Lieberman proceeds cautiously and self-critically:

> How can one explain the substantial difference between the transmission of the laws in Neziqin and those in other parts of the Yerushalmi? A different location cannot be the decisive cause, for Caesarea is only about two days journey from Tiberias and Sepphoris and communications were constant. And even though I have already explained that the editor of *Baba'ot* relied heavily on the Talmud of the South, the Talmud of the Academy at Lydda, this, too is an unsatisfactory cause for, in the last analysis, Lydda was not a great distance away.

Lieberman now suggests that the differences are best explained by dating the Talmud of Caesarea. Where Ginzberg examines "obsolete and archaic" words to date Tamid, Lieberman employs a wider variety of proofs.[2]

He counts the authorities mentioned and dates them, discovering that the majority of Amoraim mentioned are first and second generation:

Authority	*Number of times cited*
R. Ḥiyya	30
R. Hosha'y'ah Rabbah	20
Rav	many
Samuel	50

[1] *Ibid.*, p. 18.
[2] *Ibid.*, pp. 18ff.

Rav Huna	40
Yoḥanan	200
Resh Laqish	60
Elazar	60

He analyzes structure. Anonymous passages, few in number with many *beraitot* (not introduced by *tanya*) in these passages, indicate early material. The greater portion of the tractate is made up of *beraitot* and *ma'amarim* from the early Amoraim.

He analyzes language such as primitive terminology and archaic words suggesting an early text. While these investigations into the frequency with which certain authorities are mentioned or the number of occurrences of anonymous passages or unusual vocabulary are useful, they are less than conclusive evidence for the dating of the tractate under consideration. In order to use them for dating, a comparative study of other tractates must be taken to provide a control by which the character of Neziqin can be measured.

Lieberman also analyzes the form and character of Neziqin, concluding that the editing is relatively older than the rest of the Yerushalmi. He notes that the *sugyot* in this tractate are shorter and unfinished, contrasted with parallel *sugyot* in other parts of the Talmud, which are longer, with additions and explanations, displaying the sign of a later editor. Most commentators explain the brevity and peculiarities of Neziqin by relying on parallels, or by indicating that the editor of the *Baba'ot* has another, longer Talmud from which he worked.

Lieberman prefers another explanation: the character and content of Neziqin suggest that we have before us short, unordered and unreworked notes. This fact makes reasonable the conjecture that the original editor of Neziqin made use of abbreviated students' notes or the archives of the academy and did not rework them. The later editor's task was to explain and rework these notes. Lieberman summarizes his investigation in these words:

> ...it appears that the editor of the *Baba'ot* maintained the list of authorities (*reshimot*) as they were without reconstructing them, in order to maintain the complete talmud as it was taught in the academy. This explains the oddities of the abbreviated *sugyot*.[1]
>
> The omissions, the abbreviations and the references to other *sugyot* all testify to an early editing. In truth, we have no proof that the talmud

---

[1] *Ibid.*, p. 20.

> was edited after the beginning of the second half of the fourth century (i.e. not later than 360 C.E.). In all events, we may point out that, in the main, the editor of the Neziqin made use of an older Talmud.[1]

Lieberman arrives at his date and characterization of Neziqin through careful and varied analysis of the text, its language, its form, its peculiarities and the authorities cited. While in the final consideration all such attempts are conjectural, which Lieberman admits, he amasses considerable evidence to prove his conclusion. He has demonstrated the importance of the Caesarean Academy and Neziqin's relationship to it. His conclusion that original form of the tractate was student notes and academy archives is speculative, but reasonable.

xii

Comments on the Redaction of the Yerushalmi

Lieberman now applies his method and conclusions concerning Neziqin to the larger question of the redaction of the Palestinian Talmud. He begins with a refutation of I.Y. Halevy's suggestion that the Yerushalmi was not edited *at all*; the "editor" simply copied the *sugyot* as they were taught in the academies, without reworking or ordering them. If Halevy were correct, Lieberman comments, not one *sugya* would be well ordered; the entire Talmud would be confused. However, there is evidence of editing, even though the order is not always self-evident.[2]

Of particular interest is Lieberman's suggestion—with credit to Y.N. Epstein—that often Talmudic commentators incorrectly transposed *sugyot* to conform to our Mishnah, because they did not realize that there was another, different order of *mishnayot* before the editor. It is the order of our *mishnayot* which must be transposed in order to make the text intelligible.[3] To Lieberman it is clear that there was an editor for the Yerushalmi who arranged the *sugyot* according to a fixed and specific system. This editor selected whole *sugyot*, which pertained to a particular matter, and inserted them every place in the Talmud where he thought they belonged. Hence, there is much material in the Yerushalmi which does not belong to the body of the earlier Talmud, but was added by a later editor. The same editor

---

[1] *Ibid.*

[2] *Ibid.*, p. 21.

[3] *Ibid.*

eliminated all material which was not compatible with the academies in Israel.

Finally, Lieberman seeks to explain the many contradictions in the Yerushalmi, contradictions primarily embedded in the body of a *sugya*, contradictions which the editor should have sensed. For Lieberman the answer is clear. The editor juxtaposed two *sugyot* from different academies without indicating the transition from the discussion of one academy to another. In many instances *sugyot* from the Talmud of the academies of the South—Lydda, Caesarea—were placed next to *sugyot* from the Talmud of the Galilean academies—Sepphoris and Tiberias—without indication of the change The same explanation can help us to understand contradictions between parallel *sugyot*. In this respect, Lieberman suggests, the distinction between the Palestinian and Babylonian Talmuds is only relative. In Yerushalmi the number of transposed *sugyot* is relatively small, but the contradictions within a particular *sugyot* are many; in the Babylonian Talmud the reverse is true.

From his detailed analysis of Neziqin and his understanding of the role of the seperate academies, Lieberman is prepared to suggest direction for further research into the construction of the *sugya* in the Yerushalmi; we must distinguish and sort out the *sugyot* from the various academies and, first and foremost, distinguish the layers reflecting the academies at Tiberias and Sepphoris on the one hand, and the Caesarean academy and the schools in Judea, on the other.

xiii

To make use of Talmudic sources, one must begin where Ginzberg and Lieberman have begun: with an informed and critical reading of these sources. Lieberman, in particular, provides us with the first step in method worthy of emulation. He painstakingly separates the material that can be identified with the Academy at Caesarea and, accordingly, provides information concerning the development of the Talmud. His task was relatively simple, given the distinctiveness of Neziqin. Certainly the student who would use his method in other tractates of Talmud would have an even more exacting and difficult task. The student must go beyond Lieberman's effort, however, to compare the characteristics of one tractate with another. Only then can the impact of statistical analysis—upon which Lieberman relies so heavily—be felt.

The danger of broad conclusions from limited literary evidence is self evident. Both Lieberman and Ginzberg attempt to reconstruct the historical development of the literary units under discussion from the literature itself. While a thorough and comparative analysis of this literature is a first step, it is questionable whether the effort can progress sufficiently to draw positive historical conclusions.

IV

THE SUGYA

X

ḤANOKH ALBECK ON THE TALMUDIC SUGYA

BY

GARY G. PORTON

i

Ḥanokh Albeck was born in Lowicz, Poland in 1890. In 1907 he received his rabbinic ordination and in 1921 obtained his Ph.D. from the University of Vienna. He was a corresponding member and collaborator of the Akademie für die Wissenschaft des Judenthums in Berlin and served as professor on the Talmud at the Hochschule für die Wissenschaft des Judenthums from 1926 until 1935. In 1936 Albeck settled in Palestine. In 1937 he became professor of Talmud at the Hebrew University in Jerusalem. Since 1957 Albeck has been professor emeritus of the History of Halakhah and Aggada at the Hebrew University.[1] Albeck has published on all phases of rabbinic thought and literature. His editions of Genesis Rabbah and the Mishnah are definitive.

Although Albeck has published extensively about rabbinic literature, to date he has not explicitly articulated his theory about the formation of the Babylonian Talmud. However, one does find a certain consistency in Albeck's thought in reading his articles about the sources and the uses of the statements within the Talmud. Here I shall combine the main points of six articles which Albeck published between 1932 and 1958[2] and the last two chapters of his latest book,

---

[1] Isaac Landman (ed.), *The Universal Jewish Encyclopedia* (New York: 1939), vol. 1, p. 159. Harry Schneiderman and I. J. Carmin Karpman (eds.), *Who's Who in World Jewry* (New York: 1954), p. 16.

[2] This paper is based on the following articles: "The Redaction of the Babylonian Talmud," *Tarbiẓ*, XV, 1944, pp. 14–26; "The Examination of the Talmud," *Tarbiẓ*, III, 1932, pp. 1–14; "The Examination of the Talmud," *Tarbiẓ*, IX, 1938, pp. 163–178; "Variant Versions in the Mishnah of the Amoriam," *Articles in Memory of Z.P. Ḥayyot* (Vienna: 1933), pp. 1–28; "The Redaction of the Babylonian Talmud," *Sefer ha-Zikaron le Asher Gulak u Shmu'el Klein* (Jerusalem: 1942), pp. 1–12; "Sof Hora'ah," *Sinai: Sefer Yovel*, 1958, pp. 73–79.

Introduction to the Talmuds.[1] Through this combination I have constructed the main points of Albeck's theory about the formation of the Babylonian Talmud.

ii

In these articles Albeck attempts to discover the *Sitz im Leben* of the various *sugyot* of the Talmud. By studying parallel passages in the Bavli, Yerushalmi, Tosefta, traditional commentators, and Tannaitic Midrashim, Albeck hopes to discover the reasons for the differences between these parallel *sugyot.* Albeck concludes that the everyday "give and take" of the *bet ha-midrash* produced these *sugyot.* He suggests that during these school-house discussions students enlarged upon their teacher's sayings,[2] moved statements and arguments from their original context into a new context,[3] and in short created the large majority of the *sugyot* we find today in the Bavli. The following examples will illustrate Albeck's method and conclusions. In *Makkot* 10b we read:

> It was said: R. Ammi and R. Assi disagreed concerning a city which lacks elders. One said it offers asylum [for a manslaughter], the other that it does not. According to the latter we require [that there be] "elders of the city" who are lacking [in this instance]. According to the former [the presence of elders] is not obligatory.

The same discussion appears concerning the law of the stubborn and rebellious son and the law of the heifer whose neck is to be broken. Mishnah *Soṭah* 9:1 states that the law of the heifer can only be carried out by a city with a court (= elders). Hence Albeck suggests that R. Ammi and R. Assi could not have disagreed on this matter. He concludes that the rabbis' original disagreement concerned only the law of asylum *or* that of the rebellious son. During the normal "give and take" of the school-house discussions, this disagreement was moved from its original context and placed into a new context. The phrase "elders of the city" formed the basis for the transfer.[4]

Mishnah *'Eruvin* 72b states that brothers who eat at their father's

---

[1] H. Albeck, *Introduction to the Talmuds* (in Hebrew; Tel-Aviv, 1969), pp. 557–596.

[2] *Tarbiz,* 1938, p. 163

[3] *Tarbiz,* 1938, p. 163.

[4] *Tarbiz,* 1932, pp. 7–8.

table but sleep in their own houses must prepare a separate *'eruv*. The *Gemara* anonymously states:

> Then where one sleeps is decisive. Rav Judah quoted Rav: 'The Mishnah refers to people who receive their food from their father's house, but eat at their own homes...'

On page 73a we read:

> Abaye said to R. Joseph, "You were teaching us this Mishnah and we said to you, 'Then where one sleeps is decisive,' and you said to us, 'Rav Judah quoted Rav, the Mishnah refers...'"

Albeck notes that 73a is the same as the anonymous passage of 72b. He concludes that during the discussion in the *bet hamidrash* the names Abaye and R. Joseph were added, and thus an anonymous *sugya* was transformed as a result of the "give and take" of the school-house.[1]

It is essential for Albeck that the *gemara* was in a fluid state during most of the Amoraic period; it is especially important for him to prove that the *gemara* did not exist in its present "ordered" form early in the period of the Amoraim. If the *gemara* was an organized, "ordered" text early in the Amoraic period, how can one explain how the "give and take" of the schools produced changes in previous sayings, and how the school-house discussions combined and moved large blocks of material?

For this reason Albeck must deal with *'Eruvin* 32b and the term *gemara* which we find in the text.[2] He asks why did the Talmud ask, "Have you fixed it in the *gemara?*" He suggests if the term *gemara* meant the same thing for whoever composed this *sugya* as it means for us today, then this question is meaningless. Everything would have been included in the *gemara*.[3] Albeck also notes that the term *gemara* in this context means more than just a collection of "correct" or "accepted" Amoraic statements. He writes, "In many places we find that the Amoraim say *yishar vekhen 'amar rav peloni*[4] [it is correct, or acceptable, and thus said R. so-and-so] but a question such as this one [about the *gemara*] does not arise in any other place." He concludes that the term *gemara* had a more specific meaning than it has today. *Gemara* means authoritative tradition, *mesorah veqabalah*.[5] The word

---

[1] *Introduction*, p. 578.
[2] *Introduction*, pp. 576–577.
[3] *Introduction*, p. 576.
[4] *Introduction*, pp. 576–577.
[5] *Introduction*, p. 577.

gemara does not refer to an ordered text of "correct" Amoraic statements. *Gemara* only refers to an authoritative interpretation of a text or the definitive solution of a well-known difficulty.[1] Albeck states, "...there is no proof from *'Eruvin* that a fixed and ordered *gemara* existed before the first Amoraim... Before the first Amoraim we do not find the term *gemara* with the meaning of our Talmud."[2] Albeck suggests, "The term *gemara* had a more limited meaning for the author of *'Eruvin* than it has for us today." Today we use the term for our entire collection of "correct" or "accepted" Amoraic statements. The author of *'Eruvin* used the term *only* for a comment which was an authoritative interpretation of a text or the definitive solution of a well-known difficulty.

iii

Although the term *gemara* does not refer to a fixed *talmud*, "there are numerous proofs that different *sugyot* included in the Talmud were ordered [given their present form] before the final redaction of the Talmud."[3] Albeck believes that the anonymous *sugya* was formed early in the process: "...Questions and answers transmitted anonymously in the Talmud are from the early Amoraim and therefore are not the words of the last editor but rather examples of the first editors."[4] The first editors of the Talmud were the participants in the school-house discussions who formed the vast majority of the *sugyot* of the Bavli.

Albeck presents different categories of anonymous statements and *sugyot* which he believes are of an early date: "Anonymous *sugyot* placed in the Talmud directly after *mishnayot*, *baraitot*, or early Amoraic sayings are generally of an early date and are not from the time of R. Ashi."[5] Albeck also suggests that if we find a series of answers to a question, the first answer being anonymous but the rest attributed to particular Amoraim, the anonymous statement is early. Further, a generally anonymous *sugya* in which there are a few statements attributed to particular Amoraim is of an early date.[6] Also, if one anonymous *sugya* mentions another anonymous *sugya*, we must assume

[1] *Introduction*, p. 577.
[2] *Introduction*, p. 577.
[3] *Introduction*, p. 577
[4] *Introduction*, pp. 577–578.
[5] *Introduction*, p. 580.
[6] *Introduction*, p. 590.

that the one mentioned is earlier than the final redaction of the Talmud.[1] Finally, if we find comments about the style of an anonymous *sugya*, again we must assume that the *sugya* commented upon reached its final form before the final redaction of the Talmud.[2]

Some of Albeck's categories are self-evident. If one *sugya* mentions another *sugya*, we obviously must assume that the one commented upon is earlier. Albeck does present a good case for his assertion that anonymous glosses which immediately follow a *mishnah*, *beraita* or early Amoraic statement are early. His other two categories are less clear.

First, it is difficult to distinguish between "a series of answers to a question, the first answer being anonymous but the rest being attributed to particular Amoraim" and "a generally anonymous *sugya* in which there are a few statements attributed to particular Amoraim."

Second, he assumes, especially in analysis of the "series of answers" type of *sugya*, the statements in the Talmud were consistently arranged in chronological order.

Third, he believes that all comments in a sugya are related organically. Thus if a statement within a *sugya* comments upon or responds to an anonymous comment of the sugya, the anonymous saying must be the earlier. He does not allow for the possibility that the reply was to *another* statement now missing from the *sugya;* or that the saying has no real connection to the anonymous statement.

Albeck does prove one important point. We cannot assume that *all* anonymous *sugyot* are late. The anonymity of a *sugya* is not enough evidence by itself to connect a *sugya* with the final redactors of the Talmud. However, the anonymity of a *sugya* is certainly not enough proof by itself to connect it with an early period of the Amoraim.

iv

Albeck believes that the discussions in the *bet hamidrash* produced large blocks of material. During these discussions a student might quote his teacher accurately, or one might inadvertently or purposefully misquote his authority. Often a student might change his teacher's comment in order to conform to what the student thought the teacher had meant to say.[3] Sometimes a person would add his own

[1] *Introduction*, p. 591.
[2] *Introduction*, pp. 593–594.
[3] *Tarbiz*, 1938, p. 163.

gloss to a statement, and eventually the gloss became inseparable from the original statement.[1] As Albeck puts it, "...from one statement of an Amora there was born a new statement... which was passed on in his name."[2] Many well-known sayings of certain Amoraim were not actually their words, but the result of changes which occurred in the process of the "give and take" of the school-house.[3]

Not only were individual statements changed, but entire arguments or other blocks of material were moved from their original context into a new one.[4] An argument on one topic would be used in the discussion of another topic. In this process of transfer, the argument might take on a completely different connotation from its original meaning.[5] Amoraic statements that were explanations of a given *mishnah* might be used as explanations for other *mishnayot* if the discussions required it.[6] These discussions in the *bet hamidrash* combined, changed, and ordered statements and whole arguments into large blocks of material. All that the final redactors of the Talmud had to do was to combine these various blocks of material.

V

Albeck brings his ideas to their logical conclusion in his discussion of the term *sof hora'ah*. The term *hora'ah* means "explanations and reasons of the statements in the Mishnah or in other Tannaitic material."[7] Therefore, the phrase "R. Ashi and Rabina were *sof hora'ah*" means, "...in their day the explanations and the new reasons which the Amoraim gave for mishnaic statements ceased. That is, those who came after R. Ashi and Rabina did *not* create any new comments or any new reasons for mishnaic statements. We even find that they did not quote *tannaitic halakhot* in order to derive new logical conclusions from them."[8] Albeck does not claim that the Talmud received its final form during the age of R. Ashi and Rabina. He realizes that the process of the final redaction of the Talmud lasted many years.[9] He

[1] *Tarbiz*, 1938, p. 163.
[2] *Tarbiz*, 1932, p. 5.
[3] *Tarbiz*, 1932, p. 9.
[4] *Tarbiz*, 1932; most of the article deals with this problem.
[5] *Tarbiz*, 1932, pp. 1ff.
[6] *Tarbiz*, 1932, pp. 1ff.
[7] *Sinai*, pp. 73–75.
[8] *Sinai*, p. 75.
[9] *Sinai*, pp. 78–79.

does assert, however, that these last editors added nothing new or original to text of the Talmud.

vi

Conclusion: Albeck's theory follows: The discussions of the *bet hamidrash* produced large blocks of material. During these discussions quotations and even whole arguments were moved from their original context into a new one. Often these statements were changed in the process of discussion and transmission. If we find differences between two parallel *sugyot* in the Talmud, we must not assume that these differences are the result of the work of the final editors. They are the result of the give-and-take of the school-house.[1] The final editors of the Talmud did little more than sew together already existing blocks of material.

Albeck's theory attributes little or no creative activity to the final redactors of the Talmud. Were all the *sugyot* formed before the time of R. Ashi? Could not the editors who lived after R. Ashi have moved a discussion from one place to another? Could not they have added anonymous statements in order to clear up a difficulty? No doubt much of the Talmud is a result of the give-and-take of the school-house, but which schools and when? Must we assume that this creative process ceased with the death of R. Ashi and Rabina? The final editors had more material before them than those of any other age or place. They surely added comments of their own and changed and combined sections and statements in order to solve problems which they found in the text. Nothing in Albeck demonstrates the contrary. He merely asserts an alternate theory.

[1] *Introduction*, pp. 557–574 deals with this problem.

XI

DAVID WEISS HALIVNI, *MEQOROT UMESOROT*

1. *KETUVOT*

BY

ROBERT GOLDENBERG

Rabbi David Weiss Halivni was born in the Carpathian mountains, in an area now part of the U.S.S.R. During his early childhood, he received the traditional *ḥeder* training, but he left the *ḥeder* at the age of eleven. He continued his studies privately at the Yeshivah of Sighet, in Rumania, and was ordained there four years later. During most of this time, he was in the care of his maternal grandfather, Rabbi Isaiah Weiss, whose name he later formally adopted.[1] During the war years, he was interned at Auschwitz; he arrived in the United States in February, 1947.

In America, he resumed his formal education, now for the first time at secular institutions. He received his B.A. degree from Brooklyn College in 1953; his major field was philosophy. In 1956 he received an M.A. in the same field from New York University. In 1954 Weiss entered the Rabbinical School of The Jewish Theological Seminary of America. He was ordained by that institution in 1957, and one year later received from it the degree of Doctor of Hebrew Literature. In addition to a number of articles and the work presently under discussion, Weiss has published *Fragments of a Commentary on the Treatise Ta'anit by an Early Rabbinic Authority* (Jerusalem, 1959), and was the editor of the fourth volume of L. Ginzberg's *Commentary on the Palestinian Talmud* (New York, 1961). Weiss is currently Professor of Rabbinics at the Seminary.

Weiss singles out his grandfather, Isaiah Weiss, as the most significant influence on his own development. From him, Weiss inherited an overriding concern with the simple meaning (*peshaṭ*) of the Talmudic text. This desire to remove the layers of forced interpretation and to

[1] His father's name was Bezalel Wiederman. All biographical information in this essay is derived from a letter from Professor Weiss to Rabbi Shamai Kanter, dated Oct. 17, 1969.

discover what the source "really means" lies as we shall see at the very heart of Weiss's enterprise. Later, at the Seminary he discovered the published writings of H. M. Pineles (*Darkah Shel Torah*) and J. N. Epstein; he found their methods of critical literary analysis of great value in his own work.

The present volume, *Sources and Traditions*,[1] covers the third of the six orders of the Babylonian Talmud. Five companion volumes are projected. The volume contains an introduction of only thirteen pages, followed by detailed commentaries on a vast number of Talmudic passages.[2] Because the introduction sheds much light on the interests and main insights of the author, a brief summary of its contents now follows.

The title of the book reflects a distinction basic to its entire procedure. "We call 'sources' those sayings which have come down to us in their original form, as they were uttered by their author. We call 'traditions' those which were changed in the course of transmission."[3] These changes gave rise to what Weiss calls the basic problem for all Talmudic scholarship,[4] the presence in the text of forced interpretations of traditional materials. As later generations tried to make sense of the fragmentary remains of earlier teachings, they could create an organized whole only by resorting to forced interpretation of what they had received.[5] Forced interpretations (*pērushim deḥuqim*) thus are

---

[1] Tel Aviv, 1968. In these notes, referred to as ST.

[2] In a letter to Professor Jacob Neusner, dated May 7, 1969, Professor Weiss recommended a number of *sugyot* as particularly useful to the student trying to study his method. In the list that follows, the page numbers refer to Weiss's book. Those numbers in *italics* are highly recommended; those in parentheses are relatively less important. The ones unmarked fall "somewhere in between."

Yevamot: (14), *55*, 59, *63*, *85*, 93, *102*, *113*, 120.
Ketuvot: 129, 135, 146, *153*, *156*, *169*, *172*, *175*, 182, *189*, (200), *216*, (222), (225), (233), *245*, 249, *255*, *259*.
Nedarim: 279, 286, *294*, *342*.
Nazir: *355*, 383, *384*, *389*—first section, *401*, *406*, 431.
Soṭah: (459), *465*, *470*.
Giṭṭin: *485*, *493*, (502), 523, *541*, *554*, (564), *569*, *577*, 584, *599*, *600*.
Qiddushin: 613, (617), *624*, *627*, (632), 644, 649, *663*, *669*, *679*, *690*, (692), (695, 701.

NB: Both in this list and in the notes that follow, the page numbers refer to the beginning of a section. The sections are sometimes several pages long.

[3] ST, introd. p. 7, n. 1.

[4] ST, introd. p. 13.

[5] Weiss denies that the Rabbis simply had no sensitivity for the plain meaning of a text. They were compelled to depart from it. Cf. ST, introd. pp. 12–13.

the main sign of a text which has not survived in its original form.[1]

The simple interpretation of a text is defined as "the interpretation which arises from the text itself, without either adding to it or subtracting from it."[2] "Sometimes a simple comparison with parallel sources is sufficient to show that a forced explanation has its origin in an incorrect text.... In most cases, however, it is necessary to study the *sugya* in depth, to break it into its parts before the motivation for the forced explanation becomes clear."[3] The procedure followed throughout the book is based on these ideas.

Weiss distinguishes several causes for change in a source and associated distortion in its explanation. Most such changes originated with the professional reciters (*tanna'im*) in the Amoraic academies. These men, who were expected simply to memorize all received tradition and to recite it on command, occasionally tried as well to understand the materials they handled. This led inevitably to unintentional paraphrase and intentional—but sometimes erroneous—"correction" of the sources. The sources thus became inconsistent with their contexts, and later students had to invent new interpretations of the material if it was going to make sense at all.[4] Other cases can be traced to the redactors (*sadranim*) of the *sugyot*. These often worked with fragmentary materials, and in creating extended, coherent discussions they sometimes joined pieces which did not belong together. They then had to understand these fragments in terms of each other; the difficulty of this task often caused great forcing.[5] Lastly, the rabbinic leaders themselves sometimes consciously invented a forced interpretation when they felt that they had no choice. A prime motivation for so doing was their strong desire to eliminate legal disagreement among sources. Legal disputes were generally sources of difficulty, as they impeded legal decision and undermined the doctrine that no Amoraic disciple ever rejected older, more authoritative teaching.[6] On other occasions, ethical or religious considerations led the rabbis to depart from the plain meaning of their source.[7]

Finally, the introduction gives some idea of the motivation behind

---

[1] ST, introd. p. 8. It goes without saying that lack of such forcing is no proof that a text has so survived. Cf. ST, introd. p. 10, n. 11.

[2] ST, introd. p. 8.

[3] ST, introd. p. 9. n. 7.

[4] ST, introd. pp. 14–15.

[5] ST, introd. p. 16.

[6] ST, introd. p. 17.

[7] ST, introd. p. 10.

Weiss's work. The general impulse is philosophical, a strong devotion to the truth. "Any divergence from the simple interpretation," he writes, "is a divergence from the truth."[1] More practically, Weiss's interest is primarily exegetical, not historical or literary. The general thesis outlined above is offered as background to the specific comments which constitute the bulk of the volume. There is no effort to infer this conception from evidence systematically adduced; there is no effort to use it to construct a systematic description of the formation of the Talmud. Weiss himself writes that his theories had been known to earlier writers, but their main interest had not been exegetical, and therefore they had not considered it in all its aspects.[2] This exegetical interest strongly dominates the entire work.

We turn now to Weiss's detailed criticism. All examples will be taken from the comments on Tractate *Ketuvot*.

Literary Phenomena

Conflicting versions of the same material

Residence in the Holy Land was considered highly praiseworthy, and much legislation was designed to encourage it. With this aim in mind, the Mishnah on 110b stipulates that either party in a marriage may compel the other to move to the Land of Israel, stating explicitly that "this applies both to men and to women." A *beraita* in the BT adds that should the marriage break up over this issue, then the party who refused to move to Palestine, or who insisted on leaving it, should always be at a financial disadvantage in the settlement. The Palestinian Talmud, however, holds that only the husband can force his wife to move.[3] Should he refuse, she has no right to force him. Weiss shows that the PT apparently had a different reading in the Mishnah: "this applies both to wives and to slaves." The BT itself refers to this reading, and it is supported by manuscript evidence; it indicates that the husband has the right to force *all* members of his household to come with him to the Land of Israel. A slave, on the other hand, obviously cannot force his master to go, and a wife would by inference share that status. The legal difference between the Talmuds can thus be traced to different versions of the relevant Mishnah.[4]

---

[1] ST, introd. p. 10.
[2] ST, introd. p. 12, n. 13.
[3] p. Ket. 13:11, 36b.
[4] ST, p. 259.

Summary: The two Talmuds disagree over whether the wife can force her husband to migrate to the Land of Israel. This is surprising, since each apparently derives its view from the same Mishnah. Weiss shows that two versions of that Mishnah were in circulation, only one of which appears in modern printed editions. The difference between the versions explains the difference between the Talmuds.

Transfer of passages from their original location to another

Generally, a woman divorced by her husband was entitled to collect a sum of money which he had promised her when they were married (*ketuvah*). The Mishnah on 100b, however, enumerates various classes of women who do not have this right. We read there:

> A girl who [on coming of age] refuses to stay with her husband, a forbidden relative of the second degree,[1] or a sterile woman is not entitled to a *ketuvah*.... If the man had married her originally knowing that she was sterile, she is entitled to a *ketuvah*. A widow who was married to a high priest[2] ...is entitled to a *ketuvah*.

On 101b, R. Huna holds that a widow married to a high priest is always entitled to her *ketuvah*. Rav Judah, however, extends to her case the requirement that the husband know her status before marrying her. In the ensuing discussion, R. Huna is refuted. The Gemara then remarks that

> R. Huna was misled by the Mishnah. He thought that since the Mishnah states the distinction in the case of the sterile woman, but not in that of the widow, the widow always gets her *ketuvah*. But this is not so. The latter clause presupposes the earlier one.

Weiss suggests that part of the Mishnah has been transferred from M. Yevamot 9:3, which states that a forbidden relative of the second degree never collects her *ketuvah*, while a widow married to a high priest does. In this context, the question of the husband's prior knowledge does not arise. The new context, however, includes the case of the sterile woman, appropriately placed between the "always" cases and the "never" cases. The unconditional wording of the last clause has not been adapted to its new framework, and so is indeed misleading.[3]

---

[1] That is, of a relationship declared incestuous by Rabbinic, but not Biblical authority.

[2] A forbidden, but not incestuous, match. The omission lists other marriages in the same category.

[3] ST, p. 245, and introd. pp. 11–12, n. 11.

Summary: Two Amoraim differ as to the meaning of a Mishnah, and the one with the apparently simpler explanation is declared wrong. The Gemara then comments that the Mishnah itself had misled him. Weiss tries to see what was misleading in the Mishnah and how it got that way. He suggests that certain sections had been transferred from a different tractate of the Mishnah without being changed to conform to their new context. They thus seemed to imply something which was not the case and led R. Huna astray.

Interpolation of new matter in an older source

As above, we are dealing here with a list of women who cannot collect their *ketuvah* when divorced. The Mishnah on 72a concludes:

> R. Tarfon says, "Also a screamer." And what is a screamer? One who speaks in her house so that her neighbors hear her outside.

In 72b we find the following passage in the Gemara:

> What is a screamer? Rav Judah quoted Samuel: One who raises her voice concerning marital intercourse. A *beraita* teaches: One whose voice during intercourse travels from one court to another.

Weiss points out that the Talmud's question is very surprising, since the same question is raised and answered in the Mishnah itself. It is possible to understand the Talmud's question as refining that of the Mishnah ("Concerning what matters would a woman have to raise her voice to be considered a screamer?"), but this is not the usual sense of the question.

Weiss suggests that whoever asked "What is a screamer?" in the Gemara did not include that question in his text of the Mishnah. He adduces manuscript evidence that the question and answer are in fact taken from the Tosefta,[1] and supports the claim with the following passage in the Palestinian Talmud:

> What is a screamer? Samuel said, "One who speaks so that her neighbors hear her." Rav said, "One whose voice during intercourse carries from bed to bed."[2]

If Samuel were simply quoting the Mishnah, Rav could not disagree with him. Their dispute must mean, Weiss imagines, that the question and its answer were not in the Mishnah at all. By the time the Babylo-

[1] Tos. Ket. 7:7, ed. Lieberman, p. 80.

[2] p. Ket. 7:6, 31b.

nian *sugya* was edited, however, the passage from the Tosefta had found its way into the Mishnah. The editors of the *sugya* had to assume that Samuel was not merely parroting the Mishnah, and so gave his explanation a new meaning. The question which he had originally answered, however, was allowed to stand.[1]

Summary: The Gemara asks and answers the same question which is asked and answered in the Mishnah. Weiss explains this superfluity by showing that the question and answer only at a later date were added to the Mishnah from the Tosefta. When the pericope took shape, the interpolation had not yet occurred.

Weiss refers elsewhere to a different kind of interpolation. Often a legal query in the Talmud is followed by two inconsistent explanations of its basis. Weiss suggests that these may be traditional explanations of the question and its point and may have been added to the *sugya* at a later time.[2]

Breakdown of an apparently unified passage

The Bible provides that a seducer or rapist must marry his victim (should she not belong to another) and pay her father a fine.[3] The fine however could not always be collected. On 36a, we read:

> A sterile woman is not entitled to compensation for violation or seduction. A contradiction was raised: A deaf-mute, an idiot, or a sterile woman *is* entitled to compensation... What kind of contradiction is this?! One opinion is R. Meir, the other the Rabbis![4] Then how could he have raised the question at all? He had further contradictions to raise.

Weiss points out three different strata here: a) the original question, b) the challenge (What kind...), and c) the final query (How could he...). He suggests that the original question becomes astonishing only in the light of the dispute between R. Meir and the Rabbis which almost immediately precedes it. If we assume that the person who posed this question was not aware of that dispute, the question is not surprising at all. The question must have been asked *before* the portions of our Gemara assumed their present order. At a later time, they had

[1] ST, p. 216.
[2] Cf. ST, p. 154, *ad* 19b.
[3] Cf. Ex. 22:15-16, Deut. 22:28-29.
[4] Referring to the preceding discussion.

received this order, and the original question became a source of wonder.[1]

On 46b the Gemara suggests the inference that since a girl's father is entitled to receive payment of the fine, he must also receive the payment if she is betrothed. But on 40b the opposite is held, namely, that his right to the penalty can be deduced from his right to the betrothal-money! Now these two *sugyot* cannot be from the same source. Yet both contain the same extended passage in precisely identical versions. This can be explained only by assuming that each is quoting from an earlier source, which had already achieved fixed form.[2]

Philology

Lexical

On 14b, there is an extended discussion concerning the status of a young girl who had been assaulted in the *qronot* of Sepphoris. The medieval commentators assumed that the *qronot* were wagons,[3] that is, that the girl had been attacked in the market-place of the city. Modern writers among them Pineles and Kohut, interpreted the word as the Greek *krene*, well or spring. These writers found support for their view in b. Meg. 5b; R. Judah haNasi is said there to have bathed in the *qronah* of Sepphoris. Weiss, basing himself on the Munich Manuscript, reads *qronah* in one place in our *sugya* and *qronot* in another, suggesting that the two words are not related. *Qronot* here is not the plural of *qronah*, despite the common assumption. The former are truly wagons, and the latter indeed a spring. This distinction is entirely novel.[4]

Syntactical

Mishnah 4:4 deals with the rights of the father to handle various moneys belonging to his minor daughter. It proceeds:

> Should she marry, her husband's rights exceed [her father's] in that [her husband] enjoys the usufruct of her property while she is still alive. But he is obligated to support her, to ransom her, and to pay for her funeral.

---

[1] ST, p. 172.
[2] ST, p. 189.
[3] Heb. *qaron* = wagon.
[4] ST, p. 146.

The word translated "but" is in Hebrew only the letter *vav*, which normally means "and." It is impossible here to understand it in its normal sense, however, because these obligations do not represent additional advantages of the husband over the father. Weiss suggests that the *vav* be understood as explicative: "he enjoys the usufruct of her property while she is still alive, since he is obligated..."[1]

Historical

Sayings invented after the time of their "author"

The Mishnah on 38a discusses a girl who was betrothed, divorced, and subsequently violated. R. Yosi the Galilean denies that such a girl is entitled to the usual fine, but "R. ʿAqiva says, She does receive a fine, and the money is her own." On the same page, a *beraita* gives a more elaborate version of the dispute, but concludes: "R. ʿAqiva says, She does receive a fine, and the money is her father's." On 38b, the Talmud mentions this obvious contradiction, and explains that two different Tannaim had divergent traditions of R. ʿAqiva's opinion.[2] While discussing other problems which the *sugya* presents, Weiss writes that "were he not afraid," he would suggest that ʿAqiva had in fact made neither of the pronouncements attributed to him. He quotes from Midrash Ḥakhamim to Ex. 22:15,[3] where R. ʿAqiva, in discussing the penalty, says, "Even if she had been widowed or divorced." In that source, R. ʿAqiva gives no inkling as to who is entitled to collect the money. Weiss suggests that ʿAqiva simply denied the view that there is no fine at all. Later students tried to clarify his opinion and specify who was to receive the money, and these interpretations were falsely imputed directly to him.[4]

Summary: Two contradictory opinions are attributed to R. ʿAqiva. It would be simplest to say that one of them is wrong. Weiss does say that in general only one of two such contradictory traditions can be assumed to be accurate.[5] Here he goes beyond that, however, and suggests that R. ʿAqiva expressed neither opinion. He had made an ambiguous statement. When later students tried to clarify what he

---

[1] ST, p. 189, *ad* 46b.

[2] See above, p. 136.

[3] Cf. Mekhilta, ed. Horovitz-Rabin, p. 308.

[4] ST, p. 175 and introd. pp. 10-11, n. 11.

[5] Weiss does refer to the suggestion occasionally found in the Talmud that the man might have changed his mind. Cf. ST, introd. p. 7, n. 4.

meant, the various contradictory explications were all attributed directly to him. It should be noted that the Talmud itself is aware that opinions attributed to certain persons were sometimes merely inferred from other things they had said. These opinions had not been expressed, and the inferences were sometimes wrong. Weiss, however, is talking about statements, not opinions.

Misunderstood traditions

If a man ever claimed that he was of priestly descent, he naturally had to produce witnesses to verify his claim. The Mishnah on 23b discusses what kind of testimony was necessary.

> R. Judah says, "One does not elevate a man to the priesthood on the testimony of one witness." R. Eliezer said, "When the claim has been challenged; but when there are no challengers, one does elevate to the priesthood on the testimony of one witness." R. Simeon b. Gamaliel, in the name of R. Simeon, son of the Chief Priest, says, "One does elevate to the priesthood on the testimony of one witness."

The Gemara discusses this Mishnah on 26a:

> R. Simeon b. Gamaliel says the same as R. Eliezer! And should you say that they differ on the significance of a single challenger (in that R. Eliezer would admit the force of a single challenger, while R. Simeon b. Gamaliel holds there must be two), R. Yoḥanan said, All agree that a challenge must come from two people."

In Weiss's interpretation, the BT here thinks that R. Yoḥanan is offering a definition of "challenge." There is no such thing as a single challenger. Thus the proposed distinction between the two Tannaim cannot be sustained, and it does appear as if they have expressed the same opinion. Weiss points out that the PT (2:8, 26d), on the other hand, understood that R. Yoḥanan meant to say that a priest is not removed from the priesthood on the testimony of a single witness. In that case, he was not defining the term "challenge," but rather setting legal limits on the effectiveness of a certain type of challenge. Under certain particular circumstances, a challenge coming from a single witness could not be accepted. Now the suggested distinction between the Tannaim can stand. The BT had somehow lost the proper meaning of R. Yoḥanan's comment, and thereby caused itself a major difficulty.[1]

---

[1] ST, p. 158.

Summary: Two rabbis in the Mishnah seem to be saying the same thing, whereas the structure of the Mishnah suggests that no opinion in it is repeated. The Gemara suggests a possible difference between them, but an opinion attributed to R. Yoḥanan makes that suggestion impossible. Weiss shows that R. Yoḥanan's original thought had been misunderstood in Babylonia, thereby unduly complicating the understanding of the Mishnah.

Forgotten sources

The most spectacular of these cases involves the Mishnah itself. On 106a-b R. Huna asks Rav whether Temple utensils were to be purchased from funds dedicated to the upkeep of the Temple, or from funds set aside for the purchase of sacrifices. Rav answers that they were to be gotten from the latter. In the course of the discussion, a *beraita* of the School of R. Ishmael is quoted. This *beraita* explicitly supports Rav's answer. Nevertheless, an objection is raised below from a source which contradicts Rav. The *beraita* from the School of R. Ishmael, which clearly meets the objection, is not mentioned. The obvious inference is that whoever raised the objection was ignorant of the *beraita*. Weiss points out however that he must have been ignorant of M. Sheqalim 4:4 as well. That Mishnah offers several opinions concerning what was to be done with excess money in the sacrifice-fund; any of these opinions could answer the anonymous objection.[1]

Summary: Rav answers R. Huna's question, and then an objection is raised to Rav's answer. A *beraita* quoted in the *sugya* itself could answer that objection, as could M. Sheq. 4:4, which is quoted as well. Whoever raised the objection must have been ignorant of both these sources. The question of Babylonian familiarity with the Tannaitic *corpus* is generally important and interesting; this particular case of ignorance of the Mishnah is very rare.

Missing Interests

The bulk of the passages which Weiss treats have not been mentioned in this paper. In these his interest is entirely exegetical, directed at achieving clearer understanding either of the particular text or of its legal implications. In the ones we have seen, this exegetical interest

[1] ST, p. 255.

still predominates. Weiss uses a variety of literary, philological, and historical[1] means to shed greater light on the text itself. I have given examples of these above, and I have tried to arrange them in sequence, starting out with the places where Weiss's methods and findings are well within the framework of traditional commentators, and moving out toward the more novel conceptions which he employs.

There is also a smaller number of cases where Weiss's comments lend themselves to more general considerations. In a number of places, for example, Weiss cites a passage as illustrative of the methods used by the compiler of the Mishnah.[2] Instead of dwelling on these, however, I shall concentrate here on the passages where Weiss's comments seem to indicate failure to consider different orientations which might have added to his insights.

Literary

On 23a, the Talmud tells the story of Samuel's daughters, who were kidnapped by raiders and taken to Palestine. There, they went before a rabbinic court and declared that they had not been defiled. Their legal skill indicated that they had connections with Samuel, so R. Ḥanina instructed their relative R. Simeon b. Abba to see to their marriage. The latter objected that no doubt testimony concerning their true state could be found somewhere, but his objections were set aside. The story shows several seams, and Weiss[3] reluctantly suggests that the incident about the proposed marriage and the missing witnesses had in fact taken place in another connection, and had been joined by the Babylonians to the story of Samuel's daughters.[4] Weiss's reluctance indicates that he considers his conclusion radical, yet this kind of analysis into primary units is precisely what form-critics routinely perform. Here we find no recognition that other fields of study may have undergone a development similar to Weiss's, as well as an apparent reluctance to perform the analysis at all unless confirmation of its results can be found elsewhere in Rabbinic literature (in this case, the PT).[5] This isolation of Weiss's work from its contemporary analogues is striking.

[1] That is, concerning the history of the *text*.

[2] For example, ST, p. 243 (top), *ad* 96a, and introd. p. 11, n. 11. Cf. also above, pp. 138-142, *ad* 101b.

[3] ST, p. 156.

[4] The PT does in fact tell this part as a separate story. Cf. p. Ket. 2:5-6, 26c.

[5] Cf. above, p. 136, and *ib.*, n. 3.

Historical

Our first case deals with the question of marriages between priestly and non-priestly families. On 12b the Gemara refers to the fact that priests used to give their wives *ketuvah*-payments twice as large as those given by ordinary Israelites. The question naturally arises: in a marriage between a priestly family and a non-priestly family, whose custom is to be followed? In his discussion of this section Weiss suggests that the phrase "he who wishes to act like the priests" refers to marriages between high-class non-priestly families and lower-class families.[1] This suggestion, sound enough exegetically, raises a number of historical problems. Do we know anything about tendencies of families to marry within their own class? Were marriages between aristocrats and commoners considered noteworthy? Were marriages between priests and non-priests remarkable? Did the latter sort of cross-marriage function as a kind of social model for others? An exegesis of the Talmudic text can be supplied without considering these questions, but it must be wondered if its plausibility can be defended without some such investigation.

Another case is rather more perplexing. In his discussion of the difficulties caused by the first Mishnah in ch. 8 and its Gemara, Weiss suggests that the Gemara had improperly fused two separate traditions, one represented in the Mishnah and the other in the Tosefta. Again, this suggestion is exegetically successful, but then Weiss adds, almost as an afterthought, the following comment: "But it must still be clarified whether the two opposing sources were joined during the time of the BT or only after it."[2] Now since we find the conglomerate *beraita* in a *sugya* in the Talmud, it is difficult to imagine what is meant by the suggestion that it was formed only *after* "the time of the BT." But Weiss offers no hint about what he may have had in mind. This again seems to reflect a significant lack of interest in questions of history, surprising here where the history of the text itself is under discussion.

Final Comment

We return for a moment to the story of Samuel's daughters. It is striking that there seems no historical interest beyond the history of the text. The *historicity* of the incident(s) itself is nowhere discussed.

---

[1] ST, p. 158.
[2] ST, p. 220. Cf. expecially p. 222.

We do not read that we are faced with the merging of two stories into one. It is rather implied that reference to two separate, presumably historical incidents has been made into one. A literary accident may have occurred, but that is all. The two stories, once correctly separated, elicit no further questioning. This uncritical assumption of the sources' reliability underlies Weiss's enterprise. The very title of his book indicates that he thinks he can discover the "original" form of the sayings, discussions, and stories which he treats. We are working with "sources and traditions," not with early and late traditions. This terminology demands some kind of historical defense, but none is ever provided. The reliability of the tradition and the manner of its formation are to a great extent simply assumed, despite the mass of evidence of a more complicated situation that Weiss's own book reveals.

Sources and Traditions is essentially a commentary, not a work of systematic history, even text-history or tradition-history. Given its goals, it succeeds. It also reveals a number of important insights into the dynamic of the Talmudic tradition and its history, and these make it in some measure more than a commentary.

DAVID WEISS HALIVNI, *MEQOROT UMESOROT*

2. *QIDDUSHIN*

BY

SHAMAI KANTER

Traditional study of the Talmudic text involved raising questions of logical difficulty, or contradictions between quotations; it sought to harmonize the contradictions or eliminate the difficulties. For David Weiss Halivni, the source-critical approach is an added tool for dealing with the Talmudic text:

> "Source criticism seeks to differentiate between the original statements as they were enunciated by their authors and the forms they took as a consequence of being orally transmitted; that is, between the sources and their later traditions."[1]

Though a smooth logical surface is no guarantee of a perfectly-transmitted source, it is logically-forced explanation which alerts Weiss to the possibility of a faulty transmission of a rabbinical teaching. Often these logical difficulties were recognized by the early- and late-medieval commentators (especially Rabbi Yom Tov ben Abraham Ishbili, of 14th-century Seville, known by his acronym, "RYṬB'A"). But they were not concerned with the ways in which orally-transmitted statements could alter in the course of transmission, or assume new forms in different contexts.

David Weiss' commentaries upon the various *sugyot* bear out the researches of Abraham Weiss on the question of the redaction of the Talmud: each *sugya'* appears to have its own development. The editor may not know other passages dealing with his problem, in other parts of the Talmud; or he may have a different reading of the Mishnah, or of other rabbinical teachings.

In his researches into the tractate *Qiddushin*, Weiss closely analyzes about 40 textual problems in little more than 100 pages.[2] These problems are considered separately and, except in the general introduction,

---

[1] David Weiss-Halivni, "TALMUD: Source Criticism", *Encyclopedia Britannica*, 1963, vol. xxi, p. 645, quoted in David Weiss-Halivni, *Meqorot uMesorot*. p. 729.

[2] *Meqorot uMesorot*, pp. 613-719.

without methodological discussion, a strategy appropriate to the special character of almost every difficult *sugya'*. Nevertheless, certain general patterns do emerge: (i) Weiss charts the changing meaning of certain terms, and demonstrates the difficulties of interpretation arising when later authorities understand the texts in a sense different from their original meaning: (ii) Weiss shows how blocks of material, used in a *sugya'* which shows problems of logical transition, were imported from other contexts; and, (iii) Weiss discusses how contradictions originating in differing versions of original sources are harmonized through "forced interpretations" by the Amoraic rabbis, or by the anonymous editor.

I. Development of meaning

Early Mishnaic Terms: "One Precept"[1] *and* "Niqnēt"[2]

In tracing the earliest sources of rabbinical traditions, one may identify terms in the Mishnah which are understood by the Gemara according to later meanings. In the case of the term "one precept". the Jerusalem Talmud preserves the earlier meaning, unknown to the Babylonian Talmud:

> He who performs one precept—good is done to him, his days are prolonged, and he inherits the land. But he who does not perform one precept—good is not done to him, his days are not prolonged, and he does not inherit the land.
>
> (b. *Qid.* 39b)

This Mishnah is understood by the Gemara in the same sense as Mishnah *Pe'ah* 1.1. The latter lists certain commandments whose performance merits eternal life. In both instances, the term "one precept" is understood as referring to the performance of a single act. The person performing it is assumed to be equally balanced between good and bad deeds; thus the single precept can tip his scale toward a heavenly reward.

Yet this interpretation requires us to understand the phrase "he who does not perform one precept" as meaning: he who commits an evil deed. It cannot be taken literally, since the person would still be equally balanced between good and evil deeds, and undeserving of punishment.

[1] Weiss, pp. 660-663.
[2] Weiss, p. 614, and n. 10.

In the Jerusalem Talmud, however, (y. *Qid.* 1.10) R. Yosi b. R. Bun understands the term in this context as referring to a single precept which a man performs continually (e.g., honoring his parents) though he may neglect other precepts. That would explain why the listing in Mishnah *Pe'ah* includes only precepts which can be performed at all times, rather than those, like the Sabbath, which are applicable only to special occasions.

The fact that the language of Mishnah *Qiddushin* uses the phrase "inherits the land", rather than referring to the "world to come", testifies to its antiquity.[1] It took its form prior to the development of the belief in a life after death, at a period which may be called "biblical" rather than "Pharisaic", so Weiss. The phrase "performing one precept" in this Mishnah is also used in its early meaning. Though later usage comes to mean performing a single precept *once*, the Jerusalem Talmud preserves the earlier meaning.

In another case, however, concerning the use of the term *niqnēt*, Weiss rejects an hypothesis of development advanced by both Louis Ginzberg and Y. N. Epstein. The latter both hold that the first Mishnah in the tractate, reading: "A woman is acquired (*niqnēt*) in three ways..." to be quite ancient. In their view, it comes from a time when wives were considered to be property. The more common rabbinical term for marriage, *qiddushin* (sanctification), had not yet come into use, as it does in later Mishnahs. Weiss rejects this. He points out instead that wherever the Talmud discusses the laws of marriage in connection with other categories (levirate marriage, male and female servitude) the umbrella-term of aquisition, *niqēt*, is used. It is merely the term of sufficient generalization to cover such widely different cases. (In defense of Ginzberg and Epstein however, one might ask why the categories of marriage and servitude were discussed together at all, if not that they in some early time were all held to be kinds of property.)

Early Amoraic Terms: "Shoneh"[2]

Similar distinctions in linguistic development may be seen even within the Amoraic period. Terms used by early Amoraim were understood differently by late Amoraim or Saboraim who created the anonymous discussion of the *sugya'*. For example:

---

[1] Weiss, p. 663, and n. 20.
[2] Weiss, pp. 671-673.

> [If a man says: You are betrothed to me] on condition that I am learned [*shoneh*]—Hezekiah said: [Learned means] in *Halakhot* [traditional formulations of the law]. R. Yoḥanan ruled: In Torah.
>
> An objection was raised: What is *Mishnah?* R. Meir said: *Halakhot.* R. Judah said: *Midrash.*
>
> [Answer:] What is meant by Torah? The *Midrash* [exegesis] of the Torah.
>
> (b. *Qid.* 49a)

The Gemara here takes it for granted that the term *shoneh* refers to "*mishnah*", rabbinical formulations of the laws, or their exegetical derivation from Scripture: that is the basis of the objection raised, and its answer. How could R. Yoḥanan explain that someone is *shoneh*, learned in *mishnah*, by saying that he has learned Torah, the written Scripture? The answer is given: R. Yoḥanan meant by "Torah" the oral exegesis of Scripture. However, if we assume that R. Yoḥanan understood that *shoneh* could also have a less widely used reference to a knowledge of the Scriptural text, his meaning becomes immediately clear, without the necessity of answering the objection with an equation: Torah = Midrash.

Weiss cites a number of references which imply such usage of the term *shoneh*, meaning: the commitment to memory a Scriptural text (Tosefta *Shab*. 13.6; Berlin MS of Sifré *Shofeṭim*, ch 160, p. 211; Sifré *Deut*., end of sec. 4).

Thus the early Amoraim legitimately differed about whether the more-usual or less-usual meaning of *shoneh* applied in this case. But the author of our *sugya*' did not know the early, alternative meaning, and was driven to supply the equation of Torah with its oral exegesis, Midrash.

The Phrase: "Words of the Master/Words of the Pupil"[1]

In some instances, Weiss is able to demonstrate a line of development in the meaning of a phrase, and the way in which it comes to be used. A *beraita* quoted on b. *Qid.* 42b indicates that a normal person sent to commit a crime is not considered as an agent. He himself is held responsible, rather than the one who sent him, since

> there is no agent for wrongdoing; for we reason: [when] the words of the master and the words of the pupil [are in conflict, i.e., God's command not to sin vs. the human directive to sin] whose words are obeyed?

[1] Weiss, pp. 663-666.

Obviously, the agent would follow God's orders; hence we consider him responsible for his own actions.

Weiss identifies the quotation concerning the "words of master and pupil" as an addition or gloss to the discussion about agency for wrongdoing which follows. It is irrelevant to all of the examples used when the principle is questioned: (a) In the case of an agent erroneously instructed to make secular use of something dedicated as sacred property, the sender is liable for a "trespass offering". The quotation about master and pupil cannot apply here, since the context deals with an ignorant violation, not a choice between authorities. (b) The liability of a thief, for his agent's killing and selling an animal he stole, also does not apply: since once again the agent is ignorant. (c) The discussion of David's ordering the death of Uriah indicates that David was not held responsible because Joab was his agent. Yet Joab clearly had no choice: if the reasoning behind the principle were "the words of the master/the words of the pupil", David should have been held responsible.

The phrase has, therefore, been imported from elsewhere into a new context, where it does not logically fit. Weiss shows its development, and suggests how it may have arrived in its context in *Qiddushin*.

The phrase is first used by R. Ishmael b. R. Yosi (on b. *Nid.* 14b). When R. Ḥama b. Bisa asked to hear a ruling of Rabbi Judah the Prince in preference to that of R. Ishmael's own father, R. Yosi, R. Ishmael exclaimed: "How could one put down the words of the master and listen to the words of the pupil?"

Abaye makes use of the phrase (b. *Tem.* 25a) in reference to God and man: If most of the produce of a field has been harvested, and the owner declares the rest free (for both rich and poor) which law applies—the owner's designation for all, or the Torah's designation of the gleanings for the poor? "Abaye explained: What is this question? Whose word do we obey? That of the master or of the pupil? Similarly here too, whose word do we obey [God's or man's]?" Like usage is found on b. *B.Q.* 56a and b. *Sanh.* 29a.

Weiss suggests that the way the question ("Whose authority is obeyed?") came to be applied to the problem of agency in wrongdoing can be traced to the words of Ravina and R. Sama. The questions under discussion are, first, whether an inanimate object can be considered an agent, and, second, whether a decision on this question affects the ruling that there is no agency in wrongdoing:

> Ravina said: Where do we say that there is no agency for wrongdoing —where the agent is subject to responsibility... R. Sama said: Where do we say that there is no agency for wrongdoing— where if he wishes he performs it, and if he does not wish, he does not do it...
>
> (b. *B.M.* 106)

Rashi's commentary, reflecting the traditional understanding of the text, explains that the key element in agency is that the agent accepts the authority of the sender. Rashi refers back to our original passage in *Qiddushin* as an example. Weiss does not explicitly indicate the final transition. But evidently the author of our *sugya'* knew that Ravina and R. Sama focussed the problem of agency in wrongdoing on the responsibility of the agent, in his decision to obey. Our author also knew Abaye's use of the phrase about master and pupil with reference to a person's choice to obey God's command rather than man's. And he applied it to the question of agency in wrongdoing. Weiss observes that the phrase is actually not appropriate to the situation of agency at all, but rhetorical flourishes often are inappropriate to their new settings.

II. Quotations Transferred to New Contexts

A Defective Mishnah: Betrothal by Deed[1]

A greater number of Weiss' analyses deal with *sugyot* which are obscure because entire blocks of material, rather than just words or phrases, have been taken from other contexts, and used to illustrate arguments or supply lines of reasoning where they do not quite fit. In the example which follows, Weiss traces the reason for such a transfer to a defective Mishnah text in the possession of the editor of the *sugya'*.

The opening Mishnah of the tractate *Qiddushin* states that a woman is betrothed in one of three ways: "by money, by deed or by intercourse." A *beraita* quoted, *infra* 5b, explains the first phrase:

> Our Rabbis taught: How by money, If a man gives her money or its equivalent and declares to her, 'Behold, you are consecrated to me...'

Further along in the tractate, another *beraita* is quoted, in continuation of the explanation of the Mishnah:

---

[1] Weiss, pp. 624-626.

> Our Rabbis taught: By deed—how? If A writes for B on a paper... 'Your daughter is consecrated to me' ...she is betrothed. R. Zera b. Mammel objected: But this deed is not similar to a deed of purchase: there the vendor writes, 'My field is sold to you,' whereas here the husband writes, 'Your daughter is consecrated to me'!
>
> (b. *Qid.* 9a)

The latter *beraita* does not continue the line of development logically. Its predecessor deals with betrothal between a man and woman; this *beraita* describes a transaction between two men, concerning the daughter of one of them (presumably a minor). Why does not the *beraita* continue the line of explanation, as is in fact found in the Tosefta *Qid.* 1.1. and in b. *Yev.* 52a: "By deed—how? If he wrote for her on a paper... 'Behold, you are consecrated to me'..."

The *beraita* on 9a actually relates to an entirely different Mishnah:

> The father has control over his [minor] daughter's betrothal, whether effected by money, or by deed or by intercourse.
>
> (M. *Ket.* 4.4)

Our *beraita* then continues, to explain how the father's control is exercised through the deed, even though the form of the deed may be the reverse of a normal commercial transaction. The Jerusalem Talmud (y. *Qid.* 1,2) cites an incident involving R. Yosi, expressing the same view.

Having found the logically proper place for the *beraita*, in the tractate *Ketuvot*, Weiss then asks: Why was it transferred to the context of the discussion in *Qiddushin?* He offers the hypothesis that the editor's text of the Mishnah *Ketuvot* omitted the key phrase, "by money, by deed or by intercourse". It simply read, as does the text of the Mishnah *Ketuvot* quoted by the author of the Geonic legal compilation, the *She'iltot:*

> As we have learned (i.e. in the Mishnah): *The father has control over his daughter's betrothal, the works of her hands and the voiding of her vows...'*
>
> 'Her betrothal'—He betroths her by money, deed or intercourse. How do we know by money?...
>
> (Oẓar ha-ge'onim, *Ket.* par. 320)

The editor of this *sugya'*, perhaps even a contemporary of the author of the *She'iltot*, had a similarly defective Mishnah, and was constrained to insert the *beraita* beginning "By deed—how?..." into the only discussion he possessed on a Mishnah relating to betrothal by deed—*Qiddushin.*

A Defective Beraita: Acquiring Moveable/Immoveable Property[1]

In the following analysis, Weiss shows how a *beraita* passage explaining one Mishnah, having become garbled in its conclusion, was transferred from its proper place, to explicate another Mishnah containing key terms which had entered the "contaminated" source-*beraita*.

To explain a Mishnah stating that moveable property can be acquired simultaneously with real estate, by money, by deed or through possession (*ḥazaqah*). the following *beraita* is quoted in the name of Rava:

> Rava said: This was taught only if he [the purchaser] had paid the money for them all. But if he had not paid the money for them all, he acquires only to the extent of his money. It was taught in agreement with Rava: The power of money is superior to that of a deed, and the power of a deed is superior to that of money. The power of money is superior [etc.], in that *heqdesh* and the second tithe are redeemed therewith, which is not so in the case of deed. And the power of a deed is superior, for a deed can free an Israelite daughter, which does not hold good of money. And the power of both is superior to that of *ḥazaqah*, and the power of *ḥazaqah* is superior to that of both. The power of both is superior [etc.], in that both give a title to a Hebrew slave, which is not so in the case of *ḥazaqah*. And the power of *ḥazaqah* is superior to that of both: For with *ḥazaqah*, if A sells B ten fields [situated] in ten countries, as soon as B takes possession of one, he acquires all. When is this? If he has paid him for all; but if he has not paid the money for all, he gains a title only to the extent of his money.
>
> (b. *Qid.* 27 a-b)

Two difficulties are involved in this passage. First, though presumably explaining that moveable property is acquired along with the real estate, to the extent that the buyer has paid for it, the *beraita* actually makes no reference whatever to moveable property. It refers only to real estate. Second, there is a stylistic change at the end of the passage, where the form, "*x* is superior... which is not so in the case of *y*" is abandoned.

Weiss identifies the "true reading" of the last part of the passage as that found in Tos. *Ket.* 2.1 (and its parallel y. *Qid.* 1.5):

> And the power of *Ḥazaqah* is superior, since when he buys ten fields, and takes possession of one, he takes possession of all. But if he has only paid for one, or received the deed to one, he has only acquired a single field.

---

[1] Weiss, pp. 646-649.

This is closer to the form of "*x*...*y*" but could not explicitly make use of it, since its language would then imply that neither money nor deed would acquire anything at all.

Rava's statement, then, actually refers to an earlier Mishnah (b. *Qid.* 26a, and discussed there): "real estate is acquired by money, by deed or by *ḥazaqah*." This is its location, too, in the texts known to Maimonides and Alfasi. But the editor of our *sugya'*, possessing a "contaminated" text which speaks in its conclusion of a *ḥazaqah* operative only when money has been paid, could not connect this *beraita* with the Mishnah dealing with sale of real estate for money. Therefore he appended it to the subsequent Mishnah, dealing with the transfer of ownership of moveable property simultaneous with the *ḥazaqah* of real property.

A Transferred Amoraic Explanation: Honoring Parents[1]

Even Amoraic comments, in their subsequent transmission, can be rearranged by the editorial process, and seem to explain statements to which they have no direct connection. Here is a case of single Amoraic statement which has become cut loose from its original location.

R. Judah indicates that both sons and daughters are obligated to perform all those commandments for a father which Scripture mentions as a son's obligation. A *beraita* illustrating this continues:

> A man possesses the means to fulfill this, but a woman has no means to fulfill this, because she is under the authority of others. R. 'Idi b. Abin said in Rav's name: If she is divorced, both are equal.
>
> (b. *Qid.* 30b)

Presumably, R. 'Idi's statement means that the woman's obligation to her father is now equal to that of her brother. But the language here creates difficulty: (a) It implies that as a married woman her obligation is not equal to her that of her brother. Yet the reverse is true: she merely is unable to discharge her obligation. (b) The statement makes no reference to the case of a widow, which should be identical to that of a divorcee. (c) The style ("both are equal") is obscure; it would be clearer if it read: "If she is divorced (or widowed) she too can fulfill her obligation."

Weiss suggests that R. 'Idi's statement actually belongs as an explanation to the end of Mishnah *Keritot:*

[1] Weiss, pp. 651-654.

> R. Simeon says that equal honor is due both father and mother. But the Sages have said: Everywhere Scripture speaks of the father before the mother, because both a man and his mother are bound to honor the father.

R. ʾIdi is then explaining: If she is divorced, both parents claim equal honor, since the mother is no longer obligated toward the father (and obviously the case of a widow does not arise in this context). There is, however, a *beraita* (b. *Qid.* 31a) which quotes R. Joshua on this same point. Either R. ʾIdi did not know of it, or its hyperbole ("Let him pour water in a basin for them and call them like fowls!") was not taken seriously by him. Therefore he explained it himself. But someone who did understand R. Joshua in this way, assumed that R. ʾIdi could not be redundant, and hence must be referring to some other instance. He therefore transferred R. ʾIdi's words to their place in *Qiddushin*, as an explanation of the new conditions under which a married daughter becomes able to fulfill her obligation to her father.

III. Harmonizing Contradictory Traditions

Differing Mishnaic Orders: the Hebrew Maidservant[1]

From the Amoraic period onward, Talmudic discussion moves toward the elimination of as much contradiction as possible from its traditions. This is often done by reinterpreting the variant traditions to conform with accepted views. Here, for example, is a Mishnah which implies something different from the Amoraic discussion which succeeds it:

> A Hebrew slave is acquired by money and by deed; he acquires himself by completing his six years, by the Jubilee, and by deduction from the purchase price. A Hebrew maidservant is more [privileged] in that she acquires herself by signs of puberty. He whose ear is bored is acquired by boring, and acquires himself by the Jubilee or his master's death.
>
> (b. *Qid.* 14b)

Though Amoraic discussion of the Mishnah (16a, 17b) states that the Hebrew maidservant is also freed by her master's death, the order of the Mishnah itself, describing an ascending order of "privilege", implies that the maidservant is not freed by the master's death. If she

---

[1] Weiss, pp. 632-635.

were, reference to her would come last, after the mention of "him whose ear is bored". The latter is freed by the master's death.

Weiss cannot show any Tannaitic text spelling out what is implied in the Mishnah. But he draws attention to the words of R. Simeon (16b): "Four types of servants are presented with gifts upon being freed, three in the case of a man, and three in the case of a woman." The subsequent explanation, in order to avoid imputing the view, to R. Simeon, that the master's death does not free the maidservant, is driven to count the Jubilee twice: once to free a servant during the six years of service, and once to free the servant "whose ear has been bored." But the simplest understanding of R. Simeon would be that the four cases are

(a) the Jubilee—freeing male and female;
(b) expiration of six years—freeing male and female;
(c) death of the master—freeing "him whose ear was bored"; and
(d) signs of puberty—freeing the maidservant.

R. Simeon's analysis thus parallels the implication of the Mishnah, and disagrees with the accepted view that the maidservant is freed by her master's death. Weiss also finds this understanding of the Mishnah implied in the *Mekhilta deRabbi Simeon bar Yoḥai*.[1] In a passage there, contrasting the Hebrew maidservant with the Canaanite slave, one detail is missing: that she is freed upon her master's death. This agrees with the order of the Mishnah we have.

We know that the laws of acquisition are very ancient. The fact that the Schools of Shammai and Hillel differed on the interpretation of the term "money" in the discussion of betrothal, shows that the Mishnah "A woman is acquired... by money" was a fixed tradition in their day: they could only differ on its interpretation. Similarly here, says Weiss, the teachings on servants in our Mishnah were also well-established traditions by the time of R. Simeon bar Yoḥai and his contemporaries. But there was a difference in the *order* of presentation of those statements. R. Simeon's order was identical with ours, and he understood the maidservant not to be freed by her master's death, as implied by our Mishnah. But the other material on 16a and 17b must be based on a Mishnah text in different order: with the reference to the Hebrew maidservant as "more privileged" at the conclusion of the Mishnah; and thus she too (like "him whose ear is bored") is freed by the death of the master. Because of this, the Amoraim reinterpreted R. Simeon's

---

[1] Y. N. Epstein et al., eds., *Mekhilta deRabbi Simeon bar Yoḥai*, p. 165.

view to make it agree with their own, and with the clear implication of the arrangement of material in the Mishnah as they had received it.

A Defective Beraita: Title to the Not-Yet-Existent[1]

Sometimes the final editor is unaware of the differences in the traditions which reach him. He combines them, reconciling their difference, without having realized that they reflect basically the same source. The discussion, on transmitting title to something which has not yet come into existence, is analyzed by Weiss to show the stages in such a process:

> [A] Abaye said: R. Eliezer b. Jacob, Rabbi, and R. Meir, all hold that one may transmit the title to an object which has not come into the world. R. Eliezer b. Jacob, as stated. Rabbi, for it was taught: *Thou shalt not deliver unto his master a servant which is escaped from his master:* Rabbi said: The Writ refers to one who buys a slave on condition that he emancipates him. How so? Said R. Naḥman b. Isaac: E.g., if he wrote for him. 'When I buy you, you belong to yourself from now.'
>
> [B] R. Meir, for it was taught: If one says to a woman, 'Behold, thou art betrothed unto me after I become a proselyte', or, 'after thou becomest a proselyte', 'after I am freed,' or 'after thou art freed,' 'after thy husband dies,' or, 'after thy sister dies,' 'after they *yabam* performs *ḥaliẓah* for thee,' she is not betrothed. R. Meir said: She is betrothed. R. Joḥanan the sandal maker said: She is not betrothed. R. Judah the Nasi said: By rights she is betrothed, yet why did they the Sages say, she is not betrothed? Because of bad feeling. Then let R. Judah the Nasi be counted too?—Rabbi and R. Judah the Nasi are identical.
>
> (b. *Qid.* 62b–63a)

The first *beraita* (A) in Abaye's name, is problematic from several angles: first, that R. Naḥman's explanation of Rabbi's (Rabbi Judah the Prince's) view could not have been part of Abaye's teaching —R. Naḥman lived after Abaye—and must have been appended by the editor. But if so, the whole quotation from Abaye is superfluous. The following *beraita* (B) clearly shows both R. Meir and Rabbi Judah the Prince in favor of the principle that one can transmit title to the as-yet-non-existent. Why then quote Abaye at all? Second, one can argue that the case of a freed slave is a special exception in Scriptural

---

[1] Weiss, pp. 690-692.

law. If it were not for the latter *beraita*, one could argue that Rabbi Judah the Prince held as a general principle that one could *not* transfer title to the as-yet-non-existent.

Weiss concludes that the editor who quoted the *beraita* concerning Rabbi Judah the Prince's statement on the freed slave did not have the latter half of *beraita* (B), quoting R. Judah and R. Yoḥanan the sandal maker .(*Beraita* (B) is quoted without that ending on b. *Yev.* 93b, b. *Ket.* 58b and b. *B.M.* 16b.) Two points of style show the ending to be a later addition: (a) R. Judah's language repeats that of R. Meir after the opposing view of R. Yoḥanan is mentioned; (b) R. Judah's language shows that it was added to a framework which originally did not concern the cases, "after your husband dies, after your sister dies" —his reasoning applies only to those two cases and not to the other cases listed.

Thus three separate strata can be identified in this *sugya'*:

(1) Abaye's general statement;

(2) An explanation by someone after R. Naḥman, who did not know that latter half of *beraita* (B). He quoted R. Naḥman, using the example of the freed slave;

(3) Our editor who knew the end of *beraita* (B) and quoted it. Instead of identifying it as the source of Abaye's original statement, he asked why "R. Judah" was not counted, and answered that he and Rabbi (Judah the Prince) are the same.

Two Amoraic Traditions Joined: Conditional Betrothal[1]

In our final example, Weiss shows how two different interpretations of an early Palestinian Amora, Resh Laqish, were well-established in the third generation of Babylonian Amoraim, and how they were joined together in the final form of the *sugya'*:

> "If one said to a woman, 'Behold, thou art betrothed unto me on condition that I speak to the governor on thy behalf', or 'That I work for thee as a labourer', if he speaks to the governor on her behalf or works for her as a labourer, she is betrothed; if not, she is not betrothed."
>
> ...Resh Laqish said: Providing that he gives her simultaneously a coin of the value of *peruṭah*.
>
> (b. *Qid.* 63a)

The discussion that follows challenges Resh Laqish's requirement that a coin accompany that statement of betrothal, on the grounds that,

[1] Weiss, pp. 695-698.

after all, the service performed is itself of value, and therefore effects the betrothal.

The answer given traces the apparent conflict, between Resh Laqish's understanding of the Mishnah, and the *beraitot* indicating that the service performed is sufficient, to another difference of principle. The latter *beraitot* are based upon the assumption that wages become a debt only when the work is completed. Hence, the first bit of work performed functions as the value effecting the betrothal. But from the viewpoint of Resh Laqish, wages are a debt owed by the one benefitted by the work, throughout the entire process; and as such they cannot effect a betrothal (a debt cannot serve for betrothal). Hence, the requirement of the additional coin.

However, there is another understanding of Resh Laqish implicit in the words of Rava at the end of the *sugya'*:

> Said Rava: Our Mishnah presents a difficulty to Resh Laqish. Why state particularly 'on condition'? State: 'in payment for'. Hence this proves that wherever 'on condition' is taught, it means that he gives her something in addition to fulfilling the condition, to effect the betrothal.
>
> (b. *Qid.* 63a)

Weiss understands Rava in this way: The Mishnah would be redundant if it were merely stating that one must fulfill a stated condition, in order to effect a conditional betrothal. Rather, says Rava, Resh Laqish wishes to draw a distinction between the fulfillment of a condition and the financial transaction which effects betrothal. Hence, where a condition is made, in addition to its fulfillment, there must be a transfer of a coin to effect betrothal. This is the difference between the performance of a service "on condition" and the performance of a service "in payment". The alternative understanding of Resh Laqish would actually eliminate the idea of betrothal "in payment" by a service, and transform it into a conditional betrothal.

Three proofs are adduced by Weiss in support of his reading of Rava: (1) Were Rava to understand the conditional service as a payment, he would be required to state that the additional coin given is *not* a payment, something he does not state; (2) If Resh Laqish (according to Rava) were not advancing a new point, different from the idea of a betrothal through payment for services, why would Rava mention Resh Laqish's "difficulty" with the Mishnah? It is standard procedure to interpret a Mishnah in conformity with later accepted law, in this case that wages are considered a debt throughout the entire time of service; (3) Weiss quotes a reading mentioned by the RYṬB'A, in which Abaye states that the transfer of a coin is required, and that the service performed is only a condition. This, Weiss claims, must have been dropped from most texts, since it did not accord with the editor's understanding of Resh Laqish, connecting conditional-betrothal-through-service to payment.

Thus Weiss identifies the two different interpretations of Resh Laqish with two different schools. One school was responsible for the first part of the *sugya'*. It explains Resh Laqish ("Providing that he gives her simultaneously a coin of the value of a *peruṭah*") with reference to the problems of payment, and the question of when wages become considered a debt. But the schools of Rava and Abaye must have read Resh Laqish as applying the Mishnah to the question of conditional betrothal, and not to payment at all (as Weiss himself explains). Their view is seen in Rava's statement at the end of the *sugya'*.

The editor joined both views together, harmonizing them with the bridging passage as follows: "Now what compels Resh Laqish to explain our Mishnah on the basis that wages are a debt from the beginning to end, and that he gives her a *peruṭah* in addition?"

IV. Conclusion

David Weiss' source-critical commentaries are both highly complex and extremely compressed, usually no more than two pages each. In the preceeding descriptions, his line of argument has been greatly simplified, with a corresponding loss of detail and depth. Yet aside from those few cases where Weiss presents a straight interpretation of the Talmudic text itself, he seems to (a) locate a possible textual problem through subtle logical *non sequitur*, (b) present external evidence, from the Jerusalem Talmud, the Tosefta, the Munich MS of the Talmud, or Geonic literature, which suggests the existence of an alternative form of the original source, and (c) reconstruct the original source of the tradition.

What Weiss does not do, even within the limits of his own goals, is to imagine for us how the transmission of many of the metamorphosed sources might have actually taken place. This in turn might affect his uniform assumption about the oral nature of the traditions which make up the Talmud.

In what way, for example, would we come to have an Amoraic

discussion based upon an order of Mishnaic statements now lost to us, while our own Mishnah, to which that discussion is appended, reflects an alternate point of view, almost totally obscured by the editorial process? In what way would a single statement by Rav, quoted by R. ʾIdi b. Abin, only three Hebrew words in length, be detached from its original context and become appended to a Mishnah of another tractate? Such cases would seem to suggest the editing of *written* sources. In contrast, the changes in transmission of the discussion of real estate and moveable property (b. *Qid.* 27a-b) seem more likely to have occured in oral transmission. Here too, the evidence presented by Abraham Weiss for the written nature of Talmudic sources deserves careful consideration. Any analysis of sources is made stronger through advancement of a hypothetical description not only of how the sources were transformed, but also of how they were transmitted. In this respect as in others, Abraham Weiss's contribution has not yet been sufficiently exploited by David Weiss Halivni.

DAVID WEISS HALIVNI, *MEQOROT UMESOROT*

3. *GIṬṬIN*

BY

DAVID GOODBLATT

Most commentaries generally will have ramifications relevant to other texts and other issues. This is certainly the case with *Sources and Traditions. A Source Critical Commentary on Seder Nashim* by Prof. David Halivni (Weiss).[1] In the section of his commentary on Tractate *Giṭṭin* of the Babylonian Talmud I found many comments with important implications both for the exegesis of rabbinic literature in general and for the literary history of specific rabbinic texts.[2] Among the broader issues Weiss' commentary treats is that of the methods of the redactor of the Mishnah. By isolating the sources of certain sections of the Mishnah, for example, he is able to describe what happened to them in the process of redaction.[3] Other comments deal with the problem of parallel *sugyot* (pericopes), that is, *sugyot* which appear more than once in the Talmud. Weiss suggests a method for determining which context is the original one, and he applies this method to several *sugyot* in *Gittin* which have parallels elsewhere.[4] Similarly, he discusses the problem of alternate versions of the same *sugya* (*lishana 'aḥrina*). Here too he proposes and illustrates the application of a general principle for determining which version is original.[5] The largest category of comments, fittingly, is described by Weiss' subtitle: "a source critical commentary." Almost half the entries in the part of the book on *Giṭṭin* are examples of the source-critical method of exegesis.[6] I shall concentrate on the these.

---

[1] David Halivni (Weiss), *Sources and Traditions. A Source Critical Commentary on Seder Nashim* (Tel Aviv, 1968). The book is a commentary on *Seder Nashim* of the Babylonian Talmud. This paper deals with the part of the book on Tractate *Giṭṭin*, i.e., pp. 481-612.

[2] Of course, these two are interrelated. One's concept of the nature and history of a text will determine which exegetical moves are legitimate.

[3] See *Sources and Traditions*, *op. cit.*, the entries beginning on pp. 481, 527, 564, 569, 576.

[4] See *ibid.*, the entries which begin on pp. 536, 552, 567, 571, 610.

[5] See *ibid.*, the entries which begin on pp. 504 and 523.

[6] I did not attempt a systematic or thorough classification of entries, so what

Weiss' source-critical technique is based on three generally accepted facts. First, that rabbinic literature was transmitted orally (in the main) for a considerable period. In the course of oral transmission many Tannaitic and Amoraic sources were modified.[1] He gives the name "traditions" (*mesorot*) to the variant forms which a given source assumed as a result of this modification. Weiss states the second fact: "...the Talmud...primarily consists of quotations and their interpretations."[2] One might describe the Talmud as a grand orchestration of Tannaitic and Amoraic sources brought into a variety of relations with each other. Sources which conflict with, complement, or confirm one another are juxtaposed. The attempt is made to reconcile the contradictory ones and differentiate the redundant ones. Naturally, a change in one of the sources could undo these relationships. This is especially so in light of the third fact: the Babylonian Amoraim subjected the sources to the most minute analysis. Minor variations assume great significance in a work as dialectical as the Babylonian Talmud.

The source-critical method requires full cognizance of all the forms a source may have (all its "traditions") when one confronts a citation of that source. This is necessary because the "tradition" available to the author of a passage may have been different from the one in our printed texts. This last insight provides a key to the solution of numerous difficult passages. Seemingly pointless questions or apparently impertinent answers turn out to make perfect sense if one assumes that they were based on sources different from those before us. Unnecessarily forced interpretations prove inescapable, given the "traditions" confronting their authors. What one must do is locate the form of the source at the base of the difficulty or establish that such a "tradition" *did* exist.

The repository of these "traditions" is the mass of variant readings

---

follows is very rough. Since some entries deal with more than one topic, there is some overlap in the categories. Of the 53 separate entries in the section on *Giṭṭin:*

2 dealt with alternate versions of the same *sugya*.
5 dealt with parallel *sugyot*.
5 dealt with the literary history of the Mishnah.
9 dealt with the literary history of the *gemara*.
13 contained general text interpretation.
24 contained examples of the source-critical method.

[1] See ibid., pp. 7, 14-15 of the Introduction.

[2] See *ibid.*, overleaf of the English title page where this is quoted from Weiss' article in the Encyclopedia Britannica, 1963 ed., Vol. XXI, p. 645, s.v. TALMUD: Source Criticism.

for rabbinic literature. For the source-critical method such readings are not mere textual variants resulting from scribal error or the like. At least some of them represent the actual text which once was the basis of Talmudic comment and discussion. Variants of the Mishnah are attested by the several manuscripts of the latter, by the various early printings, and by the materials presented in Y. N. Epstein's *Mavo' Lenusaḥ Hammishnah*. For the Babylonian Talmud variants are available in R. Rabbinovicz's *Diqduqē Soferim*, now supplemented by M. S. Feldblum's volume on *Giṭṭin*, in the Munich manuscript, in various manuscripts of individual tractates, and in Geniza fragments. For *beraitot* quoted in the Babylonian Talmud one must determine whether parallels exist in the Palestinian Talmud, the Tosefta, or in Halakhic Midrashim. Where such parallels do exist one must then examine the variants available for the latter works (some of which have appeared in critical editions). In addition one must pay close attention to Geonic sources and commentaries by the early medieval authorities (*rishonim*). Both of these bodies of literature often preserve valuble variants.

The best way to describe the source-critical method is to illustrate it. I have selected four examples of Weiss' application of this technique to specific passages in b. *Giṭṭin*.

I. A Different Order of Cases in a Mishnah

M. *Giṭṭin* 5:8 lists several ordinances enacted "for the sake of peace" (literally: "because of the ways of peace"). Three of them concern cases in which a person does not have full legal title to certain objects. Nevertheless it is considered theft to take those objects away from him. The text is as follows:

> [Taking what is caught in someone else's] traps [which were set] for an animal, for fowl, or for fish involves theft—for the sake of peace. R. Yosi asserts that it is absolute theft [i.e., not just considered so to stop people from doing it].
>
> [Taking away] an object found by a deaf person, by a mental incompetent, or by a minor involves theft—for the sake of peace. R. Yosi asserts that it is absolute theft.
>
> [When in the process of gleaning] a poor person beats an olive tree, [taking away] what is under him involves theft—for the sake of peace. R. Yosi asserts that it is absolute theft.

On b. *Giṭṭin* 61a the middle case ("an object found by") is cited as an introduction to the following comment:

> R. Ḥisda said, "[When R. Yosi says] absolute theft [he means not that it is absolute theft under Mosaic legislation, but only] by their words [i.e., according to rabbinic legislation].

This comment is applied only to the middle case, which would imply that R. Yosi was understood to consider the first case ("traps") and the third case ("olive trees") as absolute theft according to Mosaic legislation. This is how some commentators understand the passage. However, Weiss points out, it is unreasonable to distinguish among the three cases, expecially since all follow the same verbal pattern.[1]

One commentator deletes the citation of the "object found" case which introduces the comment. However this citation (*pisqa*) is well attested. More important, R. Ḥisda's comment appears in two other Talmudic passages. In each instance it is introduced by the very same citation from the Mishnah. Weiss notes, however, that several manuscripts and some early printings of the Mishnah exhibit a different order in their text of *Giṭṭin* 5:8. They place the case of "an object found" *first*, and that of "traps" second. This explains why R. Ḥisda's comment was connected to the "object found" case: the latter was the first of the three cases listed. The Talmud usually quotes only the beginning of a passage to introduce a comment applying to the *whole* passage. R. Ḥisda's comment would thus pertain to the two other cases also.

Summary: This text had presented a dilemma. Since R. Ḥisda's explanation was introduced by a citation of the second of the three cases listed in the Mishnah, his remark apparently applied to that case alone. This in turn meant R. Ḥisda understood that R. Yosi used the exact same words to express mutually contradictory views. Alternately, one could delete the introductory citation. But this would be not only gratuitous but also contrary to the evidence of parallels. The source-critical approach then called attention to a variant form of the Mishnah from which the citation was drawn. The variation is minor: a different order in the listing of the same three cases. Nonetheless this difference explains the text both without resorting to deletion and without attributing to R. Ḥisda so perverse an understanding of R. Yosi's words. Presumably the introduction of R. Ḥisda's comment by the "object found" case is based on a Mishnah-text which gave the latter case first.

---

[1] *Sources and Traditions*, pp. 578-9.

II. A Different Text in a Proof-text

A literal interpretation of Deuteronomy 24:1 would seem to require that a husband must actually place a divorce document in his wife's hand. Otherwise the document is not validly delivered and cannot effect the divorce. However, the beginning of the eighth chapter of M. *Giṭṭin* indicates that this literal interpretation is incorrect. For example, Mishnah 8:2 deals with a case in which the husband throws the document at his wife while she is standing in the public domain. The text states that:

> if it [the divorce document] is near her [i.e., has landed near her, then it is considered validly delivered and] she is divorced; if it is near him [it is not considered delivered to her and] she is not divorced.

On b. *Giṭṭin* 78a the *gemara* asks what "near" means in the above text. Rav asserts that it means within four cubits of a person. On the following page R. Yoḥanan disagrees. He argues, "We read 'near her' in the Mishnah [which implies no such absolute figure, but rather implies that were the document] even one hundred cubits [from her, it might still be considered delivered]." He further defines "near" not in terms of proximity, but in terms of ability physically to control an object. He states, "If he can protect it but she cannot, then it is near him. If she can protect it, but he cannot, then it is near her."

A *beraita* is then cited to support R. Yoḥanan's position:

> It is taught likewise: R. ʾElʿazar says, "Whatever is nearer to her than to him [MLW], but a dog comes and takes it—in such a case she is not divorced."

This is followed by the Amoraic comment:

> "She is not divorced"?! Must she continually guard it? [i.e., the *beraita* seems to imply a *post facto* cancellation of the divorce if the document is ever lost; since this is unreasonable, its meaning must be different.] Rather he [R. ʾElʿazar] means that if it is nearer her than him, but when a dog comes and takes it, he can protect but she cannot—then she is not divorced. [Thus the criterion is physical control, not proximity.]

Even if one accepts the rather forced interpretation which this comment gives the *beraita*, the latter is still not decisive proof for R. Yoḥanan's view.[1] First of all, Weiss argues, R. ʾElʿazar may disagree with the law in the Mishnah and require a second criterion, viz., control, in addition to proximity. Instead of defining nearness as

[1] Ibid., pp. 600-602.

control (as R. Yoḥanan had suggested for the Mishnah), R. ʾElʿazar would demand *both* nearness (= proximity) and control. This interpretation of the *beraita* is no more forced than the *gemara's*, and probably less so. Weiss further argues that not only is the *beraita* not decisive for R. Yoḥanan's view, but it even appears to support the opinion of Rav. R. ʾElʿazar clearly understands nearness and control of an object to be two different concepts. He describes an instance where the document is "near" a woman but not in her control. For R. Yoḥanan such a situation by definition is impossible. In view of these considerations one wonders how this *beraita* could ever have been quoted to support the interpretation of R. Yoḥanan.

Weiss then points out that the printed texts and the Vienna manuscript of the Tosefta at *Giṭṭin* 6:1 preserve the following reading in the *beraita* of R. ʾElʿazar: "Even if it was a mile from her [literally: near her a MYL], but a dog comes etc." This form of the *beraita* does support the view of R. Yoḥanan by rejecting proximity, and selecting control, for the criterion of what constitutes valid delivery of a divorce document. Weiss speculates that the person who first cited the *beraita* in support of R. Yoḥanan knew it in the form found in the printed texts and Vienna manuscript of the Tosefta. The person responsible for the Amoraic comment following the *beraita* knew the version of the latter now in our Talmud texts. Since the *beraita* was supposed to support R. Yoḥanan's opinion (as the formula "it was taught likewise" indicates), this second person had no choice but to force the meaning of R. ʾElʿazar's words so as to yield such support.

Summary: The *gemara* had given a forced interpretation to a Tannaitic source cited to support the view of an Amora. Actually, it was only by such a forced interpretation that the source could be understood to agree with that Amora. In other words, the proof-text, if taken in its plain meaning, did not prove what it was supposed to. An examination of the variants of the Tannaitic source disclosed one reading which did support the view of the Amora in question. Presumably, this latter form of the source was originally cited. The change to the form found in our present Talmud-texts necessitated the forced interpretation given there. The source-critical method here enables us to trace the complex history of this passage.

III. A Conflation of Contradictory Sources

One section of the seventh chapter of M. *Giṭṭin* discusses conditional divorces. This kind of divorce does not take effect when it is issued, but only when the condition on which it was given is fulfilled. According to Mishnah 7:4 a couple may not cohabit in the interim between the issuance of such a divorce and the fulfillment of the condition. Engaging in intercourse could effect a remarriage, and then another divorce would be necessary. The prohibition of cohabiting prevents this complication from arising.

The Talmudic discussion of this issue begins with the following *beraita* on b. *Giṭṭin* 73b:

> The rabbis taught: If they saw her closeted alone with him at dark or sleeping with him at the foot of his bed, one does not suspect that they engaged in intercourse. One does suspect unchastity [i.e., that they did engage in intercourse, but not that they did so for the purpose of remarrying], but one does not suspect [that they had intercourse for the purpose of effecting] marriage. R. Yosi b. R. Yehudah asserts that one does suspect [that they had intercourse so as to effect] marriage.

The *gemara* immediately remarks on the contradiction between the first line (one does *not* suspect intercourse) and the second line (one *does* suspect unchastity = intercourse). Three Babylonian Amoraim offer interpretations. All of them resolve the contradiction by claiming the *beraita* presents two different cases. The first line is a case in which the witnesses only saw the couple closeted alone. The second line is a case in which the witnesses actually saw relations take place. Resolving contradictory sources by referring them to different sets of circumstances is a standard technique of the Babylonian Amoraim. However, Weiss points out, such a distinction is not present in the *beraita* itself. It appears to deal with the same set of circumstances throughout.[1]

This *beraita* has parallels in both the Palestinian Talmud and the Tosefta. Y. *Giṭṭin* 7:4, 48d has the following:

> If she was closeted alone with him for a period sufficient for intercourse to occur, one suspects [that] intercourse [took place], but one does not suspect [that the intercourse was intended to effect] marriage. R. Yosi b. R. Yehudah asserts that one does suspect marriage.

This reading, which pretty much coincides with the second line of the BT *beraita*, presents no problems of interpretation. Neither does the version in Tosefta *Giṭṭin* 5:4:

> If they saw her closeted alone with him at dark or she stayed with him at the foot of his bed... one does not suspect that they engaged in

[1] Ibid., pp. 592-4.

> intercourse—one does not suspect intercourse [not intended to effect marriage] nor does one suspect [intercourse for the purpose of] marriage. R. Yosi b. R. Yehudah asserts that one does suspect marriage.[1]

This version is just like the one in the BT, except that it adds the word *not* in the second line.

Weiss suggests that the BT version has resulted from the conflation of two contradictory sources. The first line is based on a source like the Tosefta (one does *not* suspect), while the second line drew from a source like the PT *beraita* (one *does* suspect). To make sense of the contradictory text the Babylonian Amoraim had to read two different sets of circumstances into it.

Summary: A Tannaitic source quoted by the *gemara* is self-contradictory. The source has two parallels which are internally consistent, though contradictory of each other. Each of these parallels bears a striking resemblance to one of the contradictory halves of the BT version. Weiss concludes that the latter is a conflation of the two parallels. However, this new explanation does not seem much more satisfactory than the ones offered by the Amoraim. The latter had suggested that one source was discussing two different cases. I cannot understand how two significantly different cases could be combined without any hint that this was happening. Similarly, I cannot understand how two such contradictory sources could be run together. Weiss does not explain how or why this could happen. He does not translate his literary explanation into historical terms. In fact, the failure to do this systematically is a major weakness. In some instances this failure detracts from the plausibility of the explanations the source-critical method offers.

IV. A Different Text of the Mishnah

This case is another in which the husband does not deliver the divorce document into his wife's hand, but throws it to her. M. *Giṭṭin* 8:1 states:

> He who throws a divorce document to his wife—and she is inside [WHY' BTWK] her house or inside her courtyard, behold she is divorced [i.e., the document is considered validly delivered and the divorce is effected].

[1] The last line, "R. Yosi etc.", appears only in Ms. Erfurt. Weiss suggests it dropped out of the other mss. by homoioteleuton from "marriage" to "marriage."

The Talmudic discussion at b. *Giṭṭin* 77b is introduced by a citation (*pisqa*) from the Mishnah. The passage runs:

> "And she is inside her house." ʿUlla said, "It is a case in which she is standing beside [BṢD] her house or beside her courtyard." R. ʾOshaʿya said, "Even if she is in Tiberias and her courtyard is in Sepphoris, or she is in Sepphoris and her courtyard is in Tiberias, she is divorced."

The *gemara* then objects to this last view:

> But the Mishnah states "and she is *inside* her house or inside her courtyard"?! This is what he [R. ʾOshaʿya] meant: she is like one who is inside her house or inside her courtyard. For since the courtyard is under her conscious supervision [it is as though she were there, the delivery is valid, and] she is divorced.

Weiss points out that the objection leveled against R. ʾOshaʿya applies equally well to ʿUlla.[1] The latter also does not require the woman to be inside her house or courtyard. Neither R. ʾOshaʿya's statement nor ʿUlla's conforms to the plain sense of the Mishnah. However, these two Amoraim may have had a different reading in their text of M. *Giṭṭin* 8:1. If so, one could avoid an exegesis as forced as that the *gemara* offers for R. ʾOshaʿya, Specifically, Weiss suggests that the version of the Mishnah these Amoraim knew did not contain the word WHYʾ, "and she is". It ran: "He who throws a divorce document to his wife into [LTWK] her house etc." Such a version leaves open the question of where the wife must be. The two Amoraim answered this question differently. ʿUlla asserted that the woman must be nearby, while R. ʾOshaʿya said that "even if she is in Tiberias and her courtyard is in Sepphoris" the delivery is valid.

When Weiss made this suggestion, no such reading in the Mishnah was known. Certain medieval commentators did cite the Mishnah in a way which implied that they had this reading, but no hard evidence was available. While the book was in press, M. S. Feldblum's *Diqduqē Soferim* on *Giṭṭin* appeared. It recorded a Mishnah manuscript with the exact reading Weiss had proposed: "He who throws a divorce document to his wife into her house etc."[2]

Summary: Two Amoraic comments contradicted the very Mishnah they were explaining. The *gemara* itself had recognized the more

[1] *Sources*, pp. 599-600.

[2] See ibid., p. 600, n. 9. An apparent misprint in the footnote obscures the actual text of the new reading, cf. M. S. Feldblum, *Diqduqe Soferim on Giṭṭin* (New York, 1966), *ad loc.*, folio 77b, 1. 26.

striking of the two contradictions. The *gemara* resolved it by taking the comment in something other than its plain meaning. A variant reading in the Mishnah suggests an alternate resolution appropriate for both comments. It obviates the need for a resolution since this version of the Mishnah is not contradicted by the Amoraic statements.

Conclusion

These examples illustrate the success of the source-critical method. We see here the basic procedures. First, one must maintain an independence of mind *vis-a-vis* the Talmudic discussion. Does the question of the *gemara* raise a real problem? Is an answer really to the point? Is an interpretation reasonable? A negative answer to these questions is *prima facie* evidence that "traditions" or forms of sources other than those now before us may lie behind the passage. Second, one must examine the whole range of variants attested for the sources used in the passage. Are any of the variants more compatible with the structure of the passage than the present reading? Do any resolve exegetical difficulties? If so, then these variants represent the actual sources of the passage.

Yet examples serve merely to illustrate the source-critical approach, not to explain it. Weiss in time must supply a systematic presentation of his method. Such a presentation should discuss in detail the literary and historical assumptions on which the method is based. Conversely, it should make explicit the implications of source-criticism for the question of the development of the Talmud. The issue of providing a historical account of how literary phenomena came into being, alluded to in example 3 above, must be dealt with. We ought to be able to explain, for instance, how the conflation of contradictory sources could actually have taken place. In any case, I think it safe to say that from now on the serious student of a text from *Seder Nashim* will routinely consult *Sources and Traditions* as he consults Rashi.

BIBLIOGRAPHY

Asaf, Simḥah et al., *To the Memory of Professor Jacob Naḥum Epstein* (Jerusalem, 1952).

Auerbach, Moshe, ed., *Memorial Volume for Rabbi Yiẓḥaq Isaac Halevy* (Bnē Braq, 1964).

Avi-Yonah, Michael, *Bimē Roma uBiẓantiyon* (Jerusalem, 1952).

Baron, Salo, *History and Jewish Historians* (Philadelphia, 1964).

Beer, Moshe, 'Iyyunim BeIggeret Rav Sherira Ga'on [Studies in the Letter of R. Sherira Gaon], *Bar-Ilan Annual* 4-5, pp. 181-196.

Belkin, S., ed., *The Abraham Weiss Jubilee Volume* (New York, 1964).

Cohen, Boaz (review), *The Redaction of the Babylonian Talmud* by J. Kaplan, *JQR* 24, 1933-34, pp. 263-67.

Epstein, J. N., *A Grammar of Babylonian Aramaic* (Jerusalem, 1960) in Hebrew.

——, *Mavo LeNusaḥ HaMishnah* [Introduction to the Text of the Mishnah] (Jerusalem, 1947/8).

——, ed., *Mekhilta DeRabbi Shim'on ben Yoḥai* (Jerusalem, 1955).

——, *Mevo'ot LeSifrut Ha'Amora'im* [Introductions to Amoraic Literature] (Jerusalem, 1962).

——, *Mevo'ot LeSifrut HaTanna'im* [Introductions to Tannaitic Literature] (Jerusalem, 1957).

Fein, Samuel Joseph, *Nidḥé Yisra'el* (Vilna, 1850/1).

Feldblum, Meyer S. "Professor Abraham Weiss: His Approach and Contribution to Talmudic Scholarship", *The Abraham Weiss Jubilee Volume* (New York, 1965), English, pp. 7-80; Hebrew, pp. 13-72.

Ginzberg, Eli, *Keeper of the Law, Louis Ginzberg* (Philadelphia, 1966).

Ginzberg, Louis, "The Mishnah Tamid", *Journal of Jewish Lore and Philosophy*, I, 1,2,3,4, 1919, p. 33ff.

——, *Students, Scholars and Saints* (New York, 1958).

Graetz, Heinrich, *History of the Jews*, Vol. II (New York, 1927).

Guttmann, Michael (review), *The Redaction of the Babylonian Talmud* by J. Kaplan, *Monatschrift für die Geschichte und Wissenschaft des Judentums* 80, 1936, pp. 355-358.

Halevy, Yiẓḥaq Isaac, *Dorot HaRishonim*, IIa (Frankfurt A.M., 1901).

——, *Dorot HaRishonim*, III (Pressburg, 1897).

Jawitz, Ze'ev, *Sefer Toledot Yisra'el* (Tel Aviv, 1935).

Kaplan, Julius, *The Redaction of the Babylonian Talmud* (New York, 1933).

Klein, Hyman, "Gemara and Sebara", *JQR* 38, 1947-48, pp. 67-91.

——, "Gemara Quotations in Sebara", *JQR* 43, 1952-53, pp. 341-63.

——, "Mekhilta on the Pentateuch", *JQR* 35, 1944-45, pp. 424-34.

——, "Some General Results on the Separation of Gemara from Sebara in the Babylonian Talmud", *Journal of Semitic Studies* 3, 1958, pp. 363-72.

——, "Some Methods of Sebara", *JQR* 50, 1959-60, pp. 124-46.

Lieberman, Saul, "Palestine in the Third and Fourth Centuries", *JQR* 36, 1946, pp. 329-70.

——, "The Talmud of Caesarea—Jerusalem Tractate Neziqin", *Tarbiẓ* II, 4, 1931, Supplement.

Lewin, Benjamin M., "Autobiographic Sketch", *Sinai* 14, 1944, pp. 195-7, in Hebrew.

——, ed., *'Iggeret Rav Sherira Ga'on* (Haifa, 1921).

——, *Ozar HaGeonim* [Geonic Responsa and Commentaries], I-XIII (Haifa, Vol. 1; Jerusalem, Vol 2-13, 1928-43).
——, *Rabbanan Savora'ei veTalmudam* [The Saboraic Rabbis and their Talmud] (Jerusalem, 1937).
——, *Rav Sherira Ga'on* (Jaffa, 1917).
Neusner, Jacob, *A History of the Jews in Babylonia*, IV. *The Age of Shapur II* (Leiden, 1969).
Schechter, Solomon, *Studies in Judaism, First Series* (Philadelphia, 1945).
Seligson, Max, "I. H. Weiss", *Jewish Encyclopedia*, XII (New York, 1925) pp. 495-97.
Weiss, Abraham, *Hithavut HaTalmud BiShelemuto* [The Development of the Talmud as a Literary Unit] (New York, 1943).
——, *Leḥeqer HaTalmud* [The Talmud in its Development] (New York, 1954).
——, *Studies in the Literature of the Amoraim* (New York, 1962) in Hebrew.
Weiss, Isaac Hirsch, *Zur Geschichte der jüdischen Tradition* (Vilna, 1910).
Zuri, Jacob S., *'Arikhat HaMishpat Ha'Ivri. Ḥoq Ḥevrat HaShutafut im Torat HaMishpat Ha'Ivri Ḥevrat HaShutafut* [The Editing of Jewish Laws, Laws of Partnership] (London, 1941).
——, "Hasafut 'al lo Riv" [Uncontested Judgement] *Hasolel* (Jerusalem, 1924) pp. 22ff.
——, "HaTafqidim BeVa'ad R. Ami VeRav Asi", *B. M. Lewin Festschrift*, ed. Y. L. H. Fishman (Jerusalem, 1940) pp. 174-95.
——, "Histadrut HaMishpaḥah" [Family Organization] *Hamishpat Ha'Ivri*, Vol. 4, ed. P. Dickstein (Tel Aviv, 1933) pp. 1-25.
——, *Ḥoq Mit'aseq Shelo Bireshut Im Torat HaMishpat Ha'vri—Mit'aseq Belo Reshut* [Laws of Involuntary Agency] (London, 1941).
——, *Hypotheka* (London, 1944).
——, *Mishpat HaTalmud* [Talmudic Law], Two Vols. (Warsaw, 1921).
——, "Neḥiqat HaḤuqim Bemaqom Uvizeman BeMisphat Ha'Ivri" [The Usage of Laws Concerning Place and Time in Jewish Law] *HaMishpat Ha'Ivri*, Vol. 1, eds. Eliash and Dickstein (Tel Aviv, 1926).
——, *Rab, Sein leben und sein Anschauungen* (Zurich, 1918).
——, *Rabbi 'Aqiba* (Jerusalem, 1924).
——, "Rabbi Huna bar Abbin HaKohen, Safra DeSidra" *Sinai*, I, 1938, pp. 440-459.
——, *R. Jochanan* (Berlin, 1919).
——, *Rabbi Yosi bar Hanina meQisrin* (Jerusalem, 1926).
——, *Rav* (Jerusalem, 1925).
——, *Rav Ashi* (Jerusalem, 1924).
——, "Shtei Nequdot 'al HaBa'alut BeMishpat Ha'Ivri" [Two Viewpoints on Ownership in Jewish Law] *HaMishpat Ha'Ivri*, Vol. 1, eds. Eliash and Dickstein (Tel Aviv, 1926) pp. 203-204.
——, *Tarbut HaDeromim* [The Culture of the Southerners] (Warsaw, 1924).
——, "Tefilat HaGelilim" [Prayer of the Galileans] *Alexander Z. Rabinowitz Festschrift* (Tel Aviv, 1924) pp. 50-4.
——, *Toledot Darkhē HaLimud* [The History of Methods of Learning] (Jerusalem, 1914).
——, *Toledot HaMishpat HaẒiburi Ha'Ivri* [History of Jewish Social Law] *Vol. 1. Book One: Shilton HaNesiut VeHaVa'ad* [The Rule of Patriarchate and Council] *Mavo, Kolelot* [Introduction, General Principles] (Paris, 1931).
——, *Toledot HaMishpat HaẒiburi Ha'vri* [History of Jewish Social Law] *Vol.1, Book Two: Tequfat Rabbi Yehudah HaNasi* (Paris, 1931).
——, *Toledot HaMishpat HaẒiburi Ha'vri* [History of Jewish Social Law] *Vol.1,*

Book Three, Part One: Tequfat Rabban Gamliel BeRabbi Judah HaNasi III, Tequfat Rabbi Yehuda HaNasi II (London, 1933).
——, *Toledot HaMishpat HaẒiburi Ha'Ivri* [History of Jewish Social Law], *Vol. 1, Book Three, Part Two: Yeshivat Rabbi Ḥanina bar Ḥama BeẒipori* (London, 1934).
——, *Toledot HaMishpat HaẒiburi Ha'Ivri* [History of Jewish Social Law], *Vol. 1, Book Three, Part Two: Shilton Rashut HaGolah VeHaYeshivot, Tequfat Rav Naḥman bar Yiẓḥaq Rosh Hakallah VeRosh HaYeshivah* (Tel Aviv, 1939).
——, *Toledot HaMishpat HaẒiburi Ha'Ivri* [History of Jewish Social Law], *Vol. 1, Book Five, Part Two: Yeshivot Ṣur Taḥat Roshut R. Ḥiyya bar Abba, Ḥaver HaVa'ad* [The Academies under the Leadership of R. Ḥiyya bar Abba, Member of the Council].
——, *Torat HaDeromim* [The Torah of the Southerners] (Jerusalem, 1914).
——, *Torat HaMishpat Ha'Ezraḥi Ha'Ivri* [History of Jewish Civil Law], *Mishpat HaNeziqin* [Law of Torts] *Part One* (London, 1937).
——, *Torat HaMishpat Ha'Ezraḥi Ha'Ivri, Shitat HaTa'anot* [Jewish Civil Law, Theory of Claims] (London, 1934).
——, *Torat HaMishpat Ha'Ezraḥi Ha'Ivri* [History of Jewish Civil Law], *He'Irurim* [Pleas] *Part One*, (London, 1935).
——, "Yesodot HaShilton HaẒiburi Ha'Ivri", *Sinai* VI, 13 ff., (Jerusalem, 1943).

INDEX

i. Scriptures

ii. Babylonian Talmud

* Indices were prepared by Mr. Arthur Woodman, Canaan, New Hampshire, under a grant from Brown University.

iii. Palestinian Talmud

iv. Mishnah

v. Tosefta

GENERAL INDEX

Aba b. Kahana, R., 119
Abahu, R., 119
Abaye, R., 7-8, 10, 15, 21, 99; and *sugya*, 129, 142, 152, 159, 162; bailment, 73; Epstein discusses, 77-79, 81, 83-84; Halevy and evidence of arrangement, 29, 35-36, 38, 40-41, 45-46; source criticism, 89-90
Aba b. Zavda, R., 102
Academies; Aramaic literary forms, 95-103; end of instruction, Saboraic element, 51-60; "general academy", 37-38; geographic influences, 20-25; Neziqin and editing, 114-24; *sugyot*, 127-33
Adam, Book of, 61
Adda b. Ahava, R., 67, 79
Aḥa, R., 21, 44
Aḥa b. Rava, R., 39
Aḥai, R., 58
Aḥai of bē Hatim, R., 43, 54
Albeck, Ḥanokh, 80; end of instruction, 132-33; *Introduction to the Talmuds*, 128; Talmudic *Sugya*, 127-33
Alfasi, 156
Ammi, R., 36, 128
Amoraim, 7-8; end of instruction, 51-60; influences, 5-10, 14-18, 20-25; literary forms, 95-103; literature and end of Talmudic form, 76-86; R. Ashi and Talmud, 4-9, 26-47; Saboraic element, 5-7, 10, 61-74; source criticism, 88-94; Tamid and Amoraic names, 116-22
Arab invasion, 4
Asaf, Simḥah, 75n
Ashi, R.; contributions weighed, 61-63, 65-66, 71, 73-74; editorial contributions, 4-10, 14-25; end of instruction, 51, 53-55, 57, 93-94, 132-33; Epstein discusses, 87, 83-84; Geonic tradition, 13-25; Halevy and evidence of arrangement, 36-47; property rights, 14, 16, 22-24; source criticism, 89, 91-93; *sugyot*, 130; three stages of editing, 62; two versions or editions, 14, 16, 22-24
Ashi bar Shimi, Rav, 13
Assi, R., 93-94, 128
Auerbach, Moshe, 27n
Authentic teaching: *see* End of instruction
Avi-Yonah, M., 36n

Ba b. Mina, R., 117
Babylonian masters: *see* Amoraim
Bailment, 73
Baron, Salo, 3-4
Ben Arza, 113
Brüll, N., 13, 61-62, 66

Caesarea; Neziqin and editing, 114-24; Talmudic editing, 107-24
Chariot, Works of, 100
Cohen, Boaz, 61, 65n
Commentary on the Palestinian Talmud, 134
Constantine, 9, 36